YEAR OF DESPERATE STRUGGLE

YEAR OF
DESPERATE
STRUGGLE

Jeb Stuart and His Cavalry, from Gettysburg to Yellow Tavern, 1863–1864

MONTE
AKERS

CASEMATE
Philadelphia & Oxford

Published in the United States of America and Great Britain in 2015 by
CASEMATE PUBLISHERS
908 Darby Road, Havertown, PA 19083
and
10 Hythe Bridge Street, Oxford, OX1 2EW

Copyright 2015 © Monte Akers

ISBN 978-1-61200-282-8
Digital Edition: ISBN 978-1-61200-283-5

Cataloging-in-publication data is available from the Library of Congress and
the British Library.

10 9 8 7 6 5 4 3 2 1

Printed and bound in the United States of America.

For a complete list of Casemate titles please contact:

CASEMATE PUBLISHERS (US)
Telephone (610) 853-9131, Fax (610) 853-9146
E-mail: casemate@casematepublishing.com

CASEMATE PUBLISHERS (UK)
Telephone (01865) 241249, Fax (01865) 794449
E-mail: casemate-uk@casematepublishing.co.uk

CONTENTS

DEDICATION
To Lexy and Kyle, who have made our family complete.

PROLOGUE

"Tell again," the grandsire faltered,
sitting by the farmhouse door,
"Tell again the tale unaltered,
how you rode of yore;
it will quicken the slow beating
of my pulse once more."
—*The Cavalryman's Story,* poem published
in the June 13, 1863 issue of *Harper's Weekly*

THIS BOOK IS A SEQUEL, or companion, to *Year of Glory: The Life and Battles of Jeb Stuart and His Cavalry, June 1862–June, 1863*, published by Casemate in 2012. Both books were written in an attempt to recapture and describe a unique individual who performed unique acts in a unique time. Whereas biographies of Stuart naturally cover his entire life, each of these two books focus on only a single year or major portion of a year during the Civil War, when Stuart established and lived up to his reputation, or as sometimes happened, failed to do so. This means that whereas his biographies touched on and considered the major events of Stuart's life, they could rarely delve into the details or minutiae of what he did and experienced when he was not involved in those major events. This book not only explores Stuart's battles and campaigns during the last eleven months of his life, but also gathers daily detail from wartime letters, published memoirs of Confederate officers and soldiers, post-war articles, newspaper accounts, and other veterans' recollections, so that a reader may follow Stuart on an almost day-to-day basis to explore the ordinary with the extraordinary, the normal with the remarkable.

Stuart's battles and campaigns are described, to a large degree, based on the reports written during the war by the officers who participated in them which were published in the *Official Records of the War of the Rebellion*, or "OR." Although there has been no intent on the author's part to revise the world's understanding of Stuart's military campaigns, some of the information and analysis, particular that concerning Stuart's mortal wounding at Yellow Tavern, and to a lesser degree his participation in the Gettysburg campaign, run counter to the secondary analyses of certain other authors and historians. Those differences arise from interpretation of the sometimes inconsistent primary sources, filtered through the eyes of the author.

Of necessity, a great deal of the detail about Stuart's day-to-day life came from the writings of his staff officers. Stuart left behind many letters, dispatches, and campaign reports, and although he kept personal notebooks for autographs, poems he liked, and musings, as well as a pre-war diary, he did not keep a wartime diary. During the war Stuart employed a total of at least 48 officers at different times on his staff, in addition to which there was a small crowd of couriers, scouts, escorts, and clerks. Most of those men are not even mentioned in this book, but those who kept a diary, had memoirs published, wrote of their memories to the *Confederate Veteran* magazine, or who left behind letters have become significant co-stars in a tale principally about Stuart. Readers of *Year of Glory* were introduced to many of those characters, but a brief description of some of them is appropriate in order to set the stage for *Year of Desperate Struggle*.

The first of these individuals is Heros Von Borcke, who for all practical purposes was removed from the scene on June 19, 1863 when he was wounded in the throat at the battle of Middleburg, before the period covered by this book.★ Nevertheless he continued to play a role in Stuart's life after his wounding. He was huge by1860s standards—6'4" and 240 pounds—but also handsome and hard to ignore. He was from Prussia and was therefore the target of a good deal of Southern sycophancy stemming from Confed-

---

★The previous volume left off with Jeb Stuart defending the passes of the Blue Ridge against probing Federal cavalry, fighting the battles of Aldie, Middleburg and Upperville, June 17–21, to screen the Army of Northern Virginia's passage through the Shenendoah Valley toward Pennsylvania. Chronologically the present volume begins on June 24, 1863, when Stuart decides on his own fateful route toward Gettysburg.

erate longing for recognition in Europe. He was fun-loving and boisterous as well as a warrior of ferocious formidability, and Stuart appointed him to his staff almost immediately after their first meeting. He was a devoted chronicler of his time and experiences in the Confederate army, and although he never rode with Jeb again after being wounded, he showed up from time to time during the last year of Stuart's life. His book, *Memoirs of the Confederate War for Independence*, published in 1866, was the first detailed account of Stuart and his campaigns, at least during the period 1862–63. Unfortunately he never let facts get in the way of a good story.

Henry B. McClellan was Northern-born and reared, a first cousin of Federal Major General George B. McClellan, and he had three brothers serving in the Union army. After graduating from Williams College in Massachusetts in 1858 he took a job in a rural part of Virginia and fell in love with the people and the place, such that he enlisted in the 3rd Virginia Cavalry on June 14, 1861. He soon became a lieutenant, then assistant adjutant general, then Chief of Staff for Stuart. Intelligent and insightful, he wrote *I Rode With Jeb Stuart: The Life And Campaigns of Major General J.E.B. Stuart* after the war, which is one of a handful of important books about Stuart and his cavalry containing an abundance of detail concerning military actions and movements, most of which McClellan witnessed.

William W. Blackford was Stuart's staff Engineer Officer and probably second only to Von Borcke in survivors of the war who were extremely close to Stuart. His memoirs, *War Years with Jeb Stuart,* published long after his death, strike a happy balance between Von Borcke's boisterous storytelling and McClellan's dry military history, capturing Stuart and his times in an enduring and endearing fashion.

John Esten Cooke was an aide-de-camp, ordnance officer, and inspector on Stuart's staff, as well as his cousin by marriage. Although Cooke was often too boring and bookish for Stuart's taste, Cooke worshipped him and, as a professional writer, had an eye for what he believed would capture the public's attention. The author of several books, *Wearing of the Gray* is his best known. Although his writings contain a great deal of valuable historical information—Cooke was a witness to much of what Robert E. Lee, Stonewall Jackson, Jeb Stuart and John Pelham did during the war—his writing style reflects his times and modern readers often find it stilted. Unfortunately, his mixing of historical fact with stylized fiction denigrated the value of the facts instead of enhancing the fiction.

Andrew Reid Venable joined Stuart's staff shortly after Chancellorsville and remained there until Yellow Tavern. The Venables were classic "FFVs" (first families of Virginia) and no less than four men of that name served on the staffs of well-known Confederate leaders, including Robert E. Lee. The circumstances of how he married, which occurred after Stuart's death, are one of the most unique in the annals of the war.

There were many others, Fitzhugh Lee, Wade Hampton, John S. Mosby, to name a few, who affected Stuart's life significantly and who are famous enough to need no description, many of whom have their own memoirs or biographies. Hundreds or thousands of others were witnesses and participants who left sparse or no records of what they saw and did.

There is no hidden message intended by this book. It does not revise history, attempt to justify the Confederacy's dismal record on race and slavery, or attempt to paint Stuart as flawless. Jeb Stuart had a great many flaws but he was, in the author's opinion, one of the most fascinating characters who ever lived, and the time during which he became famous was the most unusual, captivating, horrible, and charming in our nation's history. Stuart might have been nothing more than a footnote in our history but for the American Civil War, yet if ever there was a man for his time, it was Stuart and that war. Why Hollywood has not singled him out for possible block-buster material is a mystery, although now, considering that he gave his life defending America's greatest blemish—slavery—it is probably too late for that to ever happen.

Like the grandsire in the poem quoted from *Harper's Weekly* published eleven days before the opening scene of this book, what follows is intended to quicken the beating of pulses of those who enjoy hearing unaltered tales about a long ago generation who once "rode of yore."

CHAPTER 1

OUT OF THE FRYING PAN AND INTO HELL

Morning, June 24, 1863

Of a horseman born.
It is Stuart of Laurel Hill,
"Beauty" Stuart, the genius of cavalry,
Reckless, merry, religious, theatrical,
Lover of gesture, lover of panache,
With all the actor's grace and the quick, light charm
That makes the women adore him—a wild cavalier
Who worships as sober a God as Stonewall Jackson . . .
— Stephen Vincent Benét, *John Brown's Body*

I T WASN'T LIGHT, BUT they are up and moving. The lucky ones have body servants to start fires, pack up, and get horses ready, but those are considerably less common than they were in 1861. In fact, almost everyone and everything is different after two years.

The ambrotypes, tintypes and cartes de visite taken back then, of boys in battle shirts and militia tunics with big d-guards and tiny pinfires, props mostly, are safe at home. Those faces without names, "fading to yellow in a brown leather frame," will show future generations only what novice soldiers looked like. Stuart's horsemen of 1863 are veterans.

Men yawn, cough, hack up phlegm, are flatulent, and relieve themselves wherever they please. There are no latrines, not in a temporary camp like the one they've occupied the night of June 23, 1863. The wood smoke coaxed from the coals of the previous nights' fires is merciful in its masking of odors, man and horse.

Men stumble and grumble in the dark. Horses turn away, toss their

heads, resist the bit, avoid the bridle, swell up when saddle girths are tight-
ened. More than one horse gets swatted, has its ear twisted, or gets kicked.
More than one horseman has a foot stepped on by an iron-shod hoof. More
than one shouts an iridescent curse in the dark.

Precious few have coffee to boil or bacon to fry. Several fish out corn-
bread, Yankee hardtack, or a cold biscuit from a grimy haversack. More skip
the morning meal in favor of a pipe or hand rolled cigar, the smoke from
which improves the atmosphere a little more.

They are mounted within twenty minutes of waking, and they cover
two miles before the sun makes it possible to see each other plainly.

They are also not much look at. There is little fluff, a minimum of fancy.
Nearly everything they wear and carry has a practical use. Gone are the big
knives, the plumes in hats, havelocks, gaiters, and tarred kepi covers. Mostly
gone are kepis, chasseur and forage caps, state banners, company flags, and
guidons. Also gone is a lot of the romance.

The fancy tailored, individualized-by-company uniforms of 1861 wore
out months ago. Many, if not most of the coats the men wear are Type 1 or
Type 2 Richmond Depot shell jackets with nine buttons, shoulder straps
and belt loops. Types and appearance of cloth, depending on the date of
issue, range from wool to cassimere to cotton/woolen jean to English kersey,
such that there are different textures and colors: cadet gray, light gray, green-
ish-gray, yellow, and brown. Buttons might be state seal, Confederate issue
"C," U.S. eagle, wooden, flower, or bone. Belts, which are both brown and
black, are held on with state seal plates, inverted U.S. oval plates, pre-war
militia plates, tongue and wreaths, an occasional snake buckle, and often a
plain roller buckle. Pants are usually the same color and cloth as the jacket,
although some of the "trowsers" have a seat reinforced with an extra layer
of cloth. Hats are often small-brimmed, round pork-pies. Footwear, furnished by the soldier, consist of boots mostly but brogans are common,
sometimes with pants tucked into socks. At least most cavalrymen have
footwear of some kind.

Just as there is variety among the soldiers' uniforms, there is also variety
in the condition of their clothes. While some of the men wear clothes issued
to them recently, others, particularly some officers who must furnish their
own, are in tatters. A lieutenant rides by wearing a hat missing its crown, so
that his tussled, unkempt hair protrudes above the brim in different direc-

tions. Closer observation reveals that his pants have no knees and, when he stands in the stirrups, nothing covers his rear end. His boots are in ruins and his toes can be seen protruding from their fronts. Only his frock coat is reasonably complete, and yet it is so stained and grimy it is difficult to determine its original color.

At least the men look healthy. Some of the horses are in pathetic condition. Nearly all are gaunt with visible ribs. Some are sway-backed and look like the kind of nag one would find pulling a junk wagon. Many have no shoes and some are limping. The day is new, yet quite a few are already lathered and hanging their heads. Many have visible sores and healing wounds. In some regiments men are riding double on the horses that appear sound, the plan being to capture serviceable mounts in Maryland or Pennsylvania.

Saddles come in every variety from McClellan to Jenifer to Grimsley to Hope. Many of the saddle blankets are dark blue with a dark yellow stripe, others are pieces of quilts or carpet. They ride in columns of fours at a walk, alignment almost non-existent. Once the sun is up and sleep is shaken off, they begin joking and laughing, making fun of the things they pass, mooing at cows, baaing at sheep, crowing at chickens, barking at dogs and calling out to civilians or answering questions about where they are going with buffoonery and wild exaggeration.

"Ain't you heard? Old Abe done moved to Canada and Queen Victoria's asked Bobby Lee to marry her. We're the groomsmen."

"I was just on my way to town and these other fellas started following me. Makes me kinda nervous."

"On our way to put the whole Yankee nation to flight."

Couriers jangle by, trotting or galloping, and are hooted at.

"What's your hurry? Somebody chasing you?"

"Whoa, come back, I'm right here. Come bring me that letter from home I know you got for me."

"That's the biggest damned dog I've ever seen. How'd you get him broke to a saddle?"

Even officers, or at least most of them, are not immune from the jests and ribbing.

"Where we going captain and how we gonna know when we get there?"

"My butt hurts, lieutenant, can I get your mother to rub liniment on it again?"

"Hey major, let's trade horses. Yours looks just like my sister."

It is different when Jeb Stuart comes along. He doesn't do it often because he prefers being at the head of the column, leading, singing to Sweeney's banjo, joking with his staff officers, sending and receiving messages, or studying the terrain. When he does ride by, or sits his horse beside the road to watch his warriors pass, the shouts and whoops travel like a wave with the column, and the jibes are all admiration.

"Hey here's old Jeb! Hurrah for Stuart!"

"Ah boys! I feel all right now, there is General Stuart."

"Looka here, ain't he the grandest thing you ever seed?"

"We're with ya, Ginral, We'll follow you to hell and back, or just to hell if'n you tell us to stay there!"

Usually Stuart would acknowledge their shouts with a laugh, a grin, a word, a joke, or a gesture. He might take off his hat and wave it in the air, or break into song, or shout a word of encouragement to the men according to their unit.

"Is that Company C? Bully for old C! You've never failed to make the Yankees skedaddle!"

"Ah, Colonel Owens 3rd, isn't it? If I had half a dozen more regiments like the 3rd we could be in Washington City tomorrow!"

The men would eat it up, bask in his approval, certain he means every word of the praise, but this day, this particular Wednesday, he does not acknowledge their greetings.

He trots by on his big bay mare, Virginia, wearing one of his gray battle-jackets with buff-colored cuffs, the double-breasted front buttoned back on each side to reveal a gray vest and checkered shirt, head down in thought. He still wears a plumed hat, but no red-lined cape this summer day. His pants are plain gray, not the fancy dark blue pair with parallel gold stripes or the gray pair with similar stripes, and his boots are not the tall, thigh-high pair he often wears, and which can become so hot, but a pair that come only to his knees. His spurs are silver, not gold. The saber belt and pistol holster are buckled over a yellow sash, and some of his horsemen strain to see what pistol he is wearing today, wondering if it is the new double-action Trantor that Von Borcke gave him before the big Prussian was wounded five days earlier.

The gift caused a stir because Von audaciously had the case in which the English revolver was housed inscribed to "Lt. Gen J.E.B. Stuart C.S.A. Culpeper, Va. June 1863 from Heros Von Borcke," even though Stuart is only a major general. There is little doubt in anyone's mind that the promotion will come, and soon, but it still seemed like tempting fate to jump the gun, so to speak.

The general seems self-absorbed, but that is alright. Everyone knows where they are headed, at least for the most part. It's no surprise he is deep in thought, planning for what lies ahead, considering his options and selecting the best one, as he seems to have a God-given knack for doing. Only a few, a very few, think Jeb Stuart seems less like himself, even somehow diminished this Wednesday morning.

If there are any gray horsemen who think about their commander's mood and consider the subject any further, they are not mystified. The last two months have been damned hard on Jeb Stuart.

The first few days of May were taken up with the Battle of Chancellorsville, and even though the Confederate triumph was impressive and almost unbelievable, and even though Stuart took command of the Second Corps after Jackson was wounded and led it to a decisive victory, the fight took the life of Channing Price on May 1 in a tragic manner. Price was Stuart's assistant adjutant general and one of the most talented staff officers in the army. His ability to hear a lengthy command or message one time and then write it down word for word—a gift developed when tending to the business of his nearly blind father—made him irreplaceable. Add the facts that Jeb loved him and that his death was utterly preventable, caused by loss of blood because no one had a tourniquet handy, and it was a stunning blow.

Yet it paled to near-nothingness compared to the death of Lt. General Thomas Jonathan "Stonewall" Jackson nine days later. Jackson was not only the most famous and effective of all of Lee's lieutenants, a man worshipped in the South, but he was a close personal friend of Stuart's. Despite having polar opposite personalities—Jackson dour and humorless; Stuart merry and prankish—the two were famously fond of each other, and the war without Jackson would take on a more somber cast than before.

Despite the loss of Jackson, his departure provided an unparalleled opportunity for Stuart—promotion to Lt. General and command of the Second Corps. Rumor was that Jackson requested it on his deathbed. Stuart certainly relished the idea, and after the war there will be Southerners who will claim that failure to put Stuart in that command position was the reason the South lost the war.[1] Why promotion didn't come evidently bothered Jeb enough to make him write a letter to General Lee inquiring if his performance at Chancellorsville was unsatisfactory, to which Lee replied—"I saw no errors to correct."

There have been other, lesser irritations, such as the publication in the *New York Times* on May 21, 1863 of a diary written by one of Jeb's staff officers, the brother of beloved Channing Price no less, ridiculing Stuart. Granted, the author did not mean harm and never dreamed he would lose the journal and have it fall into the enemy's hands, but one passage—"Gen. Stuart was with us and prattled on all evening in his garrulous way—described how he commenced the war by capturing 50 of Patterson's advance guard on the day preceding Bull Run"—was particularly galling. It showed disrespect within his own military family, and gave Stuart's detractors, of which there are plenty, rich fodder for further ridicule.

But nothing in the previous two months was so utterly painful, and deflating, for Jeb Stuart as what happened on June 9 at Fleetwood, near the railroad stop known as Brandy Station. He had been taken by surprise, caught off guard by Federal cavalry, and although he managed to win the day, more or less, the victory was hollow. The Yankees got what they came for—information—came within a cat's whisker of defeating Jeb's scattered, unprepared brigades, and demonstrated palpably that they were no longer the easily spanked rabble on horseback they had once been. Yes, Jeb held the field at the end of the day, but it so happened that a division of Confederate infantry was on its way and the Federals knew it. Yes, Jeb held the field, but he suffered the loss of more irreplaceable members of his military family, particularly the courageous Captain William Farley, who was killed, and Lt. Robert Goldsborough, who was captured.

After the battle, instead of heaping praise on Stuart for driving off the invaders, Southern newspapers were shrill in their denunciations, and more than one high-ranking Confederate officer let it be known that they thought Stuart had been "caught napping," "whipped," "too busy rollicking, frolicking and running after girls," or "so conceited he got careless."

It stung. Stuart was a confident man, but what some took for conceit was more a love affair with life and all its possibilities than egotism. He certainly enjoyed attention, basked in praise and was ambitious, but for the most part Stuart was just what he seemed—a happy, fun-loving, friendly military commander of near-genius competence . . . who was extremely sensitive.

He'd written to his wife, Flora, to defend himself, set the record straight, accused the papers of dishonesty—which was true in some cases—theorized that there were political forces involved, undermining his reputation in order to further their goal of nationalizing the family's salt business. However, the criticism was so massive, so widespread, so unfamiliar, that it threatened, at least in a sense, to unhorse the man. He was determined to regain his reputation, to show his critics that he was every bit as marvelous and unique and praiseworthy as he'd been described after each of his two "Rides Around McClellan."

In fact, those two complete circumventions of the entire Army of the Potomac had been so notable, so popular, that it might be time to do it again. Stuart had heard, most people had, what Abe Lincoln said about the rides. The U.S. president had taken a stick, drawn an imaginary circle and said, "When I was a boy we used to play a game—three times around and out. Stuart has gone around McClellan twice. If he goes around him one more time, gentlemen, McClellan is out." Now McClellan was gone. He'd been "out" for nearly seven months, but what might a third trip around the Army of the Potomac do? Might it cause Hooker, or even Lincoln to be "out"? What could possibly be wrong with finding out?

As if all of the foregoing was not enough to make any commander of Confederate cavalry seem distracted, even diminished, there was the wounding of Heros Von Borcke on June 19 to top things off. Stuart loved Von Borcke. No man, other than John Pelham (killed the previous March on the Rappahannock) was as near and dear to Jeb as the six-foot-four, 240-pound Prussian. He had been with Stuart almost daily for a solid year, and they were like boys who had discovered a mutual passion and a mirror-image mind. They admired each other, made each other laugh, frolicked like puppies, and then rode side by side into battle and waged war with fearsome Old Testament conviction. Now Von had been horribly wounded in the throat while riding at Stuart's side, and doctors had pronounced the wound mortal. He had not died yet, but everyone expected the grim news any day.

Those daunting factors might have overwhelmed another man, but Jeb Stuart was far from overwhelmed. He was hardwired to be optimistic, and he devoted no small part of his letters to his wife attempting, to no avail, to persuade her to adopt a similar attitude. Still, the successes and consequent adoration he'd enjoyed for the previous two years were so complete, and the recent turn of events so antipathetic, that they ate at his psyche. He was not truly diminished, but for a man accustomed to nothing but laurels, the recent criticism and setbacks were a private agony, a burning psychological itch, a mental frying pan in which his thoughts hopped to find a way to escape the heat.

What he did not, could not, know was that, in terms of reputation, he was about to jump out of the frying pan . . . and into Hell.

NOTES

1. E.g., Col. Winfield Peters, speaking before the Veteran Cavalry Assoc. of the Army of Northern Virginia on June 1, 1907: "Had Stuart been kept in Jackson's place—which he'd won—Gettysburg would have been a Federal Waterloo," quoted in: "Stuart's Death; How it Occurred," in "Confederate Column" of the *Richmond Times-Dispatch,* p. E-7, September 22, 1907.

CHAPTER 2

THE WAYWARD ROAD
TO GETTYSBURG
June 24 to July 1, 1863

*We were now about to start on an expedition which
for audacious boldness equaled if it did not exceed
any of our dashing leader's exploits . . .*
—Maj. William W. Blackford, Engineer Officer,
    Stuart's staff, writing of Stuart's Gettysburg campaign

AFTER ITS SPECTACULAR victory at Winchester in the Shenendoah Valley, Richard Ewell's Second Corps of Lee's Army advanced through western Maryland and proceeded to spread out in Pennsylvania. It was followed by A.P. Hill's Third Corps, with James Longstreet's First Corps to follow. As the last week of June began, Joe Hooker's Army of the Potomac remained in northern Virginia, successfully screened by Stuart's cavalry at the Blue Ridge; however, by now reports from elsewhere had begun to reveal Lee's intentions—a full-fledged invasion of the North.

On June 24, 1863, the cavalry of the Army of Northern Virginia consisted of seven brigades and a battalion of Horse Artillery, as follows:

Hampton's Brigade—Brig. Gen. Wade Hampton
Robertson's Brigade—Brig. Gen. Beverly H. Robertson
Fitz Lee's Brigade—Brig. Gen. Fitzhugh Lee
Jenkins' Brigade—Brig. Gen. Albert G. Jenkins
Jones' Brigade—Brig. Gen. William E. "Grumble" Jones
W.H.F. Lee's Brigade—Brig. Gen. W.H.F. "Rooney" Lee (under the
    command of Col. J.R. Chambliss Jr.)

Imboden's Brigade—Brig. Gen. John Imboden
Stuart's Horse Artillery—six batteries under Major R.F. Beckham

Of those brigades, Robertson's and Jones', with three batteries of artillery, were detached from Stuart's main command and operating on the right flank of the Army of Northern Virginia, screening its northward march. Imboden's brigade, with one six-gun battery, was in the Shenandoah Valley, operating semi-independently, destroying bridges and tracks along the B&O rail line and harassing the Federals in that part of the Valley, keeping them occupied rather than focused on Lee's movements. Jenkins' brigade, with one battery, was on the right flank of Ewell's corps, and the other three brigades, plus one six-gun battery, were with Stuart near Salem's Depot.

Much has been written about the orders Stuart received from Robert E. Lee, what he did and did not obey, and what both of them did and did not intend. As with the orders that would be given to George Custer thirteen years later almost to the day, the written directions provided to Stuart have been pored over, debated, and served as the foundation for millions of written words by historians, peers, admirers, apologists, and critics. In both cases, the commanders knew and trusted their subordinates and allowed them great discretion in carrying out the orders, confident in both cases that the subordinate's judgment would prove sound if not flawless. In both cases the opposite occurred.

The most relevant portions of Lee's orders to Stuart, dated June 23, 1863 at 5 p.m., were as follows:

> If General Hooker's army remains inactive, you can leave two brigades to watch him, and withdraw with the three others, but should he not appear to be moving northward, I think you had better withdraw this side of the mountain to-morrow night, cross at Shepherdstown next day, and move over to Fredericktown.
>
> You will, however, be able to judge whether you can pass around their army without hindrance, doing them all the damage you can, and cross the river east of the mountains. In either case, after crossing the river, you must move on and feel the right of Ewell's troops, collecting information, provisions, etc.

Even with 150-plus years of hindsight, it is difficult for Stuart apologists to regard these orders as Lee's blessing for anything close to support of a frolicking ride around or through Hooker's army for the next nine days, utterly out of earshot and eyesight when Lee needed him most. Lee obviously wanted Stuart at or near Frederick, Maryland, which coincided with Lee's plans for the movement of his infantry, and specifically he wanted him to screen Ewell's Second Corps on its right.

Unarmed with either hindsight or a crystal ball, Stuart focused on three other parts of the order—"If Hooker's army remains inactive . . . ", "You will . . . be able to judge whether you can pass around their army without hindrance. . ." and "doing them all the damage you can."

It can meantime be understood if Stuart was confused by Lee's first sentence: "if Hooker's army remains inactive," followed by "should he not appear to be moving northward." Those two phrases amount to the same thing, leading one to suspect that Lee did not intend the word "not" to be in the sentence. What he meant to say was "should he appear to be moving northward."

In any case, Hooker's army wasn't inactive, but neither was it moving northward when the order was issued. Hooker's exchanges of information with General Halleck and the President during the period June 19–June 24 reflect that the Army of the Potomac was scattered, with the First Corps under Reynolds at Herndon Station; the Second Corps under Hancock at Centreville; the Third Corps under Birney at Gum Spring; the Fifth Corps under Meade at Aldie; the Sixth Corps under Sedgwick at Germantown; the Eleventh Corps under Howard between Leesburg and Aldie; the Twelfth Corps under Slocum at Leesburg; and the Cavalry Corps under Pleasonton at Aldie. Hooker was depending on his cavalry to keep tabs on Lee, and although he knew that Ewell had crossed the Potomac he believed that it was for the purpose of "plundering," and that Federal forces already in that district were sufficient to "check any extended advance of that column, and protect themselves from their aggression."[1]

He anticipated that if Lee crossed the Blue Ridge it would be for the purpose of an attack toward Washington, so his main concern was that his army be available for defense of the capital, to possibly make a slap at Ewell, and to be ready to intercept Lee when or if he "retreated" back toward Richmond. A full blown invasion of Maryland or Pennsylvania by Lee did not seem to be on his radar, and he was particularly irritated at newspaper reports that reported the strength and location of the Federal army while purporting to be more knowledgeable about the enemy than he.[2]

Hooker's messages to Halleck on June 24 included an uncharacteristically self-deprecating remark: ". . . outside of the Army of the Potomac I don't know whether I am standing on my head or feet."

The part of Lee's orders that said "You will . . . be able to judge whether you can pass around their army without hindrance . . ." must have looked like a glowing go-ahead to Stuart. Truth was, Stuart had already laid the groundwork for such a course of action. On June 18 he and General Lee had been together discussing the role of the cavalry in the upcoming campaign, and if Lee is to believed—usually a safe bet—Stuart suggested that "he could damage the enemy and delay his passage of the river [the Potomac] by getting in his rear." Lee went a step further in his after battle report, and said that "he [Stuart] was authorized to do so and it was left to his discretion whether to enter Maryland east or west of the Blue Ridge." However, he added one more phrase: "but he was instructed to lose no time in placing his command on the right of our column as soon as he should perceive the enemy moving northward."[3]

That then, at least in the mind of Robert E. Lee, was to be Stuart's signal that he should return to the army—the movement of Hooker's army northward. Until that occurred Jeb had carte blanche to use his best judgment about circling Hooker's army, doing damage, and deciding where to enter Maryland.

Further proof that Lee gave Stuart permission "to get into Hooker's rear" came from Lt. General James Longstreet. The day before Lee issued his orders, he sent Stuart a letter through Longstreet, who forwarded it with a message of his own, saying "He [Lee] speaks of your leaving, via Hopewell Gap, and passing by the rear of the enemy. If you can get through by that route, I think that you will be less likely to indicate what our plans are than if you should cross by passing to our rear. . . . I think that your passage of the Potomac by our rear at the present moment will, in a measure, disclose our plans. You had better not leave us, therefore, unless you can take the proposed route in rear of the enemy."[4] Longstreet essentially blessed and urged Jeb's plan to "get in the enemy's rear."

And if any doubt remains that Jeb had Lee and Longstreet's blessing to attempt to get behind Hooker, and all the way around him if practicable, there is Stuart's own after-battle report:

> I began to look for some other point at which to direct an effective blow. I submitted to the commanding general the plan of leaving a brigade or so in my present front, and passing through Hopewell or some other gap in Bull Run Mountains, attain the enemy's rear, passing between his main body and Washington, and cross into Maryland, joining our army north of the Potomac. The commanding general wrote me, authorizing this move if I deemed it practicable, and also what instructions should be given the officer in command of the two brigades left in front of the enemy. He also notified me that one column should move via Gettysburg and the other via Carlisle, toward the Susquehanna, and directed me, after crossing, to proceed with all dispatch to join the right (Early) of the army in Pennsylvania.
>
> Accordingly, three days rations were prepared, and, on the night of the 24th, the following brigades, Hamptons, Fitz. Lees, and W.H.F. Lees, rendezvoused secretly near Salem Depot.[5]

The "brigade or so" that Jeb left in his present front, where it would be available to screen the movements of Ewell's Corps, was that of Albert Jenkins, a former U.S. Congressman and contender for having the longest beard in the Civil War, plus Lige White's 35th Battalion of Virginia Cavalry of Grumble Jones' Brigade. The elements of Jenkins' brigade were the 14th, 16th, and 17th Virginia Cavalry regiments and the 34th Battalion of Virginia Cavalry, commanded by Lt. Col. Vincent "Clawhammer" Witcher.

The latter battalion, also known as "Witcher's Boys," may have been the least Jeb Stuart-like of all of Stuart's cavalry in the campaign. Organized in the mountainous region between Kentucky and Virginia in an area predominantly pro-Union and with a background of Indian wars involving the Mingos and the Cherokees, the battalion was originally a group of bushwhackers and "independent scouts" that the Confederacy didn't even claim. Witcher was a lawyer from what became West Virginia whose nickname was based on the style of scissor-tail coat he preferred to wear, and his boys spent much of the early part of the war focusing their wrath on similar groups of pro-Union bushwhackers and scouts. One of the Witcher's Boys' specialties was to lynch any prisoner captured from the "enemy" by roping him to a bent tree by the neck, then cutting the rope that secured the tree so that the victim was launched into eternity. On at least one occasion they killed a captive by decapitating him. Although they would serve credibly during the Gettysburg campaign, by the beginning of 1864 Witcher and his boys would be shuffled off to serve in East Tennessee.

Jenkins' command, numbering more than 1,600, must have seemed adequate to Stuart to do as Lee wanted,[6] and he knew that the commanding general had three other brigades of cavalry he could call on if the need arose, even though none were close enough to arrive on short notice. Still, Hooker seemed unaware of what was happening, and Jeb had the blessing of both Lee and Longstreet to execute the kind of bold, glorious raid, with all its attendant havoc for the enemy, that had brought him accolades before. Jeb had been blessed, in the campaign he expected would be the last of the war, to be allowed to make up for all perceived shortcomings. What could possibly go wrong? The answer is "a lot."

The specifics of Stuart's plan of march were provided him by John S. Mosby. The Gray Ghost had been behind Hooker's lines, and when he returned to Stuart's headquarters on June 23, he was able to report the positions of the different corps of the Army of the Potomac. He recalled 14 years later that he "suggested that a splendid opportunity was now offered him to strike Hooker a disparaging blow by passing through an unguarded pass of the Bull Run mountain with a portion of his cavalry and cutting right through the middle of the Federal army, destroying its transportation as he went, and crossing the Potomac at Seneca (where I had crossed some two weeks before with my command) he could unite with General Lee in Pennsylvania."[7] Cutting through the middle of the enemy's army instead of riding completely around had a nice ring to it, and would be something new and seemingly more daring than what Jeb had done to McClellan. Jeb liked the sound of it.

The three brigades rendezvoused at Salem's Depot and spent the night of June 24–25. They were up, not merely before dawn, but at 1 a.m., and headed toward Haymarket. There, a little after dawn and to Stuart's surprise, he found Winfield Scott Hancock's Second Corps on the move through the town, heading north.

Hancock was not yet on the march as part of a larger movement by the entire Federal army, but Stuart did not know that. He had, barely six hours into his "audacious expedition," encountered exactly what General Lee had intended as the trigger for him to turn back and place his command on the right flank of the northward marching Confederate infantry. Jeb either didn't realize that was Lee's expectation or just didn't see it the same way. Instead of turning back he first sent a message to General Lee advising him of what he had discovered. Then he set up artillery and began shelling the Federals.

If the message to Lee made it through, the commanding general did not mention it in his official report, which he wrote the following January, and Major H.B. McClellan wrote after the war that "It is plain from General Lee's report that the messenger did not reach him; and unfortunately the dispatch was not duplicated." That the message was important is obvious from McClellan's next observation, that it would "have gone far to disclose to him [Lee] the intentions of the enemy."[8]

The very first shot fired by the Horse Artillery hit a Federal caisson, always a desired target, and the result was satisfying. The Yankees' artillery ammunition exploded, pieces of wheels and wood flew into the air, horses stampeded, and infantrymen scattered like a flock of pigeons. Stuart was delighted, and shouted "Good shot!"

The Yankees returned the fire. There was fighting but not many casualties. One of Engineer Officer William W. Blackford's two horses, Manassas, was wounded, and Stuart took some prisoners. From them he may have learned that Hancock's Corps was only changing camps, at least as far as the prisoners knew, which was what Stuart would have wanted to believe.

He waited for a while for Hancock to get out of the way, then made a detour around the flank of the Federal column to Buckland. Already his plan for where to cross the Potomac into Maryland had to be altered. This was no small matter, and it was the first of several reasons why Stuart was absent so long from Lee's army.

It began to rain and the Rebels went into bivouac near a large mansion belonging to a doctor who was an acquaintance of Stuart's. Naturally the general and his staff were invited to dine with the family and naturally they accepted. There was an excellent meal served by attractive young ladies of the family who, after placing the bowls and platters on the table took positions, like servants, behind the chairs of the guests. Stuart noticed and declared that the universal laws of nature demanded a reversal. The young ladies were seated and the Confederate officers laughingly served them.

It was still raining and Stuart was invited to spend the night in the house but he declined and directed that his blankets be spread beneath a tree not far away. Many of his staff slept on the porch.[9]

The appearance of Hancock across Stuart's path caused yet another unexpected complication for Stuart at this point. After delivering his information and recommendations on the 23rd, Mosby had ridden back into enemy territory to do additional scouting, and was returning to report to Stuart again when he found Hancock between him and his chief. After observing awhile and rejecting the idea of trying to sneak through the masses of blue soldiers, Mosby came to the conclusion that Stuart would logically turn back and rejoin Lee's army, so that is what Mosby did. Not only did Stuart not turn back but, hoping that Mosby would soon rejoin him, he dawdled at Buckland a total of ten hours—time he did not have to waste—before moving on again.

Had he turned back in order to cross the Potomac on the west side of the Blue Ridge, there were 60 miles of mountainous road between him and Shepherdstown, the nearest ford that side of the mountains, which would take two days to reach. Instead, without consulting anyone, he moved east on the 26th of June toward Wolf Run Shoals and from there toward Fairfax Court House. In addition to having to find a different route than originally planned, fodder for the horses was short, and it was necessary to halt several times each day to allow them to graze, even though the countryside was so denuded of grass and vegetation by two years of war that there was very little grazing to be done.

Lee's army, by then, was in Pennsylvania, marching steadily. It was deep inside "Yankeedom," and whereas the majorities of the populations of various towns in Maryland were occupied by "secesh," that was certainly not the case in Pennsylvania. Lt. Col. E. Porter Alexander, riding beside the caissons, limbers and guns of Lee's artillery noted the frequent display of U.S. flags hanging from houses, and about which he philosophized in a manner as relevant in modern times as it was in 1863. Of the U.S. flags he wrote that "our men took not the slightest notice," but the same could not be said of Federal troops "everywhere and always, during the war & since—almost to this very day. It is a feeling I cannot myself understand, but it is like the feeling with which fervent believers in some religions regard the emblems of faith of other sects, & seek to insult and destroy them—as the old Spanish priests would an idol or Scotch covenanter would a cross."

Porter recorded a less weighty anecdote, recalling that at one Chambersburg house "a good looking stout Dutch girl" came to the front gate of her home and waved a small U.S. flag "defiantly . . . [and] in an excess of zeal," brandishing it in the faces of the passing Rebels until one of them, a member of Parker's battery "with quite a reputation as a wag," came along. He stopped directly in front of her, stared at her for a moment and "then gave a sort of jump at her & shouted 'Boo.'" She scampered back to her porch as a roar of laughter and cheers went up all along the Confederate column.[10]

Stuart and his men spent the night of June 26–27 between Brentsville and Wolf Run Shoals and before light on the 27th they pressed on toward Fairfax Courthouse. Along the way three of Stuart's staff officers, Henry McClellan, Andrew Venable, and John Esten Cooke, left the column to try and find a blacksmith to get their horses shod. About a mile east of Fairfax Station, a few miles short of Fairfax Court House, they found one who was not only anxious to assist, but who had a wife willing to making them a memorable breakfast. She presented real coffee, sweet meats, different kinds of bread, butter, cream and, best of all, cherry pies.

The three officers were enraptured, and were just beginning to assault the meal when riders in blue uniforms came into view. They were galloping, however, and looked to Cooke like they intended to ride right by. But Venable was taking no chances. He bridled his horse and mounted, as did McClellan, while Cooke decided to wait until his horse was shod.

That decision lasted about 20 seconds. Another group of Federals appeared from another direction, running straight for the house, pistols drawn.

Venable and McClellan selected opposite escape paths and Cooke jumped on his horse and selected a third. Demands that they halt were followed by shots, but all three reached safety, jumping fences, riding through swamps, and dashing through woods along the way.[11]

Stuart, meanwhile, was approaching Fairfax Court House, where a classic case of mistaken identity occurred. A squadron of the 11th New York Cavalry commanded by Major S. Pierre Remington was passing through the town on its way back to the Washington D.C. defenses, where they were assigned. When the advance guard of Stuart's column, consisting of about 20 men, approached the town in a stand of woods, Remington mistook them for some of Mosby's men, and he ordered a charge.

The Confederate advance guard fell back out of the woods and Remington's squadron of 82 men came roiling out, just as a squadron of the 1st North Carolina of Hampton's brigade appeared on the scene. The Yankees came on at a gallop with pistols and sabers drawn. The Tarheels were surprised, and for a few moments the Federals not only held their own but managed to shoot down or capture some of the Rebels directly in their front. Then the rest of the 1st North Carolina arrived.

Within a moment the Federals were surrounded, the Rebels opened fire and men and horses—nearly all of the Federal horses—fell. Of the 82 New Yorkers who made the charge, four were killed, 21 were wounded, and the other 57, as well as the wounded, were captured.[12] It was a gallant little affair, but now Stuart had Federal prisoners to slow him down.

At Fairfax Court House Stuart's men found much-needed provisions, and Hampton's men also captured a small train of sutler's wagons and a small enemy cavalry escort in nearby Annandale. Of particular interest in the town were two warehouses filled with luxuries—canned fruit, ginger cakes, figs, tobacco, canned sardines and oysters, sugar, lemons, cheese, crackers, butter, and molasses—as well as shoes, socks, hats, gloves, civilian clothes, and Federal uniforms. The Rebels fell on the stores like locusts on a field of wheat. A large supply of white straw hats and white cotton gloves were particularly popular and hundreds of Rebels exited the warehouses wearing both. Even Stuart accepted and donned a pair of the gloves, ate some dried figs and enjoyed some lemonade prepared by his men.

It was a grand and satisfying experience, but it ate up more precious time. In 48 hours Stuart had covered only 35 miles. The rich food and fine new clothes were no help for the horses, which were breaking down in a steady stream, littering the road behind the column with men leading limping chargers, gradually eroding the strength of Stuart's command.

After taking the town, Stuart sent another dispatch to Lee reporting, "I took possession of Fairfax C. H. this morning at nine o'clock, together with a large quantity of stores. The main body of Hooker's army has gone toward Leesburg, except the garrison of Alexandria and Washington, which has retreated within the fortifications."[13]

Again, it isn't clear whether this message reached General Lee. The fact that the main body of Hooker's army was moving toward Leesburg, which was on the Potomac River, would have been valuable news, but Lee did not mention learning of it in his official report, and while it isn't apparent how Stuart could have known such information about the entire Federal army, it is likely he had other far-ranging scouts besides Mosby to provide it. Interestingly, a duplicate of the message did reach Richmond, as its contents were recorded in the diary of War Department clerk John B. Jones on July 1.

The Rebels rode on, and finally reached the Potomac. After being absent from Lee's army for four days, they still had not crossed into enemy territory. They left Virginia and entered Maryland at a little known crossing called Rowser's Ford late that night. It was not an easy task.

The Confederates could not cross wherever they might have wanted. The river was nearly a mile wide, its banks in many places were steep, the current was swift, and the water was deep. In addition, the known crossings were well guarded by the enemy. Stuart dispatched Captain Richard B. Kennon, an assistant adjutant general who had served on his staff since April to find the best place to cross.

Kennon served with the 4th Virginia Cavalry in 1861 and acted as a courier for Stuart at First Manassas, where a bullet ricocheted off his saber scabbard which left a dent he never had repaired or replaced, as it was a nice little proof of his having been in battle. He later became a lieutenant in the 8th Virginia before joining Jeb's staff, and he shared an odd sort of coincidence with his commander. Whereas Stuart was married to the daughter of Union brigadier general Phillip St. George Cooke, Kennan was married to the daughter of Confederate brigadier general Phillip St. George Cocke.[14]

Rowser's Ford was crossable and there did not seem to be enemy pickets on the far side, but the water was two feet higher than normal, and Kennon scouted downriver to look for something better. The only ford he found was worse. Not only were the banks steep and rocky, but there was quicksand and water too deep for the artillery. Kennon returned to Rowser's Ford and swam it, but it was so deep and the river so wide that he had to stop more than once and dismount on a rock to let his horse rest, which it sometimes did while still swimming. Once across, he turned around and went back, where he found Stuart waiting for him. Jeb gave him a bear hug, saying he never expected to see him again, after which Kennon reported that the crossing was deep and swift and probably was not usable for the artillery.

Stuart didn't have many options, however, and decided to try it, but first he had six of the Federal prisoners taken earlier in the day—quartermaster and commissary clerks unaccustomed to hard campaigning—cross under the theory that if they could make it anyone could. They did, but the water was so deep in places that it swept over their saddle pommels, meaning that the artillery pieces, limbers, and caissons would become totally submerged and all of the gunpowder would be soaked and ruined during the trip over.

The solution was to park the caissons at the edge of the river and to hand each horseman—the 3rd Virginia crossed first—a shell, cartridge, or bag of powder to carry and keep dry. The troopers grumbled, but did as they were told, and as each reached the far side he handed down his ordnance so that it could be piled up to await the artillery.

The crossing took hours, but there were no Federals on the far side to oppose them, and by 3 a.m. the rear guard was across.

Had Stuart opted back in Buckland to march to and cross at Shepherd-stown he would, once across, have been only 30 miles, one full day's ride, from Gettysburg. As it was, he was then twice as far from the little town, now at least two days away and possibly three at the rate he was going. He had been absent from the main body of the army for four days during the most critical campaign of the war. However, as Jeb saw it, the real fun and the opportunity to redeem himself was just beginning.

Each of the delays, detours and decisions foreshadow what is now known—that Stuart was not going to be where he would be needed, nor even close. Contemporary accounts from Lee's headquarters were that the commanding general was already asking his subordinates if anyone had heard from Stuart or knew his whereabouts. Lee expected him to return any day. Had he known that he would not see Jeb until July 2, four more days away, he would have directed Jenkins, or possibly Robertson or Jones, to assume the role—eyes of the army—that was traditionally Stuart's. Lee was unaware of Stuart's whereabouts, however, and did not make any such arrangements. He simply expected word from Stuart at any moment and continued to do so.

Lee cannot be excused for that failure, of course. For all he knew Stuart and his command had been killed or captured and would never return. Not only did he have other cavalry available to reconnoiter, but he could have sent out any number of individual scouts who very well may have been more effective at finding and reporting the position of the enemy than three noisy, hard-to-ignore brigades of cavalry, regardless of who commanded them. Still, finding fault with Lee does not excuse Stuart.

There was no foreshadowing of doom in Jeb's mind. In all likelihood, his attitude was exactly as it was described by eighteen-year-old Theodore Garnett, a future staff officer who was then serving as a courier and a clerk from the 9th Virginia, and who was on the scene to observe Stuart's attitude: "Raiding was Stuart's hobby and one which he rode with never failing persistence. . . . What a glorious opportunity was now offered for the indulgence of his love! What a tempting prize lay within his reach. . . . Here was an undertaking which . . . would eclipse in brilliance and real importance any exploit of the war."[15]

To his credit, Stuart at least wrote in his official report a month later that on the 28th he "realized the importance of joining our army in Pennsylvania" and resumed the march northward as though heading straight for it. Lee's army, however, was west of Stuart, not north.

Once the sun came up, the visible transformation resulting from crossing the river was startling. "Oh what a change!" wrote Blackford. "From the hoof-trodden, war-wasted lands of old Virginia to a country fresh and plentiful."[16] That meant, however, that the horses were all that much more anxious to graze. As Blackford recorded, his favorite horse, Magic, had not had a mouthful of grain in days and was "thin as a snake," so much so that he rode the wounded Manassas and led Magic, "saving her for the big battle that we knew was coming."[17]

On the other side of the river was the C&O Canal, a vital supply line from Washington, D.C. to Hooker's army. It was filled with canal boats, many carrying passengers and more than a few Federal officers. It was another valuable Federal resource that could not be left intact. Stuart's method for putting it out of commission was to first assist the passengers from the boats and to help them unload their baggage, to then turn all of the canal boats sideways, or across the canal, open the sluice gates and drain the canal into the Potomac, leaving the boats stranded and the canal empty.

From one of the Federal officers they learned the interesting news that Hooker was no longer in command of the Army of the Potomac, and had been replaced by Maj. Gen. George Gordon Meade. The news was welcome. Anything that kept the enemy off-balance and potentially ill-prepared was good for the Confederates.

They rode on toward Rockville, which was on the main road to Washington, D.C., and there discovered what would prove to do more damage to Stuart, and therefore Lee and the Army of Northern Virginia, than any other factor during Stuart's raid. Oddly, it appeared to Jeb Stuart to be the single greatest accomplishment of the raid—a Federal wagon train of 140 brand new vehicles that stretched along the road for eight miles. It was bound for Hooker's army, laden with supplies—mostly oats and hay—each wagon pulled by four fat mules wearing brand new harness. It was exactly the type of item Jeb knew that the thousands of mules and horses of Lee's army needed desperately. As one of Stuart's officers recalled, "Such a train we had never seen before and did not see again."[18]

Most of the teamsters were only lightly armed, if at all, and upon seeing the gray-clad horsemen, they began whipping their mule teams into a run. Some attempted to stay on the road and outrun the Confederates while others swung around and tried to make a dash back to Washington. Still others struck out across country. Wagons and teams crashed into each other, became entangled, or overturned, winding up in dramatic wrecks of one to four wagons lying on top of or beside kicking, braying mules held in place by their harness. Drivers were yelling, cursing, and lashing their terrified teams. The scene was madness. John Esten Cooke described it as "grotesque."

Stuart shouted for volunteers to follow and then he led the charge. Rebel horsemen galloped into the middle of the scene, some shouting "Halt! Halt! Halt!" while others fired away with carbines and pistols. A lieutenant of the 2nd South Carolina, Thomas Lee, and four men dashed to the rear of the train and routed the rear guard. When Thomas overtook the last of these, he was close enough to Washington, D.C. to see its outer defenses.

When the wild chase and capture were over, 125 undamaged vehicles were in the hands of the Rebels. Of course it was then necessary to stop and feed the famished Confederate horses, and as Blackford wrote, "It did one's heart good to see the way the poor brutes got on the outside of those oats." Once the horses had eaten their fill, the troopers filled their grain bags, and sometimes saddlebags, with more grain.

In addition to the oats and fodder, some wagons contained food—hardtack, ham, bacon, and whiskey—as well as eating utensils and miscellaneous useful items. The Confederates found them "most acceptable."[19]

At that point, Stuart saw an opportunity that might do more to restore his tarnished reputation than anything else in the world—an attack on Washington, D.C. They were only six miles from Georgetown, and it was entirely possible that the capital city's defenses were lightly manned. Stuart could not know it but his approach to the city had already caused a panic, and the news on the street was that ten to twelve thousand of the enemy were on the outskirts of town, burning a huge supply train and preparing to attack, while almost all of the city's defenders had been dispatched to Meade's army. Clerks from all government departments were given rifles and rushed to the earthworks surrounding the capital. A gunboat on the river was alerted to stand by and receive the members of the President's cabinet and other ranking officials.

Stuart considered the idea seriously enough to take a courier and ride to the end of the wagon train to reconnoiter. He studied the situation and considered the feasibility, but finally rejected the idea. In his subsequent report he wrote:

> I calculated that before the next brigade could march this distance and reach the defenses of Washington, it would be after dark; the troops there would have had time to march to position to meet attack on this road. To attack at night with cavalry, particularly unless certain of surprise, would have been extremely hazardous; to wait till morning, would have lost much time from my march to join General Lee, without the probability of compensating results. I therefore determined after getting the wagons under way, to proceed directly north, so as to cut the Baltimore and Ohio Railroad (now becoming the enemy's main war artery) that night.[20]

The causes of delay were not finished. With the wagons, Stuart had captured more than 400 Federal soldiers, some of them officers, and the latter petitioned Jeb to be paroled. Jeb consented. It was the courteous, proper thing to do, never mind that the printing and processing of the paroles consumed all of the night of the 28th and part of the morning of the 29th.

While the paroles were still being processed, Fitz Lee took his brigade before dawn in the direction of Baltimore to the B&O Railroad, where he tore up the track at Hood's Mill, burned a bridge at Sykesville, and cut the telegraph line that provided direct communication between Washington and the Army of the Potomac.

Getting the wagon train back in line and ready to move was no small task. Soldiers had to be detailed as drivers and their horses assigned to a herd. Seeing the unbelievable length of the train, a decision was made to shorten it by taking two mules from each team of four and placing them in another herd which, like the herd of horses, required troopers to guard and drive.[21] While that may have seemed wise in the short run, in the long run it caused additional delay as the two-mule teams wore out more quickly and fresh ones had to be caught, harnessed and put in their place.

As the huge, unwieldy column rolled through Rockville, a different type of stampede occurred, more enjoyable but causing additional delay. The town contained a large female academy, and dozens of its fetching young scholars, or at least all who proclaimed Southern sympathies that day, congregated on the road in front of Stuart's column. Cooke described them in his characteristic manner as "the fairest specimens of the gentler sex as the eye ever beheld," consisting of "gaily coloured dresses, low necks, bare arms and wildernesses of braids and curls."[22] They clamored for souvenirs, and began snipping off buttons from uniforms, locks of hair, and hanks of mane. A girl of about sixteen happily pulled hair from the mane of Cooke's mount, declaring the animal to be "a Secession horse." Jeb delighted in the scene, this sort of thing being to his way of thinking the very object of life and warfare.

Stuart had previously calculated that he would reach Hanover by the morning of June 28, and had he done so there might never have been any recriminations for his absence, but it was then the afternoon of June 29 and he was still a day away.

The next town after Rockville was Westminster, and the Confederates arrived there about 5 p.m. The town was occupied by 95 Federals, two companies of the 1st Delaware Cavalry, commanded by Major Napoleon Bonaparte Knight, who on this occasion failed to live up to his gallant name.

The 1st Delaware had spent the war so far in the defenses of Baltimore, and in addition to being hopelessly outnumbered and having no combat experience, Knight had a dirty little secret. He had, when the war began, enlisted in the Confederate army, then deserted and joined the 1st Delaware.

On the afternoon of June 29, he was dealing with his problems by occupying a seat in a local tavern, worrying about what might happen to him if he was captured by the Confederates, and becoming progressively more intoxicated.

This meant that the titular commander of the two companies was Captain Charles Corbit, who was more pugnacious than he was cautious. Unlike Remington and the squadron of the 11th New York at Fairfax Court House, Corbit could not claim to have mistaken Stuart for Mosby. He knew who and what he was dealing with. Nevertheless, when the advance guard of Stuart's long column appeared, Corbit ordered "draw sabers," directed his bugler to sound the "Charge"—not the Hollywood version that originated in 1874, but the 1847 version consisting only of Male High C quarter notes and eighth notes—and advanced, from walk to the trot, from the trot to the gallop, from the gallop to the charge.

Corbit did not even have all 95 men of the two companies, about 25 of whom were deployed around the town as pickets, but the 70 blue horsemen charged as gallantly, and foolishly, as any cavalry ever did. His reason for attacking isn't clear. He probably hoped to slow the Confederates, and he may have become inspired by the townspeople, who were decidedly pro-Union. Women lined the streets to cheer his men on, and men gathered in windows or behind the corners of buildings facing the approaching Rebels and fired muskets and squirrel rifles at them.

The attack surprised the Confederates, who were some of Fitz Lee's men. They recoiled, confused, and then counterattacked. The result was the only one it could be. Corbit's men were overwhelmed, sent running, and then captured. Three of the 70 escaped, Corbit not being one of them. One who did get away was Major Knight.

More provisions were obtained in the town, as was more delay. After the fighting and securing of captured supplies, there being plenty of room in the wagons for them, the Confederates continued to Union Mills and camped for the night.

If Stuart was attempting to repeat his triumphs of the first two rides around the Federal army, he seemed to have forgotten how to do so. Each of his previous raids had been made by troopers specifically chosen for the expedition based on their endurance and particularly the good condition of their horses. The first of the two, in June 1862, began as a reconnaissance and evolved into the famous ride when the opportunity arose, but Stuart and his men were required to cover as much ground as possible, were closely pursued, and were nearly captured. The second, in October 1862, was partly for the purpose of information-gathering but also in order to capture as many horses and supplies as possible. It was organized specifically for the latter purpose, with the men assigned to separate groups for the purpose of fanning out and seizing mounts and foodstuffs, for herding and protecting what was captured, and for combat. It also involved quick, steady movement and close pursuit.

Now Stuart's raiders were simply the soldiers of three brigades selected with no premeditation in regard to endurance and certainly not for the fitness of their mounts. They were moving in enemy territory with no clear goal other than to do damage and then hook back up with Lee's army, and they moved along as though there was very little need to hurry. This latter fact was due in part to a lack of close pursuit, and on this expedition the only pursuers were 300 troopers from the 2nd Massachusetts Cavalry, who arrived at Rockville in time to see the 12 or 15 wagons that had been wrecked and then set afire by the Rebels, but who lacked enough strength to do more than dog the gray raiders.

Just north of Union Mills, where Stuart's men camped for the night, was a road that went directly to Gettysburg. Stuart did not have any reason to think he needed to go there, of course, as he'd received no more communication from Lee than Lee had received from him. Still, had he turned left onto that road, he probably could have reached Gettysburg on the 30th not long after Federal cavalry under John Buford arrived at 11 a.m. Maj. Gen. Henry Heth sent a portion of his division toward Gettysburg that day, so in all likelihood Stuart would have linked up with Lee's army at that place, been in a position to drive away Buford's videttes, and to then look for and discover the approach of John Reynolds' Corps on July 1. Lee could have been dug in on Cemetery Ridge, or he might have gathered his force at a stronger position nearer Cashtown and let the Federal army, now under Meade's command, batter itself to pieces in a scenario not shockingly dissimilar to Fredericksburg or Malvern Hill. That is not, of course, what happened.

Instead, on the morning of the 30th Stuart led his men to Hanover, which was even closer—fifteen miles—to Gettysburg than Union Mills, arriving about noon. There he ran into Judson Kilpatrick's division of Federal cavalry. Naturally, Stuart attacked.

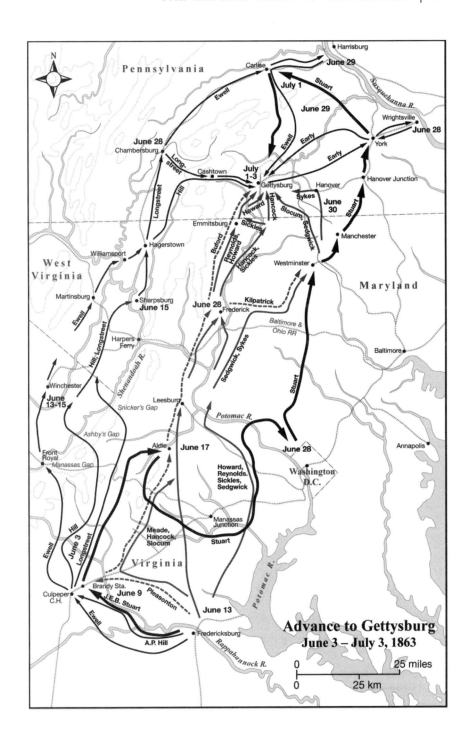

Advance to Gettysburg
June 3 – July 3, 1863

The first charge was made by the 2nd North Carolina. The Tarheels managed to drive the Federals from the town, but a brigade under Brig. Gen. Elon J. Farnsworth rallied and counterattacked, driving the North Carolinians back. Hampton's brigade was separated from the fight by the length of the wagon train and Fitz Lee was on the left flank, leaving only Chambliss, who had the smallest brigade, to engage the enemy.

Stuart, of course, was in the middle of the action, and when he saw an enemy column bearing down on him along a road lined on each side with high hedges, he laughed, shouted, "Rally them, Blackford," to his engineer, and leapt his bay mare, Virginia, over one of the lower hedges. Blackford, now on Magic, managed to follow. They were then in a field of tall Timothy grass, but there were Yankees on the other side of the hedge as well as in the road, and the two Confederates were only about ten paces away from a party of 25 or 30 of them.

Stuart and Blackford took off with the Federals in hot pursuit, and neither of the Rebel officers saw the fifteen-foot-wide, fifteen-feet-deep gully until they were almost in it. Virginia and Magic were thoroughbreds, however, and first Stuart then Blackford flew into the air and over the ditch. As Magic leaped, Blackford turned his head toward Stuart and the sight of "this beautiful animal away up in mid-air over the chasm and Stuart's fine figure sitting erect and firm in the saddle" remained captured in his mind thereafter as a Mayfly in amber.

The pursuing Yankees screeched to a halt at the edge of the gully, some nearly flying over their horses' heads.

Stuart rode to a hill in order to direct the fire of a battery of Horse Artillery at the enemy. Blackford took a path that wound around the base of the same hill at a walk, intending to cool Magic a little. He was confident he was out of danger, so that he didn't turn around to look when he heard the clatter of hooves behind him, thinking it was a companion. When the horse behind didn't slow he finally turned, almost too late, and saw a Yankee sergeant bearing down on him with his saber extended straight ahead, not more than two horse lengths away, intending to run him through. Blackford spurred Magic to the right and as she jumped the saber blade passed between Blackford's left arm and his side. By the time he had gathered his senses and control of his horse the Federal sergeant was fifty yards away, still galloping, and a little party of the Yankee's comrades on a hill not far away raised a cheer at Blackford's expense. The only thing he knew to do was shake his fist at them.

Once Wade Hampton was up, he directed dismounted sharpshooters to pick off any of the enemy who were visible. Fitz Lee, in the meantime, ran into George Custer's Union brigade and captured several prisoners, including some of Kilpatrick's staff. The wagons were gathered into a "close park," in case it became necessary to burn them. Things might have been different in the Civil War had someone done so.

Instead, late in the afternoon, Stuart sent Fitz Lee with the wagon train toward Jefferson and York, Pennsylvania, fully expecting to make contact there with Jubal Early's division. Actually he was taking his cavalry further from Lee's army. By that time nearly 400 more prisoners had been taken since the paroling of that same number after the capture of the wagon train, and they were loaded into the wagons, some conscripted as drivers. With Hampton and Chambliss, Stuart remained until he was certain that Kilpatrick was not going to take the offensive, and then departed, still heading north, toward Dover.

Fitz Lee's progress with the wagon train was neither easy nor steady. The mules were tired, hungry, thirsty and surly. The Confederate troopers were exhausted and they became careless. The Federal prisoners did not tend to be helpful. Often a driver would go to sleep on his seat, or a Yankee driver would pretend to do so, the mules would stop, and every wagon behind would do likewise. Officers, just as tired as the men, had to constantly urge the train to keep moving, which it was expected to do all night. Stuart even wrote of his prize, "Our wagon train was now a subject of serious embarrassment."[23]

Both Fitz Lee and Stuart rode all night, by then fully aware that they had been absent from Lee's army much too long. Although the Federals contented themselves with tracking their movements instead of attacking, the Rebels had no choice but to expect an assault at any time. The night was particularly dark, and as Stuart reported later, "After a series of exciting combats and night marches, it was a severe tax to their [his men's] endurance. Whole regiments slept in the saddle, their faithful animals keeping the road unguided. In some instances they fell from their horses, overcome with physical fatigue and sleepiness."[24]

Stuart arrived at Dover on the morning of July 1, hoping and expecting to find it occupied by Confederate infantry. Instead, he was told that General Early had been there but had marched off in the direction of Shippensburg. Frustrated, he dispatched Major A.R. Venable to find Early's or anybody else's Confederate infantry and, later in the day, sent Lt. Henry Lee, Fitz Lee's younger brother and a member of his staff, to Gettysburg for the same purpose.

After a brief rest the Confederate column pressed on, northwest now, through Dillsburg toward Carlisle, hoping that was where they would find the army. Despite having gotten provisions at Fairfax and Westminster, the men were again out of rations, and Jeb intended to "levy a contribution on the inhabitants" of Carlisle. Instead, he found two brigades of enemy militia—infantry and artillery—under the command of Brig. Gen. W.F. "Baldy" Smith in possession of the town and dug in as though ready for a siege.[25] Stuart sent a demand for unconditional surrender under a white flag, and when it was refused he shelled the city for several hours and set fire to the U.S. Cavalry Barracks, but was unable to take the town.

Stuart admitted in his report that "The whereabouts of our army was still a mystery," but finally, as he was about to disengage from the fight at Carlisle, he received a dispatch from General Lee. Venable had located Ewell's Second Corps and been directed to Lee's headquarters in Gettysburg, where he was then directed to return to Carlisle and summon Stuart at once. The distance between Gettysburg and Carlisle was about 30 miles, so Venable earned his paycheck that July 1st. He'd seen that the army was fighting a major battle at Gettysburg and reported it to Stuart, who immediately directed all three of his brigades to march to that place and started the ride himself that night.

That ended Stuart's pre-Gettysburg raid, and a better summary of it than Blackford's description as an expedition unequaled for audacious boldness is probably that of the commander of Company D of the 3rd Virginia Cavalry of Fitz Lee's brigade, Captain John M. Lamb. When asked to describe it, all he could think to say was "We had not slept for six nights save on horseback and horses and men were more dead than alive."[26]

A popular story is that when Stuart finally reached Lee a little before noon the next day, the commanding general was furious, and raised his hand as if to strike Stuart, demanding to know where he had been. In response Stuart, wilting, told him that he had brought him a train of more than a hundred wagons and their teams, to which Lee replied, "Yes General, but they are an impediment to me now," after which Lee softened and told Stuart he needed his help in the battle, and that they would not discuss the matter further.

In the movie version, Stuart arrived past midnight during the night of July 2–3, Lee directed his staff that he and Jeb not be disturbed, and then informed Jeb that some very fine officers in the army had concluded that Stuart had let them all down. To this Stuart demanded names so that he could defend his honor. Lee, after telling Jeb there was no time for such matters, reminded him that his orders were to protect the army from the enemy's cavalry and to keep it informed of the enemy's movements, which he had apparently not understood. He then lectured him sternly about his role and his failure, in response to which Stuart drew his saber and attempted to give it to Lee and resign his commission. This caused Lee to slam his fist on a table and shout "I told you there is no time for that," after which he calmed, told Stuart he would need his fine services, that the matter was concluded, and that they would speak no more of it.

Movies must convey a great deal of information to an audience in a short period of time with a minimum of narrative. Sometimes the writers of letters attempt to do the same thing when writing to admirers about things that happened long ago. The truth is that there is simply no reliable support in the historical record for either version of the popular story.

The first of the two versions of the Lee/Stuart meeting came from a letter written by Colonel Thomas T. Munford, commander of the 2nd Virginia Cavalry, in 1915, to a Mrs. Charles Hyde of Lookout Mountain, Tennessee, when Munford was 84 years old. Munford was not at the meeting between Lee and Stuart, being still about 20 miles away on the ride from Carlisle, but he attributed the account to Major Henry B. McClellan, who *might* have been there.

The movie version is from *Gettysburg*, based on Michael Shaara's *The Killer Angels*, but the movie departs considerably from the book, which was fiction and which had Lee telling Stuart only that they had all been worried about him.

The only part of the two scenarios that is accurate is the part about their—Lee and Stuart—speaking no more of it. They didn't, assuming there was anything of which to speak.

If any of Lee's staff were present when the two met—and Charles Marshall may have been—none left a written record. Considering that Marshall despised Stuart and blamed him for the loss of the war, it seems likely he would have gleefully reported seeing Lee chastise Stuart. Similarly, if any of Stuart's staff were present, none ever wrote or spoke of it directly. It is possible, even probable, that none of Stuart's staff were present.

Andrew R. Venable, Jr. (not to be confused with Charles S. Venable of Lee's staff) is a top contender for having been there, but if he rode all the way back to Gettysburg with Stuart, doing so would have added another 30 miles on top of the 60 or so he'd covered since departing from Dover less than 24 hours previously. He would have needed a couple of spare horses and a constitution of titanium.

Blackford wrote, "We started from Carlisle about one o'clock A.M. on July 2 and effected a junction with our army at Gettysburg early in the day." He mentions being sent to Lee's headquarters later that evening, waiting half an hour to see the general while chatting with Lee's staff officers and observing Lee come out of his tent and hurrying to the rear several times in that short period of time. Lee seemed to be weak and in pain, but in a rush, and Blackford finally asked what the problem was. He was told that the commanding general was "suffering a good deal from an attack of diarrhea."[27] Had Blackford been present when Stuart and Lee met earlier in the day, he would have recorded it.[28]

John Esten Cooke provided a little more detail, saying that Stuart and his staff passed mile after mile asleep in the saddle and at dawn Jeb dismounted in a clump of trees, said he was going to sleep for two hours and that "everybody imitated him." When Cooke was awakened by one of the couriers Stuart was already gone, having slept his two hours and ridden on alone, "a wandering Major General in the heart of Pennsylvania."[29]

Major McClellan wrote only that "Stuart withdrew from Carlisle and proceeded in the same direction [toward Gettysburg]" and "Stuart himself, with Fitz Lee's and Chambliss's commands, reached Gettysburg on the afternoon of the 2d, and took position on the Confederate left."[30]

The letter from Munford to Mrs. Hyde was written eleven years after McClellan's death. Not only does it provide information that McClellan never published, in a manner inconsistent with what the careful McClellan did record, but it included specific quotes. Lee raised his arm and demanded

"General Stuart, where have you been?! I have not heard a word from you for days, and you the eyes and ears of my army." Stuart responded, in regard to the wagons, and Lee asserted they were an impediment. Munford also wrote that McClellan said the meeting was "painful beyond description."

It might have happened. McClellan and Munford corresponded after the war at least once,[31] and McClellan included enough detail about the movements and actions of Munford in his book to make it obvious that he considered the Colonel to be reliable and to suggest that the pair exchanged additional communication. Yet McClellan, among all of Stuart's staff, wrote more and in greater detail defending Stuart against charges that he let Lee down, disobeyed orders, or had any choice in doing what he did during his June 25–July 1 escapade. Perhaps he did so because he witnessed the scene that was painful beyond description and kept it bottled up for the rest of his life, except for that one time he blurted it out to Munford. Perhaps Munford wondered for half a century what Lee and Stuart talked about, imagined what the script might have been, and by age 84 could no longer distinguish between memory and imagination. Then again, maybe the elderly Munford asked someone younger to write the letter and that person decided to jazz it up for Mrs. Hyde.

If it did happen the way Munford described, Stuart did not let it show to those around him, not even Flora, but it would have sobered him inwardly more than any newspaper article, whispered criticism, or detractor's accusations. Being chastised by Robert E. Lee would have cut the young cavalry leader to the quick.

There can be no doubt that Lee was disappointed and chagrined at Stuart's absence. His report, filed the following January, contains the statements "The movements of the army preceding the battle of Gettysburg had been much embarrassed by the absence of the cavalry," and "It was expected that as soon as the Federal Army should cross the Potomac, General Stuart would give notice of its movements, and nothing having been heard from him since our entrance into Maryland, it was inferred that the enemy had not yet left Virginia." Similarly, there can be no doubt that Stuart was aware that he had disappointed, if not outright failed Lee, and his report included the statement, "It was thought by many that my command could have rendered more service had it been in advance of the army the first day at Gettysburg, and the commanding general complains of a want of cavalry on the occasion. . . ."

However, focusing only on Lee and Stuart's reunion on July 2, the "traditional" version of what Lee said was, "Well, General, you are here at last." This account, however, appears to have its origin in John Thomason's 1930 biography of Stuart, and although Thomason was provided with a great deal of information for his book by the Stuart family, the statement must still be regarded as secondary rather than primary. Nevertheless, such words spoken by Robert E. Lee were clearly a rebuke that Stuart would have recognized.

Whatever was actually said, there are three facts that argue against Lee becoming very emotionally involved with Stuart at that particular time. First, he had a battle to fight and there was plenty on his mind about how he should do so. Second, as of July 2, early afternoon, he had no reason to be pessimistic about how the battle was going or to feel a need to blame anyone for what was happening. To the contrary, the Confederates had soundly defeated the Federals the day before, and Lee was expecting the same on July 2. His absolute confidence in the army might have become eroded by late afternoon on July 3, but it was at its zenith on the 2nd. Third, as Blackford and other officers noted, Lee was suffering from acute diarrhea. Lee may have been peckish, out of sorts and in a mood to snap or inflict a meeting that was "painful beyond belief" on Stuart or any number of people, but that particular abdominal syndrome probably made him feel more like crawling off in a hole rather than crossing swords with his cavalry commander.

The various debates over the years about whether Stuart was responsible for Lee getting into, and losing, the Battle of Gettysburg[32] were preceded by sometimes virulent exchanges between ranking former Confederate officers on the subject. During the 1870s through the early 20th Century. Henry Heth, John Mosby, Cadmus Wilcox, Charles Marshall, Walter Taylor, James Longstreet, Jubal Early, Edward P. Alexander, Henry B. McClellan and others penned criticism or defense of Stuart. Every biographer of Stuart has, of course, been required to defend, explain away, or condemn what Stuart did between June 24 and July 2, 1863. Those authors' conclusions, frames of reference, and theses are nearly as varied as the number of authors—it was clearly Stuart's fault; it was entirely Robert E. Lee's fault; Stuart failed to follow orders; Stuart followed orders to a "tee" but circumstances intervened; Lee had all the cavalry he needed but failed to utilize them; Stuart was at fault for leaving Lee with cavalry under such lackluster commanders; Stuart's activities had no bearing on the battle or its outcome; it was everybody's fault, etc. ad nauseam.

While some of Stuart's critics are fairly shrill in their denunciations— Major Charles Marshall of Lee's staff said Stuart should have been court-martialed and shot—the majority were much less vitriolic. Even Jubal Early, who was never known for reining in his tongue or giving a pass to someone he considered at fault, wrote that it was difficult for him to perceive what more Stuart could have done had he stayed with the army that could not be accomplished by individual scouts, whereas his movement through the enemy's rear area "greatly perplexed and bewildered the Federal commanders, and compelled them to move slower."[33]

Historians report history, laymen lay blame. There is not a new, startling theory to present that will change anything or make any xenophobic Rebels or hagiographic defenders of Stuart rest easy. The fact is that Lee learned to rely on Stuart to bring him vital information, expected him to do the same during the Gettysburg campaign, and was dismayed when it didn't happen. Stuart didn't disobey orders, but he was too preoccupied with restoring the reputation that had been damaged in the weeks preceding Gettysburg. He didn't intend to leave Lee in the dark, thought he'd provided him all the cavalry he needed, and thought he'd kept him informed, by courier, of his location and what he'd learned about the movements of the Army of the Potomac. Plans went awry, Hancock caused him to make a long, time-consuming detour, minor and not-so-minor events occurred that caused delay after delay, messengers got captured, killed, or lost, and he should have either burned the entire captured wagon train or sent it back to Lee's army under an escort rather than drag it along after him.

Lee's and Stuart's reports have been put under the microscope in attempts to determine how each really felt about what happened. For the most part, each report reflects the man who wrote it, and if either blame in Lee's or apology in Stuart's were in the mind of the author, neither leap off the page. However, anyone who has doubts about how General Robert E. Lee viewed the battle, its causes and the wisdom of having fought it need only read the account left by Captain Fitzgerald Ross of the Imperial Austrian Hussars. He, like Englishman Col. Arthur Fremantle, was a foreign military officer who was observing the war and who was accorded access to many of the Confederacy's significant leaders. Fremantle, Ross, and Frank Lawley, an English correspondent, had been traveling together during and after the battle, and Ross wrote that on the day Fremantle left the army to return to England that he and "L" (Lawley) visited General Lee at his temporary headquarters in Hagerstown, Maryland.

Fremantle's diary reveals that the day was July 9, 1863, just six days after the battle. The Army of Northern Virginia was still on the north side of the Potomac waiting for the river to subside enough to cross, and as Ross recorded, General Lee "spoke very openly on the subject of the late campaign."[34] Ross's memoirs were written shortly after the events he witnessed, and were published in England in 1865, long before the controversy about Stuart's role in the defeat became a common topic.

General Lee told Ross, and presumably Lawley, that if he'd been aware that Meade had managed to concentrate his whole army he would not have attacked the Federals. As it was, believing he was dealing with only a portion of Meade's army and witnessing both the enthusiasm of his troops and their success on the first day of the fight, "he had thought that a successful battle would cut the knot so easily and satisfactorily that he had determined to risk it. His want of knowledge of the enemy's movements he attributed to Stuart having gone too far away from him with his cavalry."[35]

Lee went on to explain how Stuart expected to find the Confederate army at York but that it had not advanced as far as anticipated; how Stuart was forced to make a long detour to get around the Federal army that had gotten between Lee's army and Stuart's brigades; and how Stuart had been slowed by a large train of captured wagons. He simply explained, not in a condemning or complaining manner, but as one does to account for unexpected, unintended, and undesired outcomes to the plans that people make.

Yet there it was. If Robert E. Lee was of the opinion that he would not have fought the Battle of Gettysburg had Stuart been there to provide him with better knowledge, then no further debate is necessary. The man in charge and in whom all others trusted had figured out the truth of the matter. He did not do so on July 1st, 2nd, or 3rd, but he analyzed it and recognized what happened before six more days had passed. What happened on July 2 when Jeb arrived and Lee met him is not important, particularly because it was too early for Lee to know how he really felt about Stuart's absence, meaning it is unlikely that anything happened.

What also did not happen the afternoon of July 2, 1863, and what would never happen, was the restoration of Stuart's reputation. He would continue to be "grand Jeb Stuart," he would still encourage Flora to be "happy and gay," as he would be himself. Yet there would be whispers and accusations that would become more audible as weeks and months passed. Despite appearances, he really was diminished, and he knew it. In subtle but telling ways, the "flower of the cavaliers" wilted after Gettysburg. Few people noticed, and many people would disagree with that assessment. Yet Jeb Stuart's year of glory was over and done, and a year of desperate struggle lay ahead of him, culminating in death. The struggle would be less desperate in regard to battles with the enemy than in the mind of Jeb Stuart, because more disappointment lay ahead, and after Gettysburg he came to realize, with deep regret, that his beloved Confederacy was not destined to win the war and that he was not the man destined to make it happen. Those two factors, in Stuart's mind, portended death.

NOTES

1 Message from Maj. Gen. Joe Hooker to Maj. Gen. Henry Halleck, June 24, 1863, ORs, Vol. XXVII, Part 1, p. 25.

2 Some of the more interesting of those messages were the following:

June 19, Noon, Hooker to Halleck: I have just been furnished with an extract from the New York Herald of yesterday concerning the late movements of this army. So long as the newspapers continue to give publicity to our movements, we must not expect to gain any advantage over our adversaries. Is there no way of stopping it? I can suppress the circulation of this paper within my lines, but I cannot prevent their reaching it to the enemy. We could well afford to give millions of money for like information of the enemy.

June 19, 1:55 p.m., Halleck to Hooker: I appreciate as fully as yourself the injury resulting from newspaper publication of the movements, numbers, and position of our troops, but I see no way of preventing it as long as reporters are permitted in our camps. I expelled them all from our lines in Mississippi. Every general must decide for himself what persons he will permit in his camps.

June 19: 2 p.m.: Hooker to Halleck: Do you give credit to the reported movements of the enemy as stated in the Chronicle, of this morning?

June 19, 3:55 p.m. Halleck to Hooker: I do not know to what particular statement in the Chronicle you refer. There are several which are contradictory. It now looks very much as if Lee had been trying to draw your right across the Potomac, so as to attack your left. But of that it is impossible to judge until we know where Lee's army is. No large body has appeared either in Maryland or Western Virginia.

June 24, no time recorded, Hooker to Halleck: The aspect of the enemy is not much changed from yesterday. Ewell, I conclude, is over the river, and is now up the country, I suppose, for purposes of plunder. The yeomanry of that district should be able to check any extended advance of that column, and protect themselves from their aggression.

Of the troops that marched to the river at Shepherdstown yesterday, I cannot learn that any have crossed, and as soon as I do I shall commence moving, myself, and, indeed, am preparing my new acquisitions for that event; the others are ready. General French is now on his way to Harper's Ferry, and I have given directions for the force at Poolesville to march and report to him, and also for all of Stahl's cavalry, and, if I can do it without attracting observation, I shall send over a corps or two from here, in order, if possible, to sever Ewell from the balance of the rebel army, in case he should make a protracted sojourn with his Pennsylvania neighbors.

If the enemy should conclude not to throw any additional force over the river, I desire to make Washington secure, and, with all the force I can muster, strike for his line of retreat in the direction of Richmond.

Allow me to suggest that the new troops arriving in Baltimore and Washington be at once put in the defenses, and the old ones, excepting those serving with the artillery, be put in marching condition. If this should be done quickly, I think that we may anticipate glorious results from the recent movement of the enemy, whether he should determine to advance or retreat.

I request that my orders be sent me to-day, for outside of the Army of the Potomac I don't know whether I am standing on my head or feet.

United States War Department, *The War of the Rebellion: a Compilation of the Official Records of the Union and Confederate Armies, Official Records of the Union and Confederate Armies,* Vol. XXVII, Part 1, pp. 51-56 (Washington: Government Printing Office, 1880-1901), citied hereinafter as "ORs."

3 R.E. Lee's Report, Gettysburg Campaign, Official Records, Vol XXVII, Part 2, p. 316, cited hereinafter as "ORs, Lee's Report."

4 ORs, Vol XXVII, Part 3, p. 915.

5 J.E.B. Stuart's Report, Gettysburg Campaign, Official Records, Vol XXVII, Part 1, p. 692, cited hereinafter as "ORs, Stuart's Report."

6 General Lee, in his official report of the campaign, wrote that Jenkins' force "was not greater than was required to accompany the advance of General Ewell and General Early, with whom it performed valuable service."

7 J.S. Mosby, "Confederate Cavalry Chieftain Defended By the Confederate Partisan Leader-What Were Lee's Orders-The First Day's Success Largely Due to General Stuart's Services," *Philadelphia Weekly Times,* December 15, 1877, Volume I, Number 42.

8 ORs, Lee's report;, *I Rode With Jeb Stuart* at 321.

9 John Esten Cooke, *Wearing of the Gray*, p. 231 (Bloomington: Indiana University Press, 1959), cited hereinafter as *Wearing of the Gray*.

10 Alexander, Edward Porter, Gallagher, Gary W., ed., *Fighting for the Confederacy: The Personal Recollections of General Edward Porter Alexander,* 228 (Chapel Hill: University of North Carolina Press, 1989).

11 *Wearing of the Gray* at 232-33.

12 Eric Wittenberg & J. David Petruzzi, *Plenty of Blame to Go Around,* p. 16 (New York: Savas Beatie, 2006).

13 John B. Jones, *A Rebel War Clerk's Diary*, Vol. 1, p. 366 (Philadelphia: J. P. Lippincott, 1866).

14 Robert J. Trout, *They Followed the Plume: The Story of J.E.B. Stuart and his Staff*, p. 189 (Mechanicsburg, PA: Stackpole Books, 1995), cited hereinafter as *They Followed the Plume.*.

15 Wert, Jeffry D., *Cavalryman of the Lost Cause: Biography of J.E.B. Stuart*, p. 268 (New York: Simon & Schuster 2008), cited hereinafter as Wert.

16 Blackford, W.W., *War Years with JEB Stuart*, p. 233 (New York: Charles Scribner's Sons, 1945), cited hereinafter as *War Years with Jeb Stuart*.

17 *Ibid.* at 224.

18 Richard L.T. Beale, *History of the 9th Virginia Cavalry in the War Between the States,* p. 80 (Richmond: B. F. Johnson Publishing Co., 1899).

19 *Ibid.*

20 ORs, Stuart's Report, Gettysburg Campaign, Official Records, Vol. XXVII, Part 1, p. 694.

21 J.A. Buxton "One of Stuart's Couriers," *Confederate Veteran,* Vol. 30, Sept. 1922, p. 343.

22 *Wearing of the Gray* at 236.

23 *Ibid.* at 696.

24 *Ibid.*

25 Smith had commanded a division at Sharpsburg and the 6th Corps at Fredericksburg. However, as a result of being an ally of McClellan and having alienated himself from Burnside, he lost both his corps command and his rank of Major General and was put in command of militia in the Department of the Susquehanna in Pennsylvania.

26 Eric Wittenberg & J. David Petruzzi, *Plenty of Blame to Go Around,* p. 176 (New York: Savas Beatie, 2006).

27 *War Years with Jeb Stuart* at 228.

28 On his way back from Lee's headquarters, William Blackford ran into his brother, Eugene, who was commanding a battalion of sharpshooters from the 5th Alabama Infantry. They occupied some two and three story buildings, or row houses, on Main Street which, from the back windows looked out on Cemetery Ridge. Although there is uncertainty today which houses they occupied and on what street, Blackford described that the homes were adjoining, with parlors, sitting rooms, and dining rooms on the first floor and bedrooms on the second. His brother's men had cut

passageways in the common walls so that they could walk from "one cross street to the other," and had punched or cut holes in the rear walls so that they could fire on the enemy. Beds and mattresses were piled against the shooting walls and the men were stripped to the waist and begrimed with gunpowder. They alternated firing, and those not on duty could lounge on sofas and carpets, and some of them were able to enjoy wine and "delicacies" found in the houses. The rooms were littered everywhere with feathers from shots coming through or shells bursting against the mattresses, and in places were puddles of blood and feathers where a man had been hit or laid out. Ibid. at 231-32.

29 *Wearing of the Gray,* at 246.

30 Henry B. McClellan, *I Rode with Jeb Stuart: The Life and Campaigns of Major General J.E.B.Stuart,* pp. 331-32 (Bloomington: Indiana University Press, 1958), cited hereinafter as *I Rode with Jeb Stuart.*

31 See *Ibid.* at 80-82, note 1.

32 E.g., Eric Wittenberg and J. David Petruzzi, *Plenty of Blame to Go Around: Jeb Stuart's Controversial Ride to Gettysburg* (New York: Savas Beattie: 2006); Mark Nesbitt, *Saber and Scapegoat: J.E.B Stuart and the Gettysburg Controversy* (Mechanicsburg, Pa.: Stackpole Books 1994); Warren C. Robinson, *Jeb Stuart and the Confederate Defeat at Gettysburg,* (University of Nebraska: 2007); Patricia K. Roode, *J.E.B.Stuart and the Battle of Gettysburg: Was He Responsible for Lee's Defeat?*, Seniors Honors Thesis, History Dept. Rutgers University, April 2011; Daniel Zimmerman, "J.E.B. Stuart: Battle of Gettysburg Scapegoat," *America's Civil War,* May, 1998.

33 Jubal A. Early, "Causes of Lee's Defeat at Gettysburg," *Southern Historical Society Papers,* Vol. IV, p. 270 (Richmond, December 1877).

34 Alfred Ross, *A Visit to the Cities and Camps of the Confederate States,* p. 80 (Edinburgh & London: William Blackwood & Sons, 1865).

35 Ibid. at 81.; Five years later, Lee's explanation for the loss of the Battle of Gettysburg was as follows:

"As to the battle of Gettysburg, I must again refer you to the official accounts. Its loss was occasioned by a combination of circumstances. *It was commenced in the absence of correct intelligence.* It was continued in the effort to overcome the difficulties by which we were surrounded, and it would have been gained could one determined and united blow have been delivered by our whole line. As it was, victory trembled in the balance for three days, and the battle resulted in the infliction of as great an amount of injury as was received and in frustrating the Federal campaign for the season" (emphasis added).—Letter from General R. E. Lee to William M. McDonald, Lexington, Va., 15 April, 1868. *Southern Historical Society Papers,* Vol. 7, pages 445-446 (1879).

CHAPTER 3

EAST CAVALRY FIELD AND THE RETREAT TO VIRGINIA

July 2–14, 1863

While over the fields and through the pines,
backward and forward surged the lines;
twelve thousand men in a frenzied fray;
charge and rally and mad melee.
Oh, the crash and roar as the squadrons met,
the cheers and yells—I can hear them yet!
    —From *The Cavalry Veteran* by Joseph
      Mills Hanson, *Journal of the Military*
      Service Institution of the United States,
      Vol. 49, p. 142, July–August 1911

STUART'S THREE EXHAUSTED brigades were augmented by Jenkins' brigade once they reached Gettysburg. Robertson's and Jones's brigades still had not caught up with the main body of the army after guarding mountain passes and serving as the rear guard, and Imboden's brigade was guarding ammunition and supply trains in Chambersburg.

Jenkins had done exactly what was intended by Lee and Stuart—stayed with and protected Ewell's Corps as it advanced into Pennsylvania. Now its 1,600-some troopers were reduced by several companies assigned to guard Federal prisoners. Jenkins had been knocked unconscious by an exploding shell earlier that morning, and command had devolved to Colonel Milton J. Ferguson of the 16th Virginia. However, he was with the companies in the rear with prisoners, and the portion of the brigade that united directly with Stuart's brigades was under Lt. Col. Vincent Witcher of the 34th Virginia Battalion. He reported having only 350 officers and men when he reported to Stuart during the afternoon of July 2.

Stuart's total strength is not well established. Hundreds of troopers had fallen out of the ranks during the previous few days because they or their horses or both had broken down. A study of regimental strengths published in 2005 credited Stuart with having 4,836 men under his command at Gettysburg, but he may not have been able to put as many as 3,000 in the saddle and in the field.[1] The strength of Pleasonton's cavalry corps at Gettysburg, on the other hand, is believed to have been 11,850 men.[2]

Stuart took position on the left of Ewell's Corps, which was on the Confederate army's left, and established his headquarters beneath a tree on the side of the Heidelburg Road about a mile from Gettysburg.[3] He spent the rest of the available sunlight reconnoitering, getting familiar with the ground, and determining where the enemy was positioned.

An engagement between Confederate infantry—the Stonewall Brigade—and dismounted Federal cavalry broke out on the left flank and Stuart watched it from Brinkerhoff's Ridge, which was on the far left flank of the Army of Northern Virginia. Jenkins' brigade had been operating earlier that morning where the Stonewall Brigade now was, before Jenkins was wounded. Stuart observed the Federal cavalry and made plans for what he would do the next day. During his scout he approached near enough to the railroad to be seen and fired on, after which he returned to his headquarters.

There is an enduring legend that Stuart's purpose on July 3 was to coordinate with Pickett's Charge and attack the Federal rear in order to create confusion and/or harass the broken, retreating Federals, and but for the gallantry and quick thinking of George Custer, the South might have won the battle and then the war.[4] It is only legend. The historical record does not support that interpretation.

General Lee did not bother to mention, in his report on the campaign, what Stuart was assigned to do on July 3 or to even record what the cavalry actually did that day, whereas Stuart said that "On the morning of July 3, pursuant to instructions from the commanding general (the ground along our line of battle being totally impracticable for cavalry operations), I moved forward to a position to the left of General Ewell's left, and in advance of it. . . ."

Stuart's primary if not only assignment for July 3 was to protect the

Confederate left flank. Late the previous day, two nearly simultaneous attacks by Union cavalry occurred near that left flank. Brig. Gen. David M. Gregg's cavalry division tangled with the Stonewall Brigade of Maj. Gen. Edward Johnson's division near Brinkerhoff's Ridge, as observed by Stuart, and Brig. Gen. Judson Kilpatrick's division assaulted Wade Hampton's brigade at Hunterstown, where Hampton was escorting the snake-bit wagon train captured on Stuart's raid. Accordingly Lee knew there were two divisions of enemy cavalry operating in the vicinity of his left flank, which meant that either or both might be planning an attack around that flank and into the Rebel army's rear on July 3.

Not only did Lee therefore assign Stuart and his four brigades to that sector of the battlefield, but he summoned Imboden to bring his brigade—about 2,100 men and one battery of six guns—over from Chambersburg to protect the army's rear from enemy cavalry. He arrived about noon but saw no action.

Stuart did desire to attack the Federal rear. However, the idea was his own and was not linked in any manner with what Lee and Longstreet had arranged for George Pickett and two other divisions of Rebel infantry. In fact, expecting Stuart to coordinate with Pickett's Charge ran against the grain of what Robert E. Lee intended for the cavalry to do that day.

The first part of the morning of July 3 was spent sorting out and resupplying Jenkins' men. For some reason they had been furnished only ten rounds of ammunition apiece for their Enfields, and Major McClellan wrote that the replenishing took several hours, which clashes with Jeb's report, in which he said that Jenkins' men, later in the day, had to retire after each had fired his ten rounds. It is possible that the Enfields were musketoons—Stuart called them muskets instead of rifles—but it is equally likely that the weapons were long rifles—Stuart also said they were "the most approved Enfield musket"—and that Jenkins' men were accustomed to fighting on foot like infantry. In either event, it was noon before Stuart sent messages to Hampton and Fitz Lee to follow and began moving into position with Chambliss' and Jenkins' brigades.

His plan, fully described in his report, was to occupy "a commanding ridge (that) completely controlled a wide plain of cultivated fields stretching toward Hanover."[5] This was Cress Ridge, and its north end was covered with woods, as was the road Stuart and the two brigades used to ride up the slope. The woods terminated on the southwest end of the ridge, where a stone dairy covering a spring was located. Below, on the flat about 300 yards from the bottom of the ridge, was the large frame Rummel barn.

The countryside was quiet. The battle had not extended that far and was not currently underway, so that it was, as McClellan recalled, "as peaceful as if no war existed."[6] Blackford wrote that no enemy was in sight, and Stuart, "wishing to know what was going on in the main body of the army," sent him "with a roving commission to find out."[7]

Then Stuart did an odd thing, the meaning of which is still in dispute. Two batteries of Horse Artillery, those of Capt. Thomas E. Jackson and Captain Wiley H. Griffin, were accompanying the two cavalry brigades and Stuart directed that a single cannon be rolled to the edge of the woods and, by his personal command, ordered it fired several times in random directions.

The battery the gun belonged to, the direction it was fired, the number of times it was fired, and the purpose of its being fired are all open to debate. Major McClellan, who was there, said the gun was from Griffin's battery, whereas Private H.H. Matthews of Breathed's battery, who wasn't there but who was part of the Horse Artillery and inclined to take note of such matters, wrote after the war that it was Jackson's battery. McClellan said there were a "number of shots in different directions," whereas other sources say, alternately, there were four shots, one in each direction; two shots in one direction; and even four guns, each fired in a different direction.

Those present guessed at the purpose. McClellan said he was "somewhat perplexed" by the shots, and theorized that it *might* have been a prearranged signal by which Stuart was notifying General Lee that he had gained a favorable position. Others, also including McClellan, surmised that Stuart wanted to see whether and how the Federals responded. Other speculation was that by firing the shots Stuart intended to lure Federal cavalry away from Ewell's flank and rear, so that his infantry would be unmolested when they assaulted Culp's Hill. One fuss about the shots has focused on the question of whether Stuart arrived on Cress Ridge before or after the beginning of the bombardment of the Union center, prior to Pickett's Charge, such that the shots could or could not have been heard by General Lee. The notion that Lee might have been waiting and listening for distant cannon shots on the Gettysburg battlefield and would somehow be able to divine whether they came from Stuart instead of one of the other

400 or so cannons in the area seems unlikely in the extreme.

Considering what Stuart reported—that he "hoped to effect a surprise upon the enemy's rear"—coupled with what McClellan recorded—that "not a living creature was visible on the plain below"—added to what Blackford remembered—"all was quiet as if there wasn't a soldier within a hundred miles"—it seems logical to conclude that Stuart's purpose in firing the shots was to get the enemy's attention so that they—cavalry most likely but possibly infantry—might come investigate, totally unaware of what was lurking in the woods at the top of the hill and planning to pounce in surprise.

If that was the plan and the purpose, it was short-lived, because Hampton's and Fitz Lee's brigades, not knowing they were supposed to be sneaky but complying with Jeb's orders to follow, "debouched into the open ground, disclosing the movement, and causing a corresponding movement of a large force of the enemy's cavalry," as Stuart reported, such that surprise was no longer possible.[8]

Jeb decided to come up with another plan, and summoned Hampton and Lee to come discuss the options, but before either could arrive the Federals "deployed a heavy line of sharpshooters, and were advancing" toward Cress Ridge.

Those sharpshooters, or skirmishers, belonged to the division of Federal cavalry commanded by Brig. Gen. David M. Gregg, plus a brigade of Michiganders commanded by freshly minted Brigadier General George Custer.

Custer had galloped into the war in June 1861, straight out of West Point as a 2nd Lieutenant in the 5th U.S. Cavalry. After serving with minor distinction at First Manassas as a courier between Maj. Gen. Winfield Scott and Brig. Gen. Irwin McDowell, he caught the eye of George McClellan and was invited to serve on that commanding general's staff with the rank of captain. He did so from the beginning of the Peninsula campaign through Sharpsburg, all the way to McClellan's dismissal in early November 1862, at which point Custer returned to the 5th Cavalry and his rank dropped back to 1st Lieutenant. A few months later his services as a staff officer became attractive to Brig. Gen. Alfred Pleasonton, commander of the Army of the Potomac's cavalry, and after Custer distinguished himself at Brandy Station and Aldie it was Pleasonton who arranged for Custer's meteoric promotion from 1st Lieutenant to Brigadier General of Volunteers, effective

June 29, 1863. Critics have suggested the promotion was a clerical error, but if so the same thing happened the same day to two other staff officers with the rank of captain—Wesley Merritt and Elon Farnsworth.[9]

Their sudden leap over the heads of hundreds of other officers was not particularly appreciated by those officers or by those who had labored for years to earn similar rank. An enduring story is that while Brig. Gen. John Buford was leading his cavalry to Gettysburg his men captured a spy near Frederick, Maryland, tried him, sentenced him to death and carried out the sentence, causing an outcry from local citizens. In reply, Buford supposedly said he was afraid to send the prisoner to Washington because he knew the authorities would make him a brigadier-general.[10]

Whatever the reason and circumstances of Custer being put in charge of a brigade without having any command experience, one cannot fault the wisdom of its being done. He would, on that day and many that lay ahead, work the kind of marvels in the saddle that originally made Stuart famous.

The battle that followed was not "the cavalry battle that saved the Union," nor was it a stunning Federal victory that nailed the coffin in Lee's hopes for Pickett's Charge. Though as the decades rolled by and it became obvious that Gettysburg was THE battle of the war, veterans and writers embellished what happened on that part of the field with more significance than was intended or understood on the afternoon of July 3. It was a spirited fight, and it gave George Custer the opportunity to shout "Come On You Wolverines!" a couple of times and get as many horses shot out from under him, but it only lasted 40 or 45 minutes and accomplished nothing more than preventing Stuart from pulling off the surprise attack he had wanted to achieve before Fitz Lee's and Hampton's men "debouched" into open ground.

The battle fought on East Cavalry Field[11] may be summarized as occurring in seven distinct steps.

Step one unfolded after Stuart observed the heavy line of enemy "sharpshooters" coming in his direction. He was confident in the strength of his position on Cress Ridge for defense, but he wanted to do more, which was to send his own dismounted skirmishers to occupy the Rummel Barn and engage the enemy, then send a unit of cavalry to ride around their left flank and into their rear. The former he attempted with Jenkins' men but the fact that the Federals were armed with Spencer repeaters while Jenkins' men still had inadequate ammunition for their Enfields resulted in the dismounted Confederates being pushed back and finding themselves in danger of being captured. Federal artillery shells that began crashing through the roof of the barn had an additional persuasive effect on the Rebels inside.

This led to step two. Stuart ordered a cavalry assault by a portion of Chambliss's brigade, which was joined almost immediately by the 1st Virginia of Fitz Lee's Brigade. This caused Gregg to order Custer to counterattack, and the part of the battle depicted in paintings and romance began. Custer personally led the 7th Michigan of his brigade, shouting his "Come on, you Wolverines," and the three regiments—less than 1,000 men total—charged at each other until they reached a stake and rail fence on the Rummel farm. There, with the fence separating them, they exchanged a flurry of pistol and carbine shots at point-blank range. Saddles were emptied, horses reared, bucked, and were shot down. Custer's horse was killed and he commandeered one from a bugler. Finally the Michiganders were able, under fire, to tear down a portion of the fence and the fighting intensified. The Confederates were able to capture the colors of the 7th Michigan, and the area around the fence became a killing ground. A Federal counterattack drove the Virginians back to the Rummel barn, where Jenkins' brigade, particularly Witcher's Boys, delivered a concentrated fire that sent the 7th back again.

Which gave rise to step three. Stuart saw the need for reinforcements and sent the 2nd Virginia of Fitz Lee's brigade forward dismounted, along with the 9th and 13th Virginia regiments from Chambliss's brigade, and the 1st North Carolina and the Jeff Davis Legion from Hampton's brigade. This overwhelming crowd of Confederates caused Custer and the Wolverines to retreat, nearly in a panic.

Believing he was about to prevail, Stuart launched step four by sending the rest of Hampton's brigade forward in a classic cavalry charge—draw sabers, walk, trot, gallop, charge. Supposedly some of the Federal cavalry observing what was coming at them murmured words of admiration. Federal horse artillerymen did not. They opened up with shell and canister, but not soon enough or with enough accuracy to turn Hampton's men back.

Which brought Custer back into the fray for step five. Renewing his rallying cry, he led the 1st Michigan in a counterattack. This was the climax of the battle. The two masses of cavalry crashed into each other with a racket that sounded like a forest of large trees falling at once. It was a train wreck of a collision. Horses literally somersaulted head over heels. Men flew from saddles. Some were crushed. Men cleaved each other with sabers or shot into opponents' faces.

Step six followed when, with Hampton's and Custer's men fighting horse to horse and hand to hand in the center of the battlefield, a brigade of Federal cavalry commanded by Colonel John B. McIntosh hit the Rebels on their right flank, while the 1st New Jersey and the 3rd Pennsylvania regiments hit Hampton on his left flank. Wade Hampton was seriously wounded by a saber cut to the head, Custer had another horse shot out from under him, and the Confederates, assaulted on three sides, had no choice but to retreat.

Step seven was that retreat, which was not pursued by the Federals. The way Stuart reported it, "The enemy were driven from the field, which was now raked by their artillery, posted about three-quarters of a mile off. Our own artillery commanding the same ground, no more hand-to-hand fighting occurred, but the wounded were removed and the prisoners (a large number) taken to the rear."[12]

There were, of course, a great number of more details to the battle, many gallant acts of heroism, and enough written recollections to fill a few dozen books. Yet all seven steps occupied no more than three-quarters of an hour and caused less than 500 casualties—254 Federal, of which 219 were from Custer's command, and 181 Confederate. Certainly that was a significant number of dead and wounded for a cavalry engagement, but when it is compared to what happened on other parts of the Gettysburg battlefield it is understandable why Robert E. Lee failed to even mention the East Cavalry Field battle in his report.

Summing up the day a month later, Stuart provided post-war romanticists with some additional fodder for their claims about the significance of what his cavalry did that day:

> During this day's operations, I held such a position as not only to render Ewell's left entirely secure, where the firing of my command, mistaken for that of the enemy, caused some apprehension, but commanded a view of the routes leading to the enemy's rear. Had the enemy's main body been dislodged, as was confidently

hoped and expected, I was in precisely the right position to discover it and improve the opportunity. I watched keenly and anxiously the indications in his rear for that purpose, while in the attack which I intended (which was forestalled by our troops being exposed to view), his cavalry would have separated from the main body, and gave promise of solid results and advantages.

That paragraph was not intended to communicate that he was assigned to the area for the purpose of coordinating with Pickett's assault or launching his own version of it from the opposite side of the Federal line. The notion that Stuart could have been ordered to do that, or that he thought he could do significant damage to the Federal army with only about 3,000 horsemen is completely unrealistic. Of course it did occur to Jeb that he was in the right place if the Federals came streaming back from their front in hasty retreat, and when he wrote his report he made certain to describe how he'd done the right thing—secured the left flank and exercised discretion about being in the best place to assist in the event that Lee and Longstreet were successful. Stuart wanted to leave a record to history that no matter what others did or might say about him, he was in the right place doing the right thing at the right time, and the reason it wasn't more successful was neither his fault nor was due to any worthwhile efforts by the enemy. He may never have written any other kind of report.

Blackford probably wrote for 95 percent of the soldiers on the field when he said of the evening of July 3, "At the end of the day we did not know how the result stood, for both armies held exactly the same ground they did in the morning."[13] The cavalrymen knew there had been a tremendous duel of artillery and infantry, of course, but they did not see it. Frank Robertson wrote that leaves on the trees trembled and vibrated from the effect of the artillery bombardment and later, when he saw the field across which the Confederate assault was made, he was unable to understand how any human beings could have been expected to take the Federal position. "The confidence of the Confederate army in him [General Lee] was infinite. What he said was law and right, from officers to the most homesick conscript. But it is today a mystery and a problem . . . as to why he expected and demanded the impossible. It really looked as if our grand old chief had suddenly become demented."[14]

However distracted Lee was by diarrhea or temporary dementia, he recognized when it was time to leave. He concluded that "The severe loss sustained by the army and the reduction of its ammunition, rendered another attempt to dislodge the enemy inadvisable, and it was, therefore, determined to withdraw."[15] Stuart, after pulling his brigades back to the York Road that evening, went to Lee's headquarters after dark and learned not only that the army was withdrawing but that General Lee had sent him a courier with that information who never got through—it was a recurring problem. Stuart's role, of course, would be to screen and protect the army, particularly its trains, as it began its retrograde movement.

The main withdrawal of Lee's army began on the 4th, as did the rain.

The order and direction of march was for Hagerstown, Maryland and then across the Potomac River at and near Williamsport, but by two different routes. Most of the army's long train of wagons, plus the ambulances containing the wounded, were sent over the Chambersburg Pike, through Cashtown toward Chambersburg and then Hagerstown. John D. Imboden's brigade, supplemented with a mixed command of infantry and artillery, was given responsibility for these. The artillery and three army corps took a different route—southwest through Fairfield, over the Monterrey Pass and then to Hagerstown.

Hill's Third Corps took the lead, followed by Longstreet's First Corps, followed by Ewell's Second Corps. Lee rode with Hill at the head of the long column. Fitz Lee's and Hampton's brigades moved by way of Cashtown on the road through Greenwood and Williamsport, which was the route designated for the wagon trains and ambulances. Robertson's and Jones' brigades were on the army's right, near Fairfield, in position to hold the Jack Mountain passes. Stuart rode with Jenkins' and Chambliss' brigades by way of Emmitsburg, Maryland, guarding the army's left flank.

The story of how Meade allowed Lee to escape, to Lincoln's utter horror, is well known, and it is true that the commander of the Federal army did not get a genuine pursuit up and running for a week. How he used his cavalry is a different story.

The fact that Imboden was guarding and protecting the army's wagon train did not mean that he had all of the wagons and supplies under his direction. Ewell had his own train, as well as a large herd of cattle taken from the countryside, and he sent them ahead of the main body of infantry in three different columns in order to pass through the nearby mountain passes, one to use the Cashtown Gap, one the Fairfield Gap, and one the Monterey Pass. The wagons headed for Monterey Pass were following Maj. Gen. George Pickett's division at the rear of Longstreet's Corps, and Pickett was escorting a large contingent of Federal prisoners taken in the battle.

Meade directed eight brigades of his cavalry to do all it could to disrupt the enemy's communications and to "harass and annoy him as much as possible in his retreat." Ewell's wagons had been seen from a Union signal station and were presumed to be the Confederate army's principal supply train. Accordingly, Kilpatrick left the main Federal army about 10 a.m. on the 4th on the Waynesboro-Emmitsburg Turnpike toward the village of Fountain Dale, and from there to Monterey Pass. The Confederate cavalry with responsibility for guarding that pass was the brigade of Grumble Jones. Custer took the lead of Kilpatrick's division.

The result was a sharp, back and forth, often confusing engagement between Jones' and Kilpatrick's troopers, involving more than one instance of friendly fire, near a large resort hotel called Monterey Springs. Jones' men did what they were supposed to for nearly six hours, which was enough time for more than half of Ewell's train, which was nearly forty miles in length, to move through the pass. However, the fighting continued after darkness fell, and early on July 5—about 3 a.m.—the 1st West Virginia Cavalry broke through Jones' line and had the wagon train for the taking.

The Federal troopers swarmed into the teams. Federal artillery began shelling the rear of the column. Custer became so excited that he fell or was thrown from his horse and nearly captured. Jones also barely avoided becoming a prisoner. Drivers, Rebel cavalry, and Federal horsemen fired wildly into each other, often unable to tell in the dark whether they were shooting friend or foe. The Federals kept going, taking prisoners and setting wagons afire. In the end Kilpatrick's men took or destroyed about 290 wagons and ambulances and captured more than 1,300 prisoners, including several slaves and free blacks. The incident would have later consequences for Stuart's overall command structure.

Elsewhere the night of the 4th was miserable even without having Yankee cavalry slashing at your backside. In addition to the rain and mud, it was so dark that Stuart finally ordered a halt of Jenkins' and Chambliss' brigades for a few hours out of fear that the commands would lose the road, become separated, and get lost. He also received news that a force of the enemy's cavalry had passed along the same route the previous day, and he had to calculate and make arrangements for all of the possible points at which they might strike and attempt to do damage.

There was no attack, and at Emmitsburg Stuart's men captured about 65 prisoners as well as some badly needed hospital stores that were en route to the enemy from Frederick. At the village of Cooperstown Stuart halted for an hour in order for the horses and men to feed, then moved on through Harbaugh's Valley, past Zion Church, to Catoctin Mountain. There the road split to pass through the mountain, one branch going left to Smithtown and the other right to Leitersburg. Stuart divided his command, taking Chambliss's brigade right and sending Jenkins' brigade, still under the command of Colonel Ferguson, to the left.

Before he'd gone far he found the mountain pass ahead of him held by the enemy, which turned out to be Kilpatrick's cavalry, and he ordered his command to dismount and force the Federals out, which they finally did,

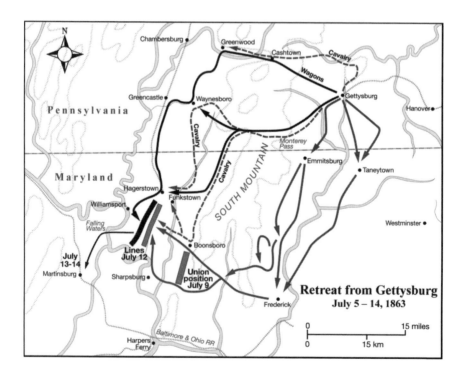

Retreat from Gettysburg
July 5 – 14, 1863

only to be met with artillery fire when they emerged on the other side of the pass. Ferguson also found his way blocked, so Stuart sent word for him to withdraw and come through along the same road he and Chambliss's command had taken. After bringing up the Horse Artillery, Stuart was able to dislodge the enemy's guns and move on toward Boonsborough on the morning of July 5.

That afternoon, about 5 p.m., there was another fight with Kilpatrick near Smithburg. A Federal soldier who was near enough to see the Rebel cavalry wrote that many were on lean horses that had no shoes and looked as though they had been ridden all the way from Virginia, while others were mounted on recently confiscated, fat farm and draft horses that were so unused to hard cavalry work that they were "well nigh unserviceable."[16]

On July 6, Stuart headed toward Hagerstown, where Jones' and Robertson's brigades joined him at Leitersburg. From there Stuart directed Chambliss to take his brigade and two regiments from Robertson's on the direct road to Hagerstown, and sent Jones toward Cavetown and thence Funktown, which was south of Hagerstown. Stuart followed Jones with Ferguson's (Jenkins') brigade.

When Chambliss arrived at Hagerstown he learned that Kilpatrick was approaching from the direction of Boonsborough. He barricaded the streets and sent word to Stuart. Soon Robertson's and Ferguson's men were spurring toward Hagerstown while Jones headed for Funktown, which would put his men in Kilpatrick's rear.

Kilpatrick attacked shortly before Confederate reinforcements arrived. The 18th Pennsylvania broke through Chambliss' barricades and routed the 9th and 10th Virginia regiments. House to house fighting followed, but by the time Jenkins' brigade and Stuart arrived the enemy was essentially in possession of the town. Jenkins attacked and Jones arrived on the left, where he opened up with artillery. A small force of Confederate infantry was also on hand, commanded by Brig. Gen. Alfred Iverson, and they, along with Robertson and Chambliss, were on the north edge of the town. Firing was going in multiple directions, and Stuart reported later that the operations in his sector were "much embarrassed by our great difficulty in preventing this latter force [the infantry] from mistaking us for the enemy."[17]

Stuart believed, correctly, that Kilpatrick's goal was to drive on to Williamsport, six miles away where the Confederate wagon trains were congregated in a narrow space at the foot of a hill near the swollen and impassable Potomac River. Accordingly he ordered all of his units to attack vigorously, even though they were outnumbered. This the dismounted Rebel cavalry did, again fighting house to house and street to street, finally clearing the town.

Hardly was Hagerstown in Confederate control again than artillery fire was heard from the direction of Williamsport, which was under assault by John Buford's brigade. The enemy had been driven out of Hagerstown toward Sharpsburg, but they had then turned on another road that took them to Williamsport. Stuart sent one column, under Chambliss, in pursuit of Kilpatrick and moved with Robertson's brigade, two regiments of Jenkins's brigade, and the Horse Artillery on a route parallel to Chambliss. Chambliss attacked the enemy's flank, the 9th and 13th Virginia regiments leading. The Horse Artillery unlimbered and opened fire, and Jenkins' brigade dismounted and fought on foot. Witcher and his "boys" distinguished themselves again and were commended by Stuart in his report.

Although the Federals were getting close to Williamsport and the Confederate wagon train, the vigorous, repeated assaults on their rear by Stuart's cavalry did the trick. Kilpatrick lifted what he'd intended to be a siege of Williamsport and was driven way on the Downsville Road. To top things off, Fitz Lee arrived with his brigade and joined in the attack.

Stuart's command bivouacked for the night in and around Hagertown, and on July 7 he rode to Downsville.

The Confederate army, its infantry, wagons, ambulances, artillery, prisoners, and thousands of wounded were stuck on the north bank of the Potomac River, which was swollen and impossible to cross, with the Army of the Potomac poised, or potentially poised, to descend on them in one great final assault that would sweep the Rebels into the river and away like the Pharoah's army in the Red Sea.

The Confederates dug in, constructing earthworks from Williamsport downriver to Falling Waters, and for five days, from July 8 to the 12th, they prepared for and expected the worst. There were cavalry fights and skirmishes every day, with the Confederates often taking the offensive. Stuart went wherever the fighting was the hottest, and on July 10 the horse he was riding, an animal captured from the enemy and apparently not given a name, was killed beneath him. Rations were sparse and becoming more so. There was no food to be purchased or stolen, and Stuart drove himself and his men to the ragged edge of disaster. It began to show.

One young lady in Hagerstown was a particular friend and Southern sympathizer, and her home became a sort of temporary headquarters, largely because she insisted on sharing all the food she could find with Stuart and his staff. One evening, probably on the 9th or 10th, Jeb and his staff arrived there about 9 p.m. after a day of incessant fighting. Jeb collapsed on the sofa in the parlor and went instantly to sleep. When it was announced that food was ready he would not awaken, but McClellan pulled him to his feet, certain that he needed food more than he needed sleep, and guided him to a place at the table. He sat, eyes open, but in a stupor, eating hardly anything. The hostess, thinking perhaps the food she'd prepared wasn't to his liking, asked if he would care for a hard-boiled egg, to which Jeb mumbled "Yes, I'll take four or five."

This startled everyone, both because it was impolite and because eggs were not plentiful, but the lady soon emerged with five eggs and placed them before Stuart, who ate one, got to his feet and staggered into the parlor. McClellan, hoping to rouse him out of his torpor, sat down at the piano and began playing and singing *Jine the Cavalry*, admitting later that the song wasn't appropriate for the occasion but hoping it would rouse the general. It did, and soon Stuart added his baritone to McClellan's tenor. After the singing ended and it was obvious that Jeb was in possession of his wits again, McClellan told him what had happened, which mortified Stuart and led to profuse apologies.

The next night or the one following, while Stuart and McClellan were riding in the dark with a single courier on the turnpike near Hagerstown, Jeb dictated some dispatches directing certain movements by his troops, and McClellan asked if they could stop at a toll house where there was a light so that he could write them out. They did so and while McClellan was writing Stuart put his head and arms on a small table and fell asleep. When he was done, McClellan woke Stuart and handed him the dispatches for his review, which was customary. Stuart read them, took a pencil and erased the names of two nearby sites and replaced them with "Sheperdstown" and "Aldie," which were in West Virginia and Virginia respectively, and were not nearby. As McClellan noted, that was absurd, and he had a fair amount of difficulty rousing Stuart into consciousness so that he could be made to understand the meaning of his own dispatches and could approve their being sent.[18] In the history of the war and the memoirs of all of Stuart's companions, there are no more striking descriptions of how totally and utterly Stuart had exhausted himself than during those days following Gettysburg before the Army of Northern Virginia was safely across the river in Virginia. His staff and his troopers were in no better condition.

Ammunition was another serious problem. Almost all of the army's stores of it had been used at Gettysburg. There was no more to be had, and on July 10, a week after his victory, Meade finally got his army moving and coming after Lee. The huge blue multitude came by way of South Mountain, an irresistible, daunting, potent mass, well fed, well rested and quite well-armed.

Then they stopped.

Nine miles from the Confederates' works at Williamsport, Meade halted on July 12 and conferred with his corps commanders about the best approach—reconnaissance in force perhaps? Probe the enemy and find his weakest points, then talk some more about where to attack? Meade even asked for a vote on whether it might be a good idea to attack the next day, but a majority of his corps commanders voted against it. Meade decided he would spend July 13 personally inspecting his enemy's position and that an attack would be made on the 14th. His staff spent the 13th drafting and circulating orders for that purpose.

After dark on the night of the 13th, the Potomac River subsided and, even though it began raining again, the Confederate army began wading across.

Stuart brought up the rear, covering the army's passage and keeping Meade's men utterly ignorant of what was happening. To add to the sound of the rain and storm, Stuart and his staff rode along the Confederate works, stoking campfires that had no one around them and singing as loudly as they could. By dawn on the 14th there were hardly any Confederates left on the north bank, and within a few hours after first light the last of the Confederate cavalry, under Fitz Lee, crossed over the river to home in Old Virginia.

NOTES

1 Wert at 285, citing John W. Busey and David G. Martin, *Regimental Strengths and Losses at Gettysburg* (Hightstown, N.J.: 2005).

2 *Stone Sentinels,* http://www.gettysburg.stonesentinels.com/AOPCavCorps.php.

3 *Wearing of the Gray* at 246.

4 An extreme example of this romantic myth is contained in Ch. 6, entitled "America's Greatest Cavalry Battle," of the book *The Cavalry Battle that Saved the Union: Custer vs. Stuart at Gettysburg,* by Paul D. Walker (Gretna: Pelican Books, 2002), which begins "To add an extra measure for success on the third day, Lee had ordered Stuart, with four brigades of cavalry and artillery, to move around the enemy's right flank, take up concealed positions, and in coordination with Gen. George Pickett's frontal attack, strike the rear of the Union line, creating confusion, panic, and a tipping of the scales in favor of the South."

5 Stuart's report at 697.

6 *I Rode with Jeb Stuart* at 338.

7 *War Years with Jeb Stuart* at 233

8 *Ibid.*; Stuart's report at 697.

9 Merritt was serving as an Aide-de-Camp for Maj. Gen. George Stoneman and Farnsworth, like Custer, was serving as Aide-de-Camp for Pleasonton.

10 H. P. Moyer, *History of the Seventeenth Regiment Pennsylvania Volunteer Cavalry,* p. 58 (Lebanon. Pennsylvania, 1911).

11 As opposed to South Cavalry Field, where Farnsworth attacked Confederate infantry and was killed in the process.

12 ORs, Stuart's report at 698.

13 *War Years with Jeb Stuart* at 237-38..

14 Robert J. Trout, Ed. *In the Saddle with Stuart: The Story of Frank Smith Robertson of Jeb Stuart's Staff,* p. 83 (Gettysburg: Thomas Publications, 1998), cited hereinafter as *In the Saddle with Stuart.*

15 ORs, Lee's report at 322.

16 Burke Davis, *Jeb Stuart: The Last Cavalier,* (New York: Rhinehart & Co. 1957), citing *Confederate Veteran,* Sept. 1922, p. 329, which cite is in error.

17 OR's, Stuart's report at 701.

18 *I Rode with Jeb Stuart* at 365-66.

CHAPTER 4

RETURN TO THE BOWER
July 15–August 26, 1863

*Had a grand time in Pennsylvania and we return
without defeat, to recuperate and reinforce, when,
no doubt the roll will be re-enacted. . . . We must
invade again—it is the only path to peace.*
   —Jeb Stuart to Flora, July 13, 1863

IT IS PART OF THE Lost Cause tradition that the men and officers of the Army of Northern Virginia did not regard Gettysburg as a significant defeat, and that they returned from
that dreadful campaign as feisty as ever, confident that with a little time to
rest and recuperate they would be back on the road to victory. In Jeb Stuart's
corner, and probably others, that was so.

Certainly there could be no admission of defeat to the public. Army and
political leaders could not admit that Lee's great invasion of the North was
only a tsunami, huge and destructive, capable of sweeping away all resistance, but once spent not capable of regeneration and repetition. Indeed, they
could not know what such regeneration was possible or within quick reach.
Southern crystal balls were just as cranky and fitful in their purpose as
Northern ones. The South certainly wasn't whipped yet, and even if the
tides of its armies were not meant to rise as high again, they didn't know
that then and besides, there were other ways to win a war than by invasion.
Anything might happen.

As for the optimistic, "I'd rather die than be whipped" Jeb Stuart, he
appeared and sounded no less confident than ever upon returning to Virginia. The last of the army was across the Potomac and on home soil by July
14, and the next day Stuart rode into Martinsburg with "a large cavalcade of

staff and couriers, and two bugles blowing most furiously." He was headed toward the one place that offered not only solace but all of the ambiance and memories of the glory of his previous triumphs—his former headquarters home, the Bower.

The old maxim "actions speak louder than words," with regard to the next few months, serve as the basis for arguing that the post-Gettysburg Jeb Stuart was a markedly changed man from the ante-Gettysburg Jeb, but that was not obvious in mid-July 1863. He wrote to Flora on the 10th that "My cavalry has nobly sustained its reputation and done better and harder fighting than it ever has since the war." He said rather euphemistically that "We got the better of the fight at Gettysburg but retired because the position we took could not be held." He directed her to pray to God for victory and said, "We have now a fresh supply of ammunition and will give battle again. May God grant us victory." On the 13th he wrote again to say that he "had a grand time in Pennsylvania and we return without defeat, to recuperate and reinforce, when, no doubt the roll will be re-enacted." He did not expect the Confederate army to remain in Virginia in a defensive position, and declared, "We must invade again—it is the only path to peace."

A very fortuitous event, at least from Stuart's perspective, occurred on July 15. One of his least favorite subordinates, Beverly Robertson, penned a letter to General Lee's chief of staff to say, "I consider it an injustice to myself and the service to remain longer in my present position. . . . I think my services would be more avail elsewhere." Following the normal chain of command procedure, Robertson submitted the letter to Stuart, who endorsed it with the statement, "Respectfully forwarded, and recommended that he be relieved from duty with this command accordingly." General Lee approved, of course, and Robertson was transferred to South Carolina to set up cavalry recruitment camps. Lawrence Baker succeeded Robertson to command of the brigade.

At the Bower the General and his staff pitched their tents in what Blackford called "the old place" around Stephen Dandridge's large home where Stuart and his staff had spent a delightful month in September and October, 1862. Blackford wrote both that "our pleasant, gay life was resumed" and that "[a] shade of sadness hung over our meeting . . . when we thought of how many who were with us during our former visit were dead or absent from wounds." He was undoubtedly thinking particularly of John Pelham,

Channing Price, and Heros Von Borcke. Both he and Frank Robertson were so worn out from the campaign that they received special treatment. Blackford was diagnosed with a case of "camp fever" that may have been malaria. He was "stuffed with quinine" and, at Mrs. Dandridge's invitation, was put to bed in the house.

Robertson and his horse had plunged off a bridge on the dark night of July 13, badly injuring his shoulder, but he had continued to carry out Stuart's order to call in the rear guard covering the army's crossing of the Potomac. Admitting that he was so "stiff and miserable that I didn't know much of anything," he then accompanied Stuart through a skirmish and rode another day to the Bower, where Stuart finally recognized the extent of his assistant engineer's plight. "Poor little fellow," Jeb said, "I will send you to the house," and had two couriers escort Robertson there, where he fell into a bed and "couldn't move for two days."

Robertson's condition did not improve quickly, and he was given a two-month furlough and transportation by government ambulance to Salem, which was located 210 miles up the Valley from the Bower. He was accompanied by Major Dabney Ball, Stuart's sometime Chief of Commissary and chaplain,[1] whose wife was in Salem and to whom Ball was delivering a large, hair-covered rocking chair. Robertson sat in the chair in the ambulance for the entire trip with his pistol ready, although not for the purpose of defense. Partridges were so plentiful along the route that the birds would perch on stone walls and roadside fences and Robertson was able to shoot enough of them to keep the little party well fed for the journey.[2]

Stuart caught up on some letter writing and gift distribution at about this time. To Flora he reported that he had made several purchases out of "the $170," which apparently had accompanied a list of items she'd sent him before the invasion of Pennsylvania began. He'd managed to obtain "most of the small items," including a shawl and a bonnet for her, an "organdie," which was a stiff transparent fabric of cotton or silk for his sister-in-law Maria, as well as "the crepe, ribbon, etc.," but he'd struck out on finding her any black silk or needles. Almost certainly not on her list, and probably not purchased with any part of the $170, but secured with Flora in mind was a "rockaway," which is a type of carriage that he'd decided "will be great for you to ride in about my headquarters."

For one of his other favorite ladies, Nannie Price, he'd acquired a cloak that he sent her with a letter on July 18, saying he'd obtained it expressly for her "in foreign parts." He waxed eloquent, or with an abundance of ornate corniness by writing that "When it encircles that form tripping over the wood lawns of 'Dundee' may it recall remembrances of one who would like once more to share the pleasure of the promenade to which fondest memories still cling with tenacity. The gift is a trifle but when she throws it over her shoulders to take a walk will she not remember 'K.G.S.'"

No sooner had the Knight of the Golden Spurs and his gray cavalrymen settled in to recuperate then a new threat arose. The heavy rains of the previous two weeks had swollen the Shenandoah River so that it could not be crossed at all by infantry, and by cavalry only by the swimming of horses. Meade recognized an opportunity and proceeded to march along the east side of the Blue Ridge to interpose his army between Lee's and Richmond.

On July 16, a large body of the enemy's cavalry was discovered between Shepherdstown and Leetown, and Stuart dispatched the brigades of Fitz Lee, Chambliss, and Jenkins toward Shepherdstown with the goal of "exposing one of the enemy's flanks," and sent orders to Grumble Jones' brigade, whose precise location was not known to Stuart, to be prepared to cooperate. Upon arriving in the Federal cavalry's presence, Fitz Lee determined that the hilly, rocky ground was not suitable for cavalry, and so dismounted his brigade and advanced in line of battle like infantry. The Union cavalry retired before them but took up a strong position at dark around the home of Colonel A.R. Boteler, a former aide de camp to Stonewall Jackson who, on August 15, 1863, would become a voluntary aide to Stuart. Both sides suffered numerous casualties in this battle near Shepherdstown, one of whom was Colonel James H. Drake, commander of the 1st Virginia Cavalry.

The Confederates prepared to attack again early on the 17th, but daylight revealed that the Federal cavalry were gone, having retreated during the night toward Harpers Ferry. The Federal cavalry's retreat was not flight from bellicose Rebels, but part of Meade's larger plan. At that place and at nearby Berlin, Maryland (now called Brunswick), Meade's army crossed the Potomac River on the 17th, intending to cut off the retreating Confederate army at Front Royal by forcing a passage through the Blue Ridge at Manassas Gap.

The Federal cavalry screened the Army of the Potomac's advance, skirmishing near Hedgesville and driving Wade Hampton's brigade, commanded by Colonel (and soon to be Brigadier General) Lawrence Baker. The leading infantry corps of the Army of the Potomac was the Third Corps, now commanded by Major General William H. French, and at first light on July 23 French advanced on Manassas Gap, which was occupied by the Stonewall Brigade and a brigade of Georgians under Colonel Edward J. Walker. The seriously outnumbered Confederates gave ground begrudgingly, and a strong Union attack at about 4:30 p.m. appeared to have the momentum to sweep the Georgians and Old Jack's veterans out of the way. The bulk of Stuart's cavalry other than Baker's brigade—Fitz Lee's, Chambliss', and Jenkins' brigades—made a forced march from the vicinity of Leetown toward Manassas Gap but did not arrive in time. Instead, infantry and artillery reinforcements under the command of Major General Robert Rodes arrived, and between the strength of his division and the poor coordination of attacks on French's part, the Federals were stopped. During the night of the 23rd the Confederates withdrew into the Luray Valley and left Front Royal to be occupied by the Yankees in the morning, but any hope Meade had of cutting Lee's army off from Richmond was abandoned. Many historians regard the Battle of Manassas Gap as the last engagement of the Gettysburg Campaign.

Stuart and the three brigades of Lee, Chambliss, and Jenkins spent the night of the 23rd below Gaines' Cross Roads, and on the 24th moved toward the sound of artillery fire in the direction of Newling's Cross Roads, which turned out to be Federal cannons shooting at Confederate infantry in Hill's Corps. Hill drove the enemy away before the cavalry arrived, and on the 25th the united Confederate forces continued on a line of march toward the Rappahannock.

Despite declaring emphatically to Flora in a letter on July 13 that his cavalry were "the finest body of men *on the planet*," Stuart apparently thought otherwise in several respects, because on July 30 he issued General Order No. 26 on "Cavalry Tactics" and had it distributed to everyone in his command. Beginning by saying that he had "endeavored in vain, by oral injunctions, to correct the defects in the mode of fighting pursued by this division," he proceeded to deliver to his horsemen four pages of a condensed manual of cavalry tactics: in preparation for action skirmishers were to be deployed quickly according to the nature of the ground; squadrons would form in distinct squadrons and regiments with distinct intervals; squadrons in rear of those deployed should ensure that no confusion occurring in front extended to them; broken squadrons must not run through the ranks of squadrons in the rear; when charging a column should begin trotting when 200 yards from the enemy and galloping at 50 yards; an enemy once broken must be followed vigorously; plundering in battle is strictly prohibited; the pistol should never be used in a charge unless the enemy is behind an impassable barrier or if a man is unhorsed; an attack should be made on either or both flanks simultaneously with the front; attacking cavalry should arrive noiselessly and then, with one loud yell, leap upon the enemy; rashness is a crime but boldness is not; when advancing in line of battle a brigade, regiment, or squadron should have its commander in front to supervise and control, but when in columns of squadrons, platoons, fours, or twos, the commander must be positioned centrally to control and communicate easily; squadron commanders will lead, "preserving in his own person coolness and self-possession, but the quickness of an eagle;" men who fail or falter in a charge "will not be lost sight of in the annals of infamy and disgrace"; should a charge be repulsed, skirmishers must direct concentrated fire on the advancing enemy to hold it in check until fresh troops arrive; only the ambulance corps will be allowed to remove the wounded . . . .and so on.

As it flowed from Stuart's pen or lips (it was signed by Major McClellan) General Order No. 26 must have seemed to its author like nothing more than a reminder list, but to a modern layman it is like an ancient and revealing stele—so that is when the cavalry begins to trot and then gallop, and that is where commanding officers were supposed to position themselves. One wonders if each of its maxims is an abbreviation of what Stuart's despised father-in-law, Phillip St. George Cooke, wrote in his 1862 *Cavalry Tactics*, or whether Jeb might have intentionally rejected Cooke's teachings simply because they were Cooke's.

At the end of July, the components of Lee's army were deployed with Longstreet's Corps in the Valley and Ewell's and Hill's Corps near Orange Court House, Gordonsville, and Culpeper, with the cavalry "holding the line of the Rappahannock. By the 30th, Stuart had decamped from the Bower and established a new headquarters—Camp Von Borcke—near Brandy Station.

Stuart's colorful and beloved former inspector and assistant adjutant general for whom the camp was named, Major Heros Borcke, was still re-covering, slowly, from a near-fatal neck wound received the previous June 19. Jeb visited him, kept track of his progress, and reported it to family and friends, and also attempted to obtain promotion, service, and an ocean voy-age for his old friend. He wrote President Davis on August 8 to recommend that Von Borcke be promoted to Brigadier General and sent to Europe to procure arms and equipment for the Confederate cavalry. Three days later, Stuart wrote his wife to say that the huge Prussian was "not improving," and was in need, according to his doctors, of "sea air."[3]

The month of August and first two weeks of September 1863, were not merely a time of rest and recuperation, but a period of great introspection as well, beginning at the top and filtering down. On August 1, President Davis issued a proclamation appointing August 21 as a day of fasting, humiliation and prayer, asking the Southern people "to unite in prayer and humble sub-mission under His chastening hand, and to beseech His favor on our suf-fering country."

There had been large religious movements in the Confederacy before, particularly after Sharpsburg in September 1862, and it does not require a degree in psychology, sociology, or theology to link a significant military tra-vail to a feeling of the need to repent and seek God's forgiveness.

On August 8, General Lee demonstrated his own repentance by sub-mitting a letter to Davis offering his resignation. He had been thinking long and hard about his performance at Gettysburg, and wrote that "I have been prompted by these reflections more than once since my return from Penn-sylvania to propose to Your Excellency the propriety of selecting another commander for this army. . . . No one is more aware than myself of my in-ability for the duties of my position. I cannot even accomplish what I myself desire. . . . I, therefore, in all sincerity, request your Excellency to take meas-ure to supply my place."

Davis did not accept, of course, writing in response, "To ask me to substi-tute you by someone . . . more fit to command, or who would possess more of the confidence of the army . . . is to demand an impossibility."

On August 13, General Lee issued General Order No. 83 in support of the President's proclamation, which began "Soldiers! We have sinned against Almighty God. We have forgotten his signal mercies, and have cultivated a revengeful, haughty, and boastful spirit. We have not remembered that the defenders of a just cause should be pure in his eyes; that 'our times are in his hand' and we have relied too much on our own arms for the achievement of our independence." With regard to August 21 he directed that "a strict observance of the day is enjoined upon the officers and soldiers of this army. All military duties, except such as are absolutely necessary, will be suspended. The commanding officers of brigades and regiments are requested to cause divine services, suitable to the occasion, to be performed in their respective commands."

Among the cadre of commanding officers in the Confederate armies, there were few more secure in their religious beliefs than Jeb Stuart,[4] yet if the national day of fasting, humiliation, and prayer caused him to exhibit any particular thoughts or actions, they have been lost to history. None of his staff officers recorded anything in particular about religious services or matters, and his letters to Flora contain no mention of it. To the contrary, his thoughts during those days were of things much more mundane—the threat of being replaced as commander of the cavalry, and a corresponding hope for promotion to Lieutenant General.

The former took the form of a rumor that Major General John Bell Hood was being groomed to replace Stuart. The historical record is not clear whether the rumor began in the War Department and was picked up by newspapers, or whether an article in the *Richmond Dispatch,* labeled "sensation news," itself permeated the War Department. Hood seemed like an odd choice for the role, considering that he was still recuperating from a serious arm wound sustained at Gettysburg on July 2, and during the war to date had not commanded cavalry.[5]

The rumor was sufficient to cause some of Stuart's admirers in the army to write letters of support to both the *Dispatch* and the *Richmond Whig,* and the sensitive Jeb probably chafed and worried about the possibility. To the extent his thoughts on the matter are preserved, however, he was dismissive of the whole affair. On August 11, he wrote Flora to say:

> I suppose you have seen mention of Hood's assignment to the command of the Cavalry as Lt. Genl. It is *all bosh*, gotten up by some malicious Scamp striving to undermine & vilify me. If there is a Lt. Genl of Cavalry appointed it will be your husband—that is if the Cav. Div. Gen Lee, the Sec'y, & Prest. Davis have a Say in the

matter. . . . Whatever defects there are in our Cav'y can not be cured by Hood.

He wrote her again on the 12th saying, "I have every reason to believe Hood's apt. is all *bosh* some malcontents are trying to get up, but will not succeed. Gen. Lee knows nothing of it & and I believe entre nous [between us] he has recommended me already for the place."

The probable basis for the Hood rumor, as well as the notion that Stuart, rather than any other officer, should be promoted to the rank of Lieutenant General, almost certainly had its origin in the decision by General Lee, revealed in a letter to President Davis dated August 3, that the Cavalry Division be reorganized into a Cavalry Corps.

The proposal was to place Wade Hampton and Fitz Lee each in command of a division, with Hampton commanding the brigades led by Grumble Jones, Lawrence Baker, and M.C. Butler, and Lee commanding the brigades of Rooney Lee (Chambliss), L.L. Lomax, and W.C. Wickham. Such an arrangement required the promotion of Hampton and Fitz Lee to Major General, effective August 3 for each, Baker to Brigadier General, which had occurred effective July 23, Butler to Brigadier General, effective September 1, Lomax to Brigadier General, which had occurred effective July 23, and Wickham to Brigadier General, effective September 1, 1863.

Thus, the newly minted cavalry corps was led by a total of nine generals, one in corps command, two in division command, and six in brigade command. At the pinnacle of this new command structure was a shoe that needed to be dropped and was expected to be, the dropping of which would be consistent with the basic command structure of the Confederate army—promotion of Jeb Stuart to the rank of Lieutenant General. Unlike the Federal army, in which major generals commanded divisions, corps, and entire armies, the Confederate arrangement was more clearly defined and religiously followed—brigades were commanded by brigadiers, divisions by major generals, corps by lieutenant generals, and armies by full generals.

But the shoe did not drop, not that August nor that September. Indeed, it never would, and the reason for its tenacious refusal to do so has never been explained. Hampton would be promoted to Lieutenant General after succeeding to command of the Cavalry Corps upon Stuart's death. His promotion was not instantaneous—it did not occur until February 1865—but it did occur. Jeb Stuart was destined to die a major general, and while no one ever made official the reason, we may assume it was because of his performance, or lack thereof, between June 24 and July 1, 1863. Just as Patrick Cleburne was never elevated beyond major general after proposing that slaves be freed, armed, and enlisted in the Southern army, Jeb Stuart was never elevated beyond that rank, most probably because of his role in the Gettysburg defeat.

No sooner had the reorganization been completed than the potential for another command change became apparent, brought on by the court-martial of Brig. Gen. Grumble Jones, Stuart's other least favorite underling. Stuart first ordered that Jones be relieved of command for his role in the loss of Ewell's wagons at Monterrey Pass on July 5. Jones then played into Stuart's hands by sending what Stuart considered "a very disrespectful letter," and he ordered that the brigadier be arrested and court-martialed. A panel was selected and a trial date was set for late August before a court was overseen by a board of six generals and one colonel.

Also during that week, Stuart and his staff relocated to "Camp Boteler," near Culpeper Court House, which was named for Alexander R. Boteler, a Confederate Congressman and patron of Stuart then serving as a voluntary Aide-de-Camp to Stuart with the rank of colonel. There Jeb had plenty to think about in addition to his duties as commander of Lee's cavalry, including the death of a sister, how much he missed his deceased daughter, little Flora, the condition and future of Heros Von Borcke, the despicable conduct of Federal cavalry Colonel John I. Gregg, the exploits of Confederate Lt. Col. Elijah V. White, and, of course, the fact that he'd still not been promoted to Lt. General.

News of the death of his sister, Victoria Augusta ("Vic") Stuart Boyden, reached Jeb in a letter from Flora received August 26, 1863. She was five years younger than Jeb, and although a brother and a sister were born between him in 1833 and her in 1838, she was his closest playmate during their childhood because both intervening siblings died early, the brother having passed away unnamed three months after being born in 1834, and the sister, Virginia Josephine, having died at age six in 1842.

Jeb answered Flora's letter immediately, the same day, calling Vic "my little playfellow and companion whose nature once chimed with my own & who always was all love and affection towards me tinged with jealousy lest I might love some one else more than herself." He regretted not having the opportunity to see her again, "but it was not so ordered by the Great Disposer of human affairs." In fact, he had been so expecting her death that he told Flora that ""I never received intelligence of the death of one so near and dear to me with less grief," and that "she was so much happier and better off than when in this world of pain and sorrow." He asked that Flora secure a good picture of her for him.

Details of Vic's demise are sketchy. Jeb wrote that he was prepared for her death because, when he heard of her sickness, he expected that she would not recover. Yet he also wrote in his letter of August 26 that "sister Lummie died the same way," which was in childbirth. Columbia Lafayette "Lummie" Hairston passed away on August 2, 1857 while giving birth to a daughter, Agnes, who also died.[6] It is unclear how Jeb could have been long-prepared and resigned to his sister's death if she died giving birth, but apparently she suffered from other serious ailments, which he referred to in saying, "I never felt she could be happy under the circumstances surrounding her."

However prepared for her death Stuart may have been, Vic's passing was one more link in a growing chain of regrets and losses that Stuart seemed determined to carry with ease, even though it might have pulled another man under.

NOTES

1 He held those positions from October 2, 1861 to July 15, 1862 and again from December 1863 until May 13, 1864. *They Followed the Plume* at 49-56.

2 *In the Saddle with Stuart*, at 87.

3 Letter of August 11, 1863, *J.E.B. Stuart Papers*, http://6whitehorses.com/cw/index.html, cited hereinafter as "Whitehorse letters."

4 Stuart may be the only Civil War commander whose Christian faith has been the basis for a book, *viz,* T. Perry, *The Christian Life of J.E.B. Stuart* (Ararat, Va.: Laurel Hill Publishing, 2008).

5 Hood did serve in the 2nd U.S. Cavalry, as a lieutenant, from March 1855 to April, 1861.

6 Sister Lummie was married to Peter Wilson Hairston, who was a cousin as well as a brother-in-law to Jeb. He served as a civilian volunteer aide-de-camp to Stuart from May to October, 1861, and was in the Battle of First Manassas, but returned home to care for his plantation, "Cooleemee," and his second wife, Fannie McCoy Cald-

well, before returning to the army and serving on the staff of Jubal Early from late 1862 until early in 1865. He and Lummie had four children between 1850 and 1857, but all were deceased by 1867, whereas Peter lived until 1886. Vic and her husband, Nathaniel A. Boyden, an attorney, had one child, a daughter named Columbia Stuart Boyden, who was born in 1860, and after her mother's death was raised by Jeb Stuart's widow, Flora, in Saltville, Virginia.

CHAPTER 5

SEASON OF SPARRING
August 27–October 9, 1863

Spur on! Spur on! We love the bounding
Of barbs that bear us to the fray.
The charge our bugles now are sounding
And our bold Stuart leads the way!
  —*Cavalier's Glee,* first stanza,
    by Major William W. Blackford,
    Engineer Officer, Stuart's staff

IT IS REASONABLE TO think that the loss of his younger sister was a reason that Jeb's thoughts returned, all the more heavily, to Little Flora, who had died the previous November. Two days after learning of Vic's death, on August 28, he wrote his wife and asked if she'd received "the love of a picture I sent you from the Valley of a little girl putting a doll to sleep, so much like our dearest Flora."[1] On September 11 he waxed more sentimental in a letter to Nannie Price, who was at "Dundee." Thinking of the place, which he'd described before as "the most lovely place on Earth," he recalled a period when his family had stayed there with the Price family in 1862, and lamented:

> [D]o you remember how Little Flora ran out to me, climbed up on my stirrup, clung around my neck with her dear little arms, with tearful kisses till forced away. Ah, Nannie, can I ever forget that picture! that parting! that embrace! Can you wonder at the tears that fill my eyes as I write. The thought flashed through my mind at that moment "we may not meet again." It is now vividly remembered and the gloomy apprehension rose and kindled tears in my

80

eyes. I was just starting on the campaign against Pope and I knew that *my life* hung by a thread ready to be severed by one of the thousands of death's missiles which sweep the battle plain. All this flashed through my mind for there are *moments* which are like a *century*. I thought of the widow (there she stood before me) and the fatherless little sylph in my arms, and breathed a prayer that he who tempers the wind to the shorn lamb, would deal tenderly with mine. Ah! little did I think *I* was to be *spared* and *she* taken!

I feel it is all gain to her but my grief admonishes me that earth has lost its chief attraction, and while it does not make me reckless, I go forth at the summons of duty and of danger with that cheerful resignation which the cold world calls rashness.

Excuse me, dear Nannie, for obtruding my grief upon you. You feel so near to me. I talk to you as if communing with myself. I dare not write to Flora as I have written to you. I have to restrain my grief, my feelings, my language on that subject (little Flora) and she little dreams what agony in the lone bivouac and even on the march those choking memories have caused me.[2]

Another event that occurred at the end of August left Jeb with mixed feelings, though with disappointment outweighing joy. The court martial of Grumble Jones ended with a verdict that he was not guilty of disobeying orders or acting in a manner that was prejudicial to military order and discipline, but that he was guilty of behavior with disrespect to his commanding officer. He was sentenced to be "privately reprimanded by the Commanding General."[3] Lee did not act on the verdict quickly, and gave a great deal of thought to what form the private reprimand should take. While Lee was still pondering, Stuart sent him a letter dated September 10 in regard to Colonel Thomas Munford, in which he took the opportunity to remind Lee that the previous assignment of Jones to brigade command instead of Munford was "highly prejudicial to the service," and that Jeb now urged Munford for command of the brigade again.[4]

The commander of the nearest Federal cavalry force was not grieving, having sentimental thoughts, or thinking about the Confederate command structure. Instead John I. "Long John" Gregg, was obsessing about John Mosby and his partisan rangers. Although only a Colonel, Gregg commanded a brigade of cavalry in the Army of the Potomac,[5] and on September 1, 1863 he addressed a letter to "the officer commanding Confederate troops near Gaines Crossroads, Virginia," in which he warned that civilians who aided the Confederate military would be treated as combatants. Gregg had been plagued by Mosby, and had assigned a brigade of 1,200 cavalry troopers, with artillery, to hunt down and capture the Gray Ghost and his sixty men.

The letter was forwarded to Stuart, who responded by writing back to Gregg on September 3 that the Federal officer's warning "caused no surprise," and that:

> I expect such from those who, baffled in legitimate warfare, seek to turn their weapons against helpless women and children and unarmed men. Your *threat* is harmless. For any acts as you propose, I will know whom to hold responsible. My government knows how to protect her citizens; and justice though sometimes *slow* will be *sure*, to reach the perpetrators of such barbarities as you desire to inaugurate. Our citizens are accustomed to your bravado. Our soldiers know their duty.[6]

Adding to Gregg's consternation and Stuart's satisfaction during those days were the actions of Lt. Col. Elijah White, who commanded the 35th Virginia, aka "White's Comanches." Although a part of Jones' Brigade of Stuart's command, he was operating independently, having been dispatched by Stuart to operate in the rear of the enemy. Despite White having clashed with Stuart during the Sharpsburg Campaign in September 1862, the cavalry commander was now singing his praises. In late August White had crossed the Potomac River and attacked a force of Federal cavalry ensconced in strong fortifications on a farm belonging to a man named William Pooles, at Edwards Ferry on the river. Despite the existence of an eight-foot-wide ditch, or moat, around the Federals' position, into which several mounted Confederates fell, White drove the enemy from their position, took 16 prisoners and 35 horses and mules, with the loss of only one man wounded.

Then on September 1, the date of Gregg's letter, White attacked Federal cavalry commanded by Kilpatrick on the Barbee and Orleans Road, killed six, wounded 10, captured 24, and seized 30 horses without losing any of his men. Of the first action, Stuart reported to his superiors on September

5 that "Colonel White and his command in this daring enterprise, which struck such terror to the enemy, deserves high praise. Every day brings new proof of his activity." As proof of the efficacy of his closing remark, on September 6 Stuart forwarded White's report on the action against Kilpatrick as proof of "the untiring activity and energy of Colonel White and his command."[7]

The matter of Stuart's promotion, or lack thereof, resurfaced in a letter to Flora dated September 4, when Jeb's expectation for advancement was still high. Apparently one of his staff officers had drawn a fanciful caricature of how Jeb would outfit himself once he was elevated to Lieutenant General. He enclosed it with his letter, described as "a first rate picture of the Lieutenant General as he appears when he has just gotten a new rig, or joke on one of the Staff." To Nanny Price a week later he commented that "Wade Hampton and Fitz Lee are Major Generals Commanding Divisions in my Cavalry Corps, but I am not yet Lieutenant General. I command the Corps as Major General."

Stuart, ever ambitious, ever desiring of recognition and reward, ever generous to those he commanded who garnered his praise, may have been heartbroken but he tried not to let it show. To Flora naturally he confided, writing on September 11:

> The cavalry has been divided into two divisions under Hampton & Fitz Lee as Major Generals, and the whole under my command, but I am not promoted—Whether I am or not remains to be seen. Gen Lee says nothing to me about it nor I to him, of course. Every one seems to think it will come—I am not sanguine.

The word "sanguine," meaning cheerfully optimistic, was commonly used in 1863 but is rarely heard today, except occasionally as a synonym for "ruddy," "bloody," or "red." It is not a word characteristic of Stuart, who was usually naturally optimistic. The subject, and Stuart's hope of promotion for a job well done and duty met, would not end that mid-September, but neither would it ever become more real. The situation was, in Jeb's mind, the same as Mammie's analysis of Scarlett O'Hara's behavior at the Wilkes' party at the beginning of *Gone with the Wind:* "not fittin,' not fittin,' just not fittin.'"

Before sunrise on September 13, 1863, Dr. J.M. Hudgin, formerly of the 9th Virginia Cavalry, arrived at Stuart's headquarters at Camp Boteler with important news. Hudgin had previously been employed as a surgeon at cavalry headquarters, but his wife had died recently, supposedly "from fright caused by the conduct of some of Kilpratrick's men,"[8] and Hudgin had been at his home in Jeffersonton, some 12 miles from Culpeper, for several days. From there he had seen a large force of the enemy's cavalry—three entire divisions as it turned out—advancing toward Culpeper, and he set out in the dark to cross the Rappahannock River "at an obscure ford" and alert Stuart.

The enemy's cavalry was supported by infantry, such that the movement had all the trappings of a concerted advance. Stuart immediately alerted Colonel Lunsford Lomax, who was then in temporary command of Grumble Jones' brigade and in the best position, near Brandy Station, to intercept the invaders. He also ordered all wagons, equipment, supplies, and disabled horses away from Culpeper toward Rapidan Station where they would be beyond the reach of the enemy if their movement was as ambitious as it appeared.

Stuart could not know that the Federal advance was only a reconnaissance in force, ordered by Meade on the 12th after Federal scouts reported "a southerly movement of the enemy" that could have been associated with the rumored transfer of Virginia troops to Bragg's army or any number of other possibilities. Meade's orders were for Gen. Pleasonton to move on Culpeper with his cavalry, and Warren, commanding the Second Corps of infantry, to follow.[9] Both were cautioned that "their movement was to be restricted to a reconnaissance for obtaining information of the enemy's position and they were not to compromise matters so as to force on a general engagement."[10] In the event they encountered a superior force they were "to retire to the line of the Rappahannock." Only if the enemy had, in fact, withdrawn from the Rapidan or "should he permit of its being done without too great a sacrifice" was Culpeper Court House to be retained in Federal hands.

Major Henry McClellan, Stuart's Assistant Adjutant General and Chief of Staff, did not interpret the Federal advance as a mere reconnaissance, and wrote that they came on "with great spirit and rapidity." They collided loudly with Lomax's badly outnumbered brigade near the old Brandy Station battlefield.[11]

September 13 turned out to be a busy, and dark, day for the Stuart Horse Artillery, now commanded by Major Robert Beckham and consisting of batteries commanded by Captain James Breathed (1st Stuart Horse Artillery), Captain William M. McGregor (2nd Stuart Horse Artillery), Captain Roger A. Chew (Ashby's Battery), Captain James F. Hart (Washington South Carolina Battery), Captain Marcellus M. Moorman ((Lynchburg Battery), and Captain Wiley H. Griffin (Baltimore Light Artillery).

At Fleetwood Hill, McGregor's Battery and one gun from Chew's Battery, commanded by Lt. James Thompson, made a stand, banging away at Kilpatrick's cavalry, which had crossed the river at Kelly's Ford along with a section of Battery K of the 1st U.S. Artillery. When a brigade of Buford's division arrived from its crossing at the Rappahannock Bridge and linked up with Kilpatrick, McGregor and Chew limbered up and retreated rapidly. Along with Lomax's horsemen they beat a path for Culpeper, some six miles away, the enemy in hot pursuit.

Chew's lone gun became separated from the rest of the retreating Rebels and, seeing enemy cavalry closing in, Chew directed the limber to leave the road and take a course due west in the direction of the court house, bouncing over fields at a full gallop, the gunners clinging to the limber chest or riding the four horses pulling the gun. Private Benjamin Holliday, fresh from VMI and having served with the horse artillery only eight days, claimed later that he expected the gun to overturn at any moment and that he stayed aboard the limber chest only by "holding onto the trunnions." The latter is highly unlikely, as trunnions are the sidepieces of the gun's barrel by which it is secured to its carriage, and they would have been beyond the reach of anyone riding the limber chest. He may have meant the iron handles on the side of the chest.

Once they were out of sight of the enemy, Chew ordered the gun to halt at "a fine old Colonial mansion" belonging to the John Minor Botts estate, and, while the ladies of the household watched from the front porch, they fired a single shot at the distant enemy before limbering up and continuing their retreat. When they arrived at the north end of Culpeper, they unlimbered again on a hill from which they had an unbroken view of the countryside and saw, coming their way in plain view, what Holliday estimated to be five or six thousand enemy cavalry, "and behind them came the infantry of Meade's army." The lone gun opened fire again, with Captain

Chew sitting erect beside it on his horse, directing the fire. "At every discharge of the gun," Holliday recalled, "I could see men and horses go down, but they would close up and continue to advance."[12]

Soon the enemy found their range. A Federal shell hit the chimney of a burned house nearby, scattering bricks. Another shell burst above the gun, wounding a horse. Chew ordered cease fire and as the men prepared to limber up again, Holliday requested and was given permission to go through Culpeper on foot and meet the gun on the south side of town. When he was about sixty yards from the cannon he heard a commotion and turned to see a squadron of Federal cavalry charging in column of fours at the rear of the gun, having slipped around the Confederates at the base of the hill, where it was too steep for Chew's men to see them.

Lieutenant James Thompson, who commanded the gun, ordered his men to scatter and abandon the cannon to the enemy. Chew and Thompson were already mounted and Chew escaped. Thompson, however, seeing the officer commanding the squadron of Yankees riding some fifty yards in advance of his men and shouting at Thompson to surrender, rode out alone to meet him. The two men began exchanging pistol shots as they neared each other and continued dueling until one of Thompson's bullets found its mark. The Federal officer fell from his horse, which continued galloping toward the Confederate officer. Thompson seized its loose reins, turned and galloped away, leading the prize and escaping, despite close pursuit.

Another gun of the Horse Artillery, of Moorman's Battery, was also captured, along with 16 of its gunners, three of whom were wounded. Loss of one of Stuart's cannon was a rare event. Losing two in a row was unbelievable, and yet the Horse Artillery was still not out of the woods. Both the Federal cavalry and its artillery were demonstrating their mettle.

The battery commanded by Captain Wiley Griffin, alternately known as the 2nd Maryland Artillery or the Baltimore Light Artillery, had three pieces on the field and took a position near Culpeper after falling back from a position near Brandy Station called Muddy Run. Soon they were drawing fire from six enemy cannon, and when the sparse, supporting cavalry of Lomax's brigade melted away, Griffin limbered up and made a dash for it. Racing through Culpeper, they were suddenly t-boned by the 1st Vermont Cavalry, which galloped headlong into the battery from a side street. Ten of the battery's men, including a lieutenant and a musician, were captured.

In another part of the little town, a section of McGregor's battery commanded by Lieutenant Charles Ford was nearly cut off, and escaped only by turning down a side alley that emptied into open ground. Seeing Confederate cavalry riding to his support, Lieutenant Ford ordered the guns to halt, unlimber and deliver one devastating blast into the pursuing Yankees before limbering up again and continuing the flight toward the Rapidan.

The Confederates would retreat, halt, unlimber, fire, limber up and fall back further. In doing so, another of Moorman's guns, commanded by Sergeant Lewis T. Nunnellee, took position at the edge of a wood. Just as they were preparing to fire, a squadron of blue riders charged out of the woods toward the cannon, coming on so rapidly that the gunners did not have time to turn the gun toward them. Just as the enemy was almost on them, with the gunners preparing to fight hand to hand, a small band of Confederate cavalry, none other than Stuart and his staff, dashed in, firing pistols, driving the Federals back, and giving Nunnellee and his men time to hitch up the gun and flee.

Confederate cavalry and artillery attempted another stand on a 400-foot elevation grandiosely called Pony Mountain. Rooney Lee's brigade, commanded by Colonel Richard Beale, arrived. Lomax was able to rally and reform his brigade and make a concerted stand, but the Federals continued to press them. Several Rebels were killed or wounded, and once again the gray troopers fell back.

Stuart and his exhausted men reached Rapidan Station and crossed the river to safety at nightfall on the 13th. Confederate infantry were there in force, and when the Federals arrived in the morning, the two sides squared off on either side of the river. The Federals had not brought any artillery from Culpeper, and in the morning a section of Moorman's Battery recrossed the river and shelled the enemy, wreaking a little revenge for the beating they'd taken the day before.

Otherwise, neither side attacked until just before dark, when Major C.E. Flourney of the 6th Virginia requested permission to cross over and attack a few squadrons of the enemy that were visible. Stuart approved and Flourney crossed the river, formed in column of squadrons, and drove the Yankees away. It was, as Major Henry McClellan observed, a "movement . . . of no consequence," but it was witnessed by spectators in all three branches of the army, and was accomplished skillfully. Once the Federals were dispersed, Flourney reformed his regiment and walked it back to the Confederate position.

The Federals had accomplished what they intended—reconnaissance—and then some. Culpeper Court House was in their hands. Perhaps more importantly, they'd demonstrated loudly and clearly that neither Federal cavalry nor Federal horse artillery remained even slightly inferior to their Confederate counterparts, as they had been less than a year earlier. Neither Brandy Station nor Gettysburg's East Cavalry Field had been a fluke. Excellent Yankee horsemen had arrived, and they would not be leaving any time soon.

As of September 15, the two armies were aligned along opposite sides of the Rapidan and Robertson's Rivers. The cavalry and Horse Artillery were posted to cover the fords and, as will be discussed in more detail in the next chapter, Lee, Davis, and Longstreet organized a major offensive movement, but it consisted of sending the bulk of Longstreet's First Corps west to reinforce Bragg's Army of the Tennessee rather than a movement against Meade's Army of the Potomac.

On September 16, Stuart made a reconnaissance across the river, taking one gun each from Ashby's and the Lynchburg batteries. On the 17th he was back in camp, which he had not named and which he referred to only as "Outpost." There he wrote Flora about something that was becoming ever nearer and dearer to his heart—finding a permanent home.

At some point during the previous three days he had learned of and visited a farm on the Rapidan that had been the residence of the grandfather of a Dr. Madison. "It . . . is in a charming neighborhood," Jeb wrote, "not far from the Railroad, beautiful woods, flowers, hills and picturesque view of the Blue Ridge." Before contacting Flora or giving her a chance to see it he wrote his brother, Alick (William Alexander), who ran the family salt business, and urged him to buy it as an investment. The place was, he asserted to Flora, "such as you and I have often pictured in our imaginations."[13] It would never be more than that.

On September 21, Stuart took time to write to Lt. Frank Robertson, his staff assistant engineer, who had been so exhausted and ill after the Gettysburg retreat that he had first been taken into the big house at the Bower to recuperate, then been given a two-month furlough and taken by government ambulance to Salem in the Valley. The two months were up but Robertson was still not recovered. Jeb sent his regrets and took the opportunity to reflect on the "fiery ordeals" he had sent Robertson into, particularly at Chancellorsville, saying, "You will never forget those trials and I hope the kind Providence which so signally favored you will soon see you restored to the field and your much attached comrades."[14]

That night a courier reported to Stuart that Federal cavalry had been sighted moving from Madison Court House against the army's left. Stuart ordered Hampton's entire division to be prepared to move at first light and, with Hampton still recovering from his Gettysburg wound, Jeb took personal command of the three brigades, which comprised approximately 2,000 men.

Soon after their pre-dawn departure, they ran into a brigade of John Buford's Union division at Jack's Shop, a small community about five miles south of Madison Court House. Skirmishing and exchanges of artillery fire escalated into all-out battle early in the afternoon when Buford launched an attack against Stuart's right flank and, simultaneously, a theretofore undetected brigade commanded by Brig. Gen. Henry Davies, of Kilpatrick's division, came at Stuart's left flank and rear.

Once again the Federal cavalry was proving to be not merely a force to be reckoned with but one to be feared. The 1st and 5th North Carolina regiments counterattacked Davies but were repulsed. Stuart, realizing that he was almost surrounded, ordered another charge by the 9th Virginia and the 5th North Carolina and fell back with the rest of his command to a small hill in the rear. There, with Jeb calmly directing the defense, the Horse Artillery was required to fire in three directions and the cavalry to attack in two. Davies now had his men across and holding the road by which Stuart had arrived, and Buford was hammering at the Confederates' right and front. Stuart and an entire division were essentially surrounded.

With his staff, Stuart led a charge of the 7th, 11th, and 12th Virginia regiments against Davies in order to create an escape route. Jeb was riding a newly acquired horse named Highflyer (sometimes recorded as Highfly) that was shot from beneath him as the attack was repulsed. At one point the two sections of Hart's Washington South Carolina Battery were side by side but blasting in opposite directions while regiments in sight of each other charged in the same manner. Buford and Davies were alternately pressing with vigor and defending stubbornly. Even Major McClellan reached the conclusion that "It seemed for a time that Stuart had at last been caught where he could not escape serious damage."[15]

An attack by two Rebel regiments on Davies' position across the road finally opened a means of escape, but only because Confederate cavalrymen dismounted in the middle of the fray, tore down a fence which Davies' dismounted men were defending, and then desperately defended the passage. The rest of the Confederate division poured through the gap and kept going, all the way to Liberty Mills on the Rapidan, where Cadmus Wilcox's division of infantry from Hill's Corps arrived and put an end to the turmoil.

An entertaining sidelight of the Battle of Jack's Shop involved one of history's more colorful, idiosyncratic, and unfortunate characters—Lt. Col. George St. Leger Grenfell.

Grenfell was a British soldier of fortune, born in 1808, who claimed to have fought in Algeria and Morocco in the 1830s against the Barbary Pirates, under Garibaldi in South America in the 1840s, and in the Crimean War and the Sepoy Mutiny in the 1850s before coming to the United States to cast his lot with the Confederacy. He served with John Hunt Morgan and Braxton Bragg in the Western Theatre, and then came east to serve as Inspector General of Cavalry. He seemed to be more of an oddity, or pet, than a valued member of the staff. Major McClellan wrote that Jeb "employed him somewhat as an inspector," and that "his eccentricities were the source of much good-natured amusement."[16]

Theodore Garnett provided an additional portrait of Grenfell later that autumn, when Stuart headquartered near Orange Courthouse at "Camp Wigwam." He wrote that Grenfell's tent was set off from the rest of the staff's, and that "he was a curious compound of soldierly qualities and personal idiosyncrasies; at times he would talk with officers & couriers in a sort of general harangue, relating some of the most wonderful anecdotes that were ever heard, and again, he would avoid all society, confining himself closely in his tent, in company with his big yellow Bull-dog, and appearing only at meals." He had two particularly fine horses that he combed and brushed frequently, allowing no other groom to touch them.[17]

At Jack's Shop, however, Grenfell found himself in some of the hottest fighting of his experience and he became demoralized. Riding beside Major McClellan in one of the Confederate regiments' attacks on Kirkpatrick that was repulsed, Grenfell decided the day was lost. "He took to the bushes," McClellan recalled, "swam the river, returned to Orange Court House and reported that Stuart, his staff, and the whole command were surrounded and captured." When he learned he was mistaken, and that Jeb and his command had extricated themselves, his mortification was, according to McClellan, "so great that he did not again show his face in our camp,"[18] which was an obvious exaggeration considering that he was there the following November.

Grenfell, according to Garnett, "disappeared from our midst about X-mas, 1863, and I heard no more until his arrest somewhere in the North, by the Yankee Gov't, charged with an attempt to burn Chicago." In fact, the "Chicago Conspiracy" was a plot hatched by Chicago Democrats, aided by Confederate agents, to free the Confederate prisoners held at Camp Douglass. It was an utter failure, 100 Democrats were arrested, eight men were tried and convicted of treason in Cincinnati in January 1865, and one was sentenced to be hanged—George St. Leger Grenfell. The British Minister in Washington intervened and convinced President Andrew Johnson to commute the sentence to life imprisonment, after which Grenfell was confined at Fort Jefferson in the Dry Tortugas in the Gulf of Mexico along with 526 other prisoners, including Lincoln assassination conspirators Dr. Samuel Mudd, Edmund Spangler, Samuel Arnold, and Michael O'Laughlin. William Felton, a custodian at Fort Jefferson, described Grenfell during those days.

He was a queer bird altogether. Grenfell was sure one tough lookin' customer, six foot tall, black-haired, an' with black eyes under big, bushy eyebrows. He had a tremendous black beard, too, an' wore a red flannel shirt open at the neck, an' his pant legs tucked in high boots. Folks said he was a son of Sir Roger Grenfell, an earl, or somethin' swell like that.[19]

In April, 1867, Dr. Mudd wrote of Grenfell to his brother-in-law, saying:

Colonel St. Ledger Grenfel is kept in close confinement under guard. A few days ago, being sick, he applied to the doctor of the Post for medical attention, which he was refused, and he was ordered to work. Feeling himself unable to move about, he refused. He was then ordered to carry a ball until further orders, which he likewise refused. He was then tied up for half a day, and still refusing, he was taken to one of the wharves, thrown overboard with a rope attached, and ducked; being able to keep himself above water, a fifty pound weight was attached to his feet. Grenfel is an old man, about sixty. He has never refused to do work which he was able to perform, but they demanded more than he felt able, and he wisely refused. They could not conquer him, and he is doing now that which he never objected doing.[20]

Grenfell was one of several prisoners who contracted Yellow Fever in September 1867. He was cared for by Dr. Mudd, who wrote his wife that he did not expect the old soldier to survive. Not only did he recover, the following March he bribed a guard and, with three other prisoners, escaped in a small boat. When pursuit by steamship failed to discover them, it was assumed they were lost at sea, but according to a newspaper account the following June he showed up in Mobile, Alabama, and from there sailed back to England, although he was never heard of again and the newspaper article may have been a fabrication.

Stuart must have been shaken by the close call at Jack's Shop, but if so it was not reflected in his letter to Flora dated September 26. In fact, that letter causes one to wonder if the battle Jeb observed was the same event that McClellan, Grenfell, and others attended. The purpose of the Federal advance, Jeb wrote, was a raid on the central railroad, so that Stuart "put after him to attack & frustrate his purpose." That attack he described as "very effectual," and although the enemy "endeavored" to get in his rear, so that he had to fight both Kilpatrick and Buford at the same time, the result was that the Confederates "drove Kilpatrick to the south side of the Rapidan where our Inf. ought to have annihilated him but instead of attacking him remained on the defensive."

Jeb said he then "crossed at Liberty Mills (*didn't 'fall back'* as the papers have it)" in order to get reinforcements and "moved upon him driving back to his artillery an advance regiment." It then being dark, Stuart moved to get on the south side of the enemy in order to attack the next morning, only to discover that "he had taken to his heels." He mentioned having had High-flyer shot beneath him, but said it happened on the 22nd, as if that date were not when the recent, desperate battle was fought.

The affair was, he concluded, "a grand success to turn back so much larger force than mine & defeat its object independently of the loss inflicted."[21] Apparently the old saying about there being as many different descriptions of the same automobile wreck as there are witnesses was accurate long before there were automobiles to wreck.

However, Stuart's embellishing was probably motivated by another reason—Flora was obsessing and needed reassurance about his safety. She was in her ninth month of pregnancy and would give birth to Virginia Pelham Stuart on October 9, 1863. Although her letters to Stuart have not survived, it is apparent from Jeb's next to her, on October 3, that her communications to him were filled with expressions of worry. "I have been thinking of you almost constantly for several days," he wrote. "Your anxiety about me pending a battle is not unlike that I feel for you in your impending trial." Stories in the newspapers were not to be believed, and to prove it he enclosed two articles, one from the *Richmond Whig* and another from the *Richmond Enquirer*, that contained Stuart-friendly news.

Turning to less sensitive subjects, he mentioned a humorous incident that had recently occurred. He and his staff "had a grand drinking," not of liquor, which Jeb never touched, but of raspberry vinegar. He did not elaborate on the origin of the beverage, which is used principally as a salad dressing today but which was popular as a beverage then. However, by referring to it as *"the* raspberry vinegar," one may infer either that Flora sent it or that she knew who did. Two bottles made the rounds, were consumed, and a third followed. Possibly by accident but more likely by design of a practical joker, this one contained catsup rather than raspberry vinegar which Jeb described as creating "a mixture anything but palatable." Jeb did not say how many were partaking, but he reported that "all but two of us," he and Surgeon John Fontaine, "got sold."[22]

Fontaine was not an official member of Stuart's staff at that time but he soon would be. Talcott Eliason had been the Cavalry's Medical Director since January 1862, but following the Gettysburg Campaign his health, like that of Robertson and Blackford, deteriorated and Fontaine was brought on board, first to assist and then to replace Eliason, who went to Richmond to recuperate and who would resign from active service on July 9, 1864. Fontaine had served as surgeon of the 4th Virginia, then for Fitz Lee's brigade. He was destined to be Stuart's tending physician after the general's mortal wounding seven months hence.

Stuart wrote Flora again on October 5. He had by then christened his headquarters "Camp Chickamauga," in honor of the singular Confederate victory in the west, made possible in large part by the addition of most of Longstreet's Corps to the Army of the Tennessee. This camp was at Brampton, the home of Dr. Andrew Grinnan, outside of Orange Court House, described in more detail below. The letter was chatty and newsy, perhaps masking Jeb's concern over Flora's condition and the fact that he'd not heard from her for several days. He sent more cavalry-favorable newspaper articles, some captured letters for Flora's sister, Maria, and he described a local lady named Miss Glasselle "who danced a jig with my great uncle [Sam Pannill] at my mother's wedding." The lady was noted for wearing a turban, being "an elegant old lady," but "never happy unless she was miserable."

Of this latter trait Jeb remarked, "It reminded me of my darling when she will insist on looking on the dark side in preference to the bright." He also reported that Von Borcke was "still quite low with fever," asked if she had the words to the song *When This Cruel War is Over*, and enclosed the lyrics to *Cavalier's Glee*, which he said was "now a great cavalry song."

Cavalier's Glee was not merely a cavalry song, but THE song of Stuart and his cavalry, second only to *Jine the Cavalry*, having been written by Stuart's engineer and faithful chronicler, William W. Blackford, as follows:

Spur on! Spur on! We love the bounding
of barbs that bear us to the fray.
The charge our bugles now are sounding
and our bold Stuart leads the way!

CHORUS: The path of honour lies before us.
Our hated foeman gathers fast.
At home, bright eyes are sparkling for us,
and we'll defend them to the last!

 Spur on! Spur on! We love the rushing
of steeds that spurn the turf they tread.
We'll through the northern ranks go crushing
with our proud battle flag o'erhead.

Spur on! Spur on! We love the flashing
of blades that battle to be free.
'Tis for our sunny south they are clashing,
for household, God and liberty!

Spur on! Spur on! We love the bounding
of barbs that bear us to the fray.
The charge our bugles now are sounding
nd our bold Stuart leads the way!

It was at "Brampton," Dr. Grinnan's estate, that Blackford wrote the poem.[23] The time Stuart and his staff spent at Brampton was not as memorable as the time spent at The Bower, but it was pleasant. The home was built in 1846 and was a "two-tier portico, temple-form Greek Revival-style residence," that, while popular in the north and deep south was rarely seen in Virginia.[24]

Stuart and his staff did not stay in the house, but they took their meals there with the family, which consisted only of Dr. Grinnan, his wife, and his sister, and also occupied two of the rooms as offices. Stuart's tent was pitched under a young tulip poplar, just to the right of the house as one approaches it. He called it his tree and once said to Dr. Grinnan: "I am never as much at home anywhere as when in my tent under this tree and many a hard ride I have had to take to get back to it. I shall be killed in this war, and you must remember this is my tree, 'Stuart's tree.'" Sadly, the tree fell during Hurricane Hazel in 1954.[25]

Meantime, General Lee finally came to a conclusion about what to do with Brig. Gen. Grumble Jones. Lee had a good deal of respect for Jones but he was also fully aware of Stuart's and Jones' dislike of each other. In a letter to President Davis, Lee wrote, "I consider General Jones a brave and intelligent officer, but his feelings have become so opposed to General Stuart that I have lost all hope of his being useful in the cavalry here. . . . I understand he will no longer serve under Stuart and I do not think it would be an advantage for him to do so, but I wish to make him useful."

On October 9, 1863, the matter was finally decided. Jones received an order from the War Department assigning him to command cavalry in the Department of Western Virginia and East Tennessee.[26] At long last Stuart was free of the two subordinate officers, Robertson and Jones, he had most longed to divorce. Thomas Rosser, one of Stuart's favorites, replaced Jones as a brigade commander, there also being some reorganization of regiments between his and Lomax's—previously Robertson's—brigade.

It was then autumn, "a closing off and a gathering in time; a putting away and a covering up time." It was not, however, quite time to go into winter quarters. Some more of Stuart's 1863 adventures lay just ahead.

NOTES

1 Mitchell, Adele H., ed., *The Letters of Major General James E.B. Stuart* , p. 337 (Stuart-Mosby Historical Society: 1990), cited hereinafter as Mitchell letters.

2 Mitchell letters at 343-44.

3 Wert at 305, citing H. B. McClellan–George W. Davis, February 1, 1896, Stuart Papers, VHS; General Orders, AIGO, October 8, 1863, Jones File, CSR, CSA Generals, NA.

4 Mitchell letters at 340-41.

5 Although he did not command the 2nd Division of the Federal Cavalry Corps, as Stuart addressed him in his letter of September 3, 16 (Mitchell letters at 337).

7 Mitchell letters at 343-44.

8 Wert at 305, citing H. B. McClellan–George W. Davis, February 1, 1896, Stuart Papers, VHS; General Orders, AIGO, October 8, 1863, Jones File, CSR, CSA Generals, NA.

9 Mitchell letters at 863.

10 Mitchell letters at 337-38.

11 ORs, Vol. XXIX, Part 1, p. 91.

12 *I Rode with J.E.B. Stuart* at 372.

13 The First Corps, commanded by Maj. Gen. John Newton, was closer to Culpeper than the Second Corps and it isn't clear why Meade called on Warren to accompany Pleasonton instead of Newton. Newton certainly noticed, got his nose out of joint and sent Meade a letter on the 13th expressing his dismay at the slight and saying: "Under such circumstance, you must not be surprised to learn that the officers and men of the First Corps are disappointed and mortified at an occurrence from which others will not fail to draw the inference that the Second Corps was selected and brought from some distance to perform an act for which the First Corps was not qualified. I cannot believe any such imputation was intended by the major-general commanding, but an ordinary regard for the reputation of the corps which I have the honor at present to command enjoins upon me the duty of forwarding this communication." O.R.s, Vol. XXIX, Part 2, p. 176.

14 *Ibid.* at 175.

15 McClellan at 373.

16 Robert J. Trout, *Galloping Thunder: The Stuart Horse Artillery Battalion*, p. 350 (Mc-Chanicsburg, PA: Stackpole Books, 2002).

17 Mitchell letters p. 345

18 *With Pen & Saber,* p. 217.

19 *I Rode with Jeb Stuart* at 375

20 *Ibid. at* n. 1.

21 Theordore Standford Garnett, Robert J. Trorut, ed., *Riding with Stuart: Reminiscences of an Aide-De-Camp*, p. 9 (Shippenburg, PA: White Mane Publishing Co., 1994), cited hereinafter as *Riding With Stuart.*

22 *I Rode with Jeb Stuart* at 376, n. 1

23 Quoted from a 1926 *Saturday Evening Post Article* by George Allan England, at http://en.wikipedia.org /wiki/George_St._Leger_Grenfell

24 Letter dated April 16, 1867, from Dr. Samuel Mudd to Tom Dyer, New Orleans, quoted at http://en.wikipedia.org/wiki/George_St._Leger_Grenfell

25 Whitehorse letters, Sept. 26, 1863.

26 *Ibid*, Oct. 3, 1863.

CHAPTER 6

THE BRISTOE CAMPAIGN AND THE BUCKLAND RACES
October 9–22, 1863

This limp I got as my horse went down
when Fitz Lee ran us through Buckland town.
Out of the woods with a spurt of flame,
driving backward our van, he came.
Custer struggled to turn the thrust,
but they whirled him off like a fleck of dust;
Davies, shattered in front and flanks,
took to the fields with flying ranks,
and off we scampered, like boys at play,
over the hills and far away.
Crack! A shot through my good steed's knee;
down he tumbled on top of me,
and I crawled to a thicket, right glad to lie
till the jubilant rebels had thundered by.
　　　—From *The Cavalry Veteran*
　　　　by Joseph Mills Hanson[1]

T HE MILITARY SEASONS OF 1862 and 1864 in Virginia continued as long as decent weather would permit and sometimes when it didn't, whereas popular history might have us believe that the season of 1863 petered out in mid-July after Gettysburg, at least in the sense of featuring great battles and campaigns of lasting fame. That was, however, neither the intent of leaders on either side nor the actual circumstance. Instead, there were two major Virginia campaigns fought in the autumn of that year, the Bristoe Campaign and Mine Run Campaign, although both are often overlooked or given short shrift by chroniclers of the war. Sandwiched as they were between Gettysburg and the Wilderness among titanic Civil War battles, the two campaigns are sometimes mere footnotes or are referred to as a series of ineffectual maneuvers and counter-maneuvers by the two armies. Nevertheless, they involved ambitious stratagems and spirited contests that killed men and wrecked families every bit as totally as Gettysburg.

The Bristoe Campaign was motivated by four factors. The first was Lincoln's nearly constant urging of Meade to take the offensive and move against Lee's army. The second was Lee and Davis's decision, in early September, to dispatch Longstreet and most of the First Corps of the Army of Northern Virginia to Georgia to reinforce the Army of Tennessee in the hope of scoring some war-changing victories in that theatre. The third was the Lincoln administration's decision to send two army corps from the Army of the Potomac to reinforce the Army of the Cumberland in order to counter-balance the increase in strength brought about by Longstreet's transfer. The fourth was the innate willingness of Robert E. Lee to boldly seize every real or perceived opportunity for an offensive swipe at the enemy.

Longstreet had been advocating a move west since early spring, prior to Chancellorsville. It is probable that he sincerely believed it to be the best course of action for the Confederacy, and with the benefit of 20/20 hindsight, we now know that it could hardly have been worse than the defeats at Vicksburg and Gettysburg. It is also possible that Longstreet was hoping to exercise independent command in the west, free from the looming shadow of Robert E. Lee, and thereby demonstrate his worth as an army commander.

Following Chancellorsville and the loss of Stonewall Jackson, Longstreet again urged Lee to send all or part of his corps to Tennessee. Old Pete's theory was that by reinforcing Bragg, he could defeat his West Point roommate, William S. Rosecrans, and then proceed north to the Ohio River, forcing Grant to turn his attention from the Mississippi and Vicksburg. If Lee happened to invade Pennsylvania at the same time, any number of wonderful things might happen for the nascent Confederacy.

But Lee saw it otherwise. He was determined to launch an invasion of the North with his full army. As Longstreet wrote later:

His plan or wishes announced, it became useless and improper to offer suggestions leading to a different course. All that I could ask was that the policy of the campaign should be one of defensive tactics; that we should work so as to force the enemy to attack us, in such good position as we might find in our own country, so well adapted to that purpose—which might assure us of a grand triumph. To this he readily assented as an important and material adjunct to his general plan.[2]

That grand triumph is not what happened, of course, and one might wonder whether Lee's decision to endorse Longstreet's plan when he raised it again in mid-August carried with it a desire to make things up to his Old War Horse. Unlikely. Longstreet had not limited his proposal to the army commander this time. He had written a letter to Secretary of War James Seddon, requesting that he be transferred to serve under Joseph E. Johnston, and he'd engaged support from an ally in the Confederate Senate, fellow South Carolinian and now Senator from Texas, the fire-eating Senator Louis Wigfall.

Wigfall had already let it be known that he considered Longstreet to be an ideal replacement for Braxton Bragg.[3] Accordingly, Lee and President Davis agreed to the request on September 5, and Longstreet immediately began the process of transferring the divisions of Lafayette McLaws and John Bell Hood, plus Porter Alexander's 26-gun artillery battalion, to Bragg's army in Georgia. The expedition covered 775 miles and required the use of sixteen different railroads, but the lead elements of his corps arrived on September 17, 1863, just in time to participate in the Battle of Chickamauga on September 19–20. Chickamauga was, thanks in no small part to Longstreet's presence, the single greatest Confederate victory in the western theatre. It was, however, the only positive outcome for the Confederacy of Longstreet's great Tennessee road trip.

Anything as monumental as the transfer of one-third of Lee's army to another part of the country did not go unnoticed in the Union army, but it wasn't discovered immediately. In fact, it took a little while to convince George Meade that such a thing could be happening.

It was apparently "Old Rosie" who first got wind of what was afoot. At 12:30 p.m. on September 6, 1863, General Halleck notified General Meade that "General Rosecrans seems apprehensive that re-enforcements to Bragg have been sent from Lee's army to East Tennessee by Lynchburg. Employ every possible means to ascertain if this be so. If Lee has sent any troops to Tennessee, I must re-enforce Burnside."[4] Meade replied at 3 p.m. that the only thing he'd heard had come from a deserter the day before, who reported seeing the brigade of infantry commanded by Stuart's brother-in-law, John R. Cooke, at Hanover Junction, on its way to Richmond. Meade didn't think that was noteworthy because Cooke "has always been stationed in the vicinity of Richmond," but had been sent to Fredericksburg earlier, so that he was apparently just heading back home.

Cooke's brigade belonged to Heth's division of Hill's Third Corps, and its movement was not related to the massive transfer of Longstreet's Corps. Meade actually had more information about the latter than he knew, and he reported to Halleck that McLaws' Division of Longstreet's Corps had been seen a few days earlier moving toward Walters Tavern, some ten miles north of Fredericks Hall Station on the Gordonsville railroad, but that "the object of this movement was said to be for the convenience of supplies." Meade said that if any movement other than Cooke's was taking place that he "should have been advised," but admitted that reliable information was difficult to obtain and promised to try to get some scouts (spies) across the lines to find out what they could.[5]

About sundown on September 6 a free black man named Wesley Norris, identified as being a former slave of George Washington Custis, of Arlington, came into the Federal lines and to General Meade's attention.

Norris was destined to receive a degree of fame, or infamy, in 1866, by testifying about Robert E. Lee's treatment of the Arlington slaves following the death of Custis in 1857. He reported that despite the direction in Custis's will that all his slaves be freed, that Robert E. Lee, son-in-law of Custis and executor of his estate, decreed that each slave would remain in bondage for another five years. Seventeen months later, Norris, his sister Mary, and a male cousin ran away, making it as far as Westminster, Maryland before being apprehended and sent back to Arlington. There, Norris stated, Lee had all three tied to posts and stripped to the waist. He ordered the overseer, a Mr. Gwin, to give the two men fifty lashes each and Mary twenty, but Gwin "had sufficient humanity to decline whipping us," and a county constable named Dick Williams was called upon to deliver the strokes while Lee looked on. As added punishment—literal rubbing of salt into their wounds—Lee directed Gwin to wash the slaves' lacerated backs with brine and then put them in jail for a week.[6]

On this occasion in 1863, however, Norris reported leaving Richmond the previous Friday, which would have been September 4, with a pass from Maj. General G.W. Custis Lee to go through Federal lines via Culpeper. Arriving by train at Gordonsville, having seen no troops on the march before, he observed a camp of some four or five thousand Confederates to the right of Gordonsville who appeared to have been there "some little time." During the two hours Norris was in Gordonsville he didn't see any troops moving through and nobody he talked to mentioned having seen any either. At Orange Court House he saw "many troops" in camp, but they were not on the march, and when walking from Orange to Culpeper he saw more, also in camp.

The Federals were not convinced that Norris could be fully trusted, and when they put him on a horse to move him through their camp to their pickets at Rappahannock Station, they blindfolded him.

Meade continued to fail to detect Longstreet's movement, the single largest, longest transfer of troops at any time in the war. On September 8 he notified General Halleck that a citizen of Tennessee named John Wilson had come into their lines to report seeing no troops moving through Lynchburg, Charlottesville, Gordonsville, or other areas where Confederates enroute to reinforce Bragg would be seen.

In reality, General Meade and others had failed to put two and two together. There was a very good reason why they had not observed Longstreet's movement. Although the most direct route for transfer by rail from Lee's to Bragg's army was through Gordonsville and Lynchburg into Tennessee, the Confederates knew that General Burnside and the Army of the Ohio were rattling about in east Tennessee. Accordingly, Longstreet's corps made the trip through the Carolinas to Atlanta and thence to join Bragg. It was a longer, more circuitous route, but it was veiled to prying Yankee eyes. Perhaps Rosecrans' message on September 6, in which he opined that the Confederate troops were coming via Lynchburg, had caused everyone to focus only in that direction.

Following the Confederate victory at Chickamauga, Maj. Gen. Joseph Hooker was dispatched to the western theatre with two army corps, the Eleventh and Twelfth, and Lee, rather than feeling undermanned due to the absence of Longstreet, decided to take the offensive and attempt to flank Meade's army at Culpeper. The fact that his army numbered only about 45,000 compared to Meade's 76,000 was of no particular consequence. Willingness to take the offensive at considerable risk was a basic part of Lee's nature, certainly a characteristic that explained his success and the devotion of his countrymen. He had demonstrated how longshot offensives could win victories at Second Manassas and Chancellorsville. Of course he'd also demonstrated how the practice could snatch defeat from the jaws of victory at Malvern Hill and on day three of Gettysburg.

Lee's confidence was also buoyed by recent reports of low morale among the new conscripts in the Federal ranks. The draft riots in New York City during the summer, rumors of mass desertions from the Federal army, and the Rebel victory at Chickamauga gave Lee the hope that Meade was vulnerable, and that another offensive might deliver favorable results. His plan of attack was to leave a cavalry division and two infantry brigades to hold the Rapidan line while his two corps under Lieutenant Generals A.P. Hill and Richard S. Ewell marched their men in a wide arc around Meade's right flank with the other division of Stuart's cavalry screening the movement. If successful, Meade would be forced to retreat and Lee would be presented with an opportunity to attack the Federal army while it was in motion or, alternatively, to seize and hold ground that was ideal for defense and to force Meade to attack.

On October 9, 1863, in compliance with Lee's orders, Stuart took Hampton's division to Madison Court House, where he bivouacked for the night, Hampton still being out of action due to the wounds he sustained at Gettysburg. As further directed by Lee, the division of Fitz Lee was left on the line of the Rapidan, supported by one brigade of infantry under Robert T. Johnston of Robert Rodes' Division, and another under James T. Walker of Edward Johnson's division, both of Ewell's Second Corps, to watch the enemy on that front. Stuart's movement was made in secrecy, and prior to leaving Orange he dispatched Major Andrew R. Venable, his assistant adjutant general, along with a "select body of men" to capture the Federal signal station on Thoroughfare Mountain, which overlooked Stuart's line of march.

Divisions from Ewell's and Hill's Corps were moving in parallel columns toward Woodville, and on the morning of the 10th, Jeb dispatched Jones' brigade, under the command of Colonel O.R. Funsten, to serve as the infantry's advance guard, while Stuart continued with Baker's North Carolina Brigade, commanded by Brigadier James B. Gordon, and Butler's Brigade, commanded by Colonel P.M.B. Young. Stuart's intent was to move on James City and occupy the enemy's attention while the infantry's flank movement developed.

Contact with the enemy was made at Russell's Ford on Robertson's River, first pickets and then a regiment of infantry and a small force of cavalry. They were driven back toward Bethesda Church, and Stuart decided to attack them in front and on the right flank simultaneously. Directing General Gordon to push forward with a dismounted force, followed by the rest of his brigade, Jeb took Young's brigade through the woods to his left in order to hit the enemy on their right. He found the Federals in line of battle, prepared for a fight, but when they were attacked in flank and rear by the 1st South Carolina Cavalry, under Lieut. Col. J.D. Twiggs, with Gordon pressing them simultaneously in their front, they broke and fled. Young's brigade captured 87 of them and Gordon even more, while those not captured were scattered in every direction.

Stuart's two brigades pursued the enemy to James City, which they found occupied by two brigades of Kilpatrick's cavalry, a division of French's infantry, and six pieces of artillery. As Stuart approached, the Federals fell back to a stronger position on hills overlooking the village, in the vicinity of Bethel Church, and once arrayed in line of battle they presented Jeb an opportunity to smash his gray horsemen against them with as much effect as waves lapping at rocks.

Instead, Stuart placed Young's brigade in their front, Gordon's brigade on their right, and two guns from Griffin's battery of Horse Artillery at the edge of the village from where they could lob an occasional shell into the Federal artillery positions. About 4:00 in the afternoon, this arrangement lured part of Kilpatrick's cavalry out of the hills. A battalion of the 5th Michigan, under Custer, made a dash at Griffin's guns and, when within about 200 yards of the pieces met a withering fire from a contingent of sharpshooters, about 150 in number, "ensconced" behind a stone fence, emptying several saddles and driving the Federals back. Stuart reported that the Confederate fire caused the Yankees to "beat a speedy retreat." Custer reported that the assault "failed for want of sufficient support."[7]

The exchange of artillery and small arms fire continued until dark, and in making his report on the incident four months later, Jeb recalled with regret the suffering of the citizens of James City, who "were thus brought between two fires," but one wonders if Jeb's decision to place his Horse Artillery at the edge of town wasn't a key factor in that suffering.

Daybreak on October 11 revealed that the enemy was gone, so Stuart left Young's brigade to hold the position at James City while he moved on with Gordon's brigade to Griffinsburg, where he found Colonel Funsten and his brigade, which had arrived there at 10 the previous night.

Federal pickets were on the edge of the town, and had been all night, but Stuart was hoping to overtake the Federals who had been at James City. Accordingly he sent the 11th Virginia Cavalry, under Lt. Col. Matt D. Ball, down the Warrenton Road in order to ascertain if they had gone that direction, sent Gordon and his brigade down the pike toward Culpeper, and sent Funsten and his brigade to the right in order to reach the Sperryville and Culpeper Court-House turnpike at Stone-House Mountain.[8]

Jeb was so intent on pursuing the enemy he'd driven away from James City that he completely overlooked a regiment of Federal infantry that was marching parallel to his cavalry on his right, heading toward and closing in on Culpeper Court House. When they were discovered, his three brigades were busy moving in other directions, and the only cavalry he could lay his hands on was Company B of the 12th Virginia commanded by Lieutenant George Baylor, who flew at the Federal foot soldiers with drawn sabers. When the company was 20 or thirty yards from the enemy, however, they discovered an impassable ditch, and the Rebels had to content themselves with putting away their sabers and firing a volley into the enemy regiment, which returned fire but, according to Jeb, then broke and ran, dropping guns, knapsacks, and blankets, but escaping.

Leaving Young's brigade at James City, Stuart and the other two brigades of Hampton's division continued to advance toward Culpeper Court House, and as they did, they came upon deserted Federal camps, clearly indicating that the enemy was fleeing before him. One may wonder why that was the case, if Stuart had only three brigades while the Federals had at least an entire division of infantry plus two brigades of cavalry plus artillery in Jeb's immediate front. The reason was simply that Kilpatrick, and apparently other Federal leaders, were estimating the Confederate force to be larger than it was. Kilpatrick reported the next day to Pleasonton, "It was Stuart in person who attacked our left as we moved on Brandy Station. Hampton was with him. Fitz. Lee was in our front. Stuart's corps must be, therefore, at or near Brandy. I send you this information, that you may know that we fought Stuart's entire cavalry yesterday."[9] The tide had turned against the Confederate cavalry in many ways, but through skillful maneuver they still had the ability to appear twice as numerous to their enemy as they really were.

When Stuart and his three brigades reached Culpeper Court House, they found that the Federals had fallen back to the Rappahannock, and were massed there with artillery on the hills and Kilpatrick's cavalry in the front. After a demonstration with Gordon's brigade, including an attack by the 4th North Carolina Cavalry that dispersed a column of enemy cavalry in its front, Stuart decided to move toward Brandy Station, where he expected to meet Fitz Lee's brigade.

Fitz had held the Rapidan line after his uncle's army and his commander's cavalry moved out on the 9th, and on the 10th John Buford's division of Federal cavalry approached and crossed the Rapidan at Germanna Ford. Fitz promptly attacked him, drove him back across the ford,[10] and continued to press him, driving him from two positions at which Buford offered resistance, first at the ford and then at Stevensburg. Buford, a hero of Gettysburg, who had only one month of military duty and two months of life ahead of him, then fell back toward Brandy Station.

Accordingly, Stuart was almost, but not quite, delivered a rare opportunity. With Kilpatrick in position on his left, and Buford coming from his right rear with Fitz Lee's Division in pursuit, he had only to insert his three brigades between Brandy Station and Buford's front and he would have had the latter's division trapped between Stuart the anvil and Lee the hammer.

Four factors prevented that outcome. First, Kilpatrick's artillery was in a position to sweep the area into which Stuart would be attacking. Second, Buford was moving too rapidly for Jeb to get in front of him. Third, Kilpatrick began moving to unite with Buford before Stuart could get between the two blue divisions. Fourth, two regiments of Stuart's force, the 4th and 5th North Carolina, failed when given the chance to attack and delay Buford's oncoming column. Instead they were driven off by a battalion of the 5th New York Cavalry that Major McClellan estimated to number less than half that of the two Tarheel regiments.

A great deal of attacking and counter-attacking followed, but Jeb was unable to either reach Fleetwood Hill before Buford nor strike a punishing blow against Kilpatrick, and once the two Federal divisions were united, General Pleasonton assumed overall command and the Federal cavalry fell back across the Rappahannock.

Stuart went into bivouac that evening near Brandy Station.

On the 12th, Stuart sent word to Young, left behind at James City, to bring his brigade forward to occupy Culpeper Court House, and then he took the rest of the Cavalry Corps, except one regiment and one piece of artillery, and rode toward Warrenton, where Lee's infantry was headed.

The single regiment was the 5th Virginia, commanded by Thomas Rosser, which numbered only about 200 men, and the single cannon was a gun from Chew's Battery. They were left behind on Fleetwood Hill to simultaneously keep watch on Pleasonton in the event he decided to come back across the river, and to give the impression that the Confederate position of the evening before was still strongly occupied. Watching the rest of the cavalry ride away, some of the 5th probably complained that they were being left behind and would miss out on the action, while others probably welcomed the idea of getting some rest. Both were mistaken.

The location of General Lee's two corps was unknown to Meade, but believing they were at or nearing Culpeper Court House, he sent the Second, Fifth, and Sixth Corps of the Army of the Potomac, with Buford's division of cavalry in the lead, moving in that direction during the afternoon of the 12th. They came in sight of Rosser's lone regiment about 2 p.m.

Chew's lone gun began banging away gamely, hoping to sound larger and more ferocious than it was. The blue horsemen came on, thousands of Federal infantry in their wake. Rosser and Chew had no choice but to limber up, saddle up, and double quick away in the direction of Culpeper Court House.

Chew unlimbered once and unloaded some additional shells at Buford as the badly outnumbered Confederates fell back, but it slowed the Federals only slightly.

As evening approached, Rosser and Chew arrived at Slaughter's Hill, a wooded ridge north of Culpeper Court House, and were heartened to discover Young's brigade and five pieces of artillery arriving from the other direction. Dismounting every man and placing the six cannons in the best positions possible, Rosser and Young commenced the type of bluff that

Confederates employed numerous times at numerous places during the war.

A long but not particularly well-populated line of battle was formed. Large and extensive campfires were lit, and Young ordered his single regimental band to strike up a song, hurry to a new position and play a different one, then move rapidly to yet another position and play another tune. Thus the Rebels passed an anxious night, during which Meade mercifully received reliable information about the actual location of Lee's infantry, which was by then approaching the Orange and Alexandria Railroad. Accordingly he withdrew in that direction, leaving Rosser, Chew, and Young safe with an abundance of extra campfires and some fagged out musicians.

Stuart's column, meanwhile, had headed toward Warrenton Springs. Along the way Fitz Lee was detached across the river at Foxville while Stuart, with Funsten's and Gordon's brigades, continued. Arriving at Jefferson, they found the 11th Virginia under Ball, which had been detached from Funsten's brigade the previous day to search for the Federals who had retreated from James City. Ball had found some of them, or they him, particularly the 13th Pennsylvania and 10th New York Cavalry Regiments.

One might expect that if two Federal regiments encountered a single Confederate regiment that the latter would be forced to take the defensive, but that was not the case. The Federals were holed up in the village and Ball was attempting to dislodge them. The arrival of Stuart and a few thousand reinforcements assisted considerably in that effort, and soon both Union regiments were routed and retreating toward the Rappahannock.

Stuart sent two regiments in pursuit across the river, and proceeded on to Warrenton Springs, where he found at least a brigade of Gregg's cavalry dug into rifle pits, with artillery support at the bridge across the Rappahannock. Ewell's Corps was nearby, and Stuart begged eight cannons from Brig. General Armistead Long, who commanded the Second Corps artillery. The artillery drove Gregg's horsemen back, and with the Rebel infantry as spectators, the 12th Virginia charged into and emptied the rifle pits to the cheers of the foot soldiers.

By then it was nearly dark, and Stuart, with Funsten and Gordon, proceeded on to Warrenton, where they camped for the night.

On October 13, Stuart received orders from General Lee to make a reconnaissance toward Catlett's Station on the Orange and Alexandria Railroad. Accordingly he sent Lomax's brigade toward Auburn, which was at a crossroads about two miles from the railroad, and followed soon thereafter with Funsten's and Gordon's brigades plus seven guns of the Horse Artillery under Beckham.

William W. Blackford, Stuart's staff engineer, described what happened next as "one of the most extraordinary events of the war." Considering that Blackford was witness to and chronicler of numerous extraordinary events, this is no small boast. What happened certainly was noteworthy, almost surreal, and it showcased Stuart's ability to know exactly what to do in a dangerous situation as well as it revealed his cunning and courage. It is of interest, however, that Stuart did not so much as mention the event, even in passing, in his report of the Bristoe Campaign. That was because, for him, it was less extraordinary than it was embarrassing.

When Stuart caught up with Lomax at Auburn, he pushed on toward the railroad, leaving Lomax and his brigade behind as his rearguard. He also sent Blackford ahead to the railroad, which was southeast of Auburn, to reconnoiter.

Blackford took three men with him and when they came in sight of the open area around the railroad station, he saw that it was filled with a vast collection of parked wagons and idle enemy troops, sufficient in number to comprise an entire corps. The four men dismounted and one was detailed to hold the horses while the other three crept forward to a clump of trees on a knoll overlooking the enemy's camp. Blackford owned a pair of particularly powerful fieldglasses, and although he did not mention using them on this occasion, it is almost certain they were utilized to good advantage. Discovering a large concentration of the enemy and the enemy's supply train, all unaware of Rebels in their midst, offered all sorts of opportunities as well as risk, and Blackford decided that Jeb needed to see the situation for himself.

He wrote a note and sent it back to Stuart telling him where he was and what he was seeing, and before long Stuart arrived with Funsten's and Gordon's brigades, and crept forward to the wooded knoll in order to examine the situation in person, probably through fieldglasses borrowed from Blackford. He'd barely begun his analysis, however, when a courier arrived, "in hot haste," and reported that the enemy was now in Stuart's rear.

During the brief passage of time between Stuart's receiving Blackford's summons and his arriving at the wooded knoll, less than two miles away, two entire Federal infantry corps, the Second and the Third, had come swinging along, driving Lomax away from his rearguard position at Auburn, and continuing on their way, marching directly across Stuart's rear, to his west, and cutting him off from Lomax and further contact with the rest of the Confederate army.

Stuart, Blackford and the rest of the command doubled back to see for themselves. Sure enough, seemingly endless columns of marching Federals were passing by, unaware of whom they had within their grasp. The famous commander of Lee's cavalry and approximately 2,000 horsemen were trapped between three corps of the enemy's infantry, which might have numbered 30,000 soldiers.

To make matters worse, the ground to the north of their position was steep, broken and wooded, and on the south, running parallel to the road they were on and a hundred yards from it, was a wide, deep canal that ran all the way from Auburn to the railroad. By Blackford's reckoning, it was impossible to escape either north or south, and going east or west would require them to cut their way through thousands of enemy infantry, an option that Blackford wrote "could not be thought of, except as a last resort."[11]

Jeb didn't ponder or hesitate. He was prepared for such a problem, without having any prior or preconceived inkling that he would need to be.

As Stuart rode it was his habit to do more than just chat with his comrades, sing songs, and ponder strategy. He routinely eyed the countryside for its military value. It was an important part of the training and the secret of many successful Civil War leaders. Just as, six months earlier he had ridden with John Pelham to what would become the Battle of Kelly's Ford and the two men had discussed passing topography for possible use as artillery positions, Jeb that morning had taken note of landscape features that might prove useful for other military purposes, and he'd noticed something that would serve his needs to meet the sudden, unusual, and unwelcome set of circumstances.

He led his two brigades back the way they'd come to the mouth of a little valley not far from Auburn and short of the enemy infantry in his rear. It opened onto the road but was heavily wooded and large enough to hold his entire command. It was now almost dark, and once both brigades were inside the basin and out of sight, Jeb set up two separate sets of dismounted pickets on the road, about twenty yards apart. The men in each picket were told to conceal themselves behind bushes and to stay there if any large body of the enemy happened along, but if a single horseman approached, the first picket was to let him pass, then step into the road to block his retreat while the second picket halted and captured him. During the night several couriers and their messages thus fell into Stuart's hands.

That being the best show in town, Blackford stretched out where he could watch, and was pleased to observe a column of about 150 Federals, each holding a lantern, parade by. The scene, he wrote "gave a very picturesque effect in the dark, still night," as it would certainly do if witnessed today. Blackford and the other Rebel spectators could hear the Yankees talking to each other. In turn, it was necessary for the hiding cavalrymen to place a soldier at the head of every mule in the brigades' ambulances to keep them from braying and giving away their location. Off and on during the night "an incipient bray" would break out from one location or another, followed almost immediately by a "whack" that was the sound made by a metal saber scabbard coming into forceful contact with a mule's forehead.

Additionally, Jeb personally selected six men to find General Lee, report the predicament he was in, and request that the commander launch an attack as soon as it was light to serve as a diversion so that Stuart and his men could escape.[12] It was learned later that all six made it through to deliver their reports, which no doubt became a topic of high glee among the wags of the army and Stuart's detractors. It also explains why Jeb conveniently forgot to include the incident in his battle report.

Perhaps some small part of the extraordinary nature of that night, in Blackford's mind, stemmed from the fact that Stuart came over and threw himself down beside him, placed his head on Blackford's stomach, and instantly went to sleep. "Hour after hour passed and the General's head on my middle became rather heavy for comfort but I was reluctant to disturb him. It got so bad that at last I was compelled to move it gently to another part of my body but this awoke him and I then snatched a few hours' sleep." The staff engineer's dilemma sounds like the setup for a modern hidden camera episode, but for Blackford it became a lifelong recollection of hopeful youth, when he was so intimate with the powers of change in the world that one of its makers used him for a headrest.

The morning of October 14 finally came and the Federal column was still streaming by, but instead of hearing the sound of Lee's guns and the requested diversion, Stuart and his men saw the Federals halt, fall out on the sides of the road, and proceed to build fires to cook breakfast. They were, Blackford recalled, only 250 yards away,[13] and it was merciful that there was sufficient wood for the fires in between, so that none of the infantry stumbled into the Rebel hiding place. As one of the Federal soldiers described it, "After reaching the top of the hill the boys began making fires, got water, put on coffee cups, pulled off shoes and stockings, stood them around to dry and sat waiting for breakfast."[14]

Stuart had his seven artillery pieces[15] lined up on the backside of the valley, arranged so that they could quickly be pulled to the highest point and unleashed on the breakfasting Federals when the signal was given. In position in front and to both sides of the guns were some 2,000 Confederate cavalry, standing to horse, prepared to attack the instant the command was given.

Thirty minutes ticked by as the Yankees relaxed and the Confederates worried. Then the booming of distant artillery was heard and Stuart gave the signal. The Rebel cannons were pulled into position and fired simultaneously. Coffee cups and blue kepis flew into the air. "We could see coffee pots upset and men running hither and thither from the storm of shells pouring upon them. . . . Gordon charged and scattered them and then Stuart marched the command out and moved off."[16]

The distant cannon fire that Jeb heard came from artillery supporting an attack by Robert Rodes' division of Ewell's Corps, which may have been made to honor Stuart's request for a diversion. However, if so, that wasn't how it was understood by the general in overall command of the artillery that made the noise. In his report on the Bristoe Campaign, dated January 30, 1864, Brigadier General William Pendleton recalled that "Early on the morning of the 14th, a portion of the enemy's forces was discovered to be in position near Auburn, occupying a commanding ridge extending on both sides of the road passing through that place. . . . After an examination of the position, Carter's battalion was directed to a position on the right and ordered to occupy it, being supported by Rodes' division . . . [which] . . . made a flank movement to the left to gain the enemy's rear."[17]

Assuming Rodes' attack was merely serendipity that favored Jeb and was not ordered by Robert E. Lee, the commanding general may be forgiven due to his having his hands full with other matters. His flanking movement had had its desired effect, causing Meade to retreat, but so far it had not offered the Confederates an opportunity to deliver a punishing or decisive blow. Instead, it now appeared that the Army of the Potomac was falling back on Centerville, which was heavily entrenched. If Meade could not be cut off from that place Lee, whose army was moving northeast from Warrenton toward Gainesville, knew it was unlikely he would be able to use his outnumbered force to bring on a battle according to his own terms. Similarly, Meade understood that in order for an attack by Lee's army to be effective, it would need to occur soon.

The point at which a decisive blow by Lee's army might have the desired effect was Bristoe Station, a railroad depot up the line northeast from Catlett's Station. The Confederate Third Corps, under A.P. Hill was in the vicinity of Gainseville, northwest of and generally parallel to Meade's army, and driving toward Bristoe, hoping to get there first. In response Meade sent orders to Maj. Gen. Gouverneur K. Warren, whose Second Corps was near Auburn and Catlett's Station, to ""move forward as rapidly as you can as they may send out a column from Gainesville to Bristoe."

It looked like there was going to be a footrace, but for the most part the Federals had already won. The Union Fifth Corps, commanded by Maj. Gen. George Sykes, was already at Bristoe Station, whereas Warren was the army's rear guard. Hill was essentially moving blind toward an area chock full of the enemy, thinking that he might get there first and thereby pulling off another of the kind of hard marching miracles for which he'd become famous at Cedar Mountain and Sharpsburg.

Confederate army corps are not supposed to move blind, particularly not at top speed. Hill needed Confederate cavalry to be in his front, ascertaining the enemy's position and passing back reliable information, which was exactly what Jeb Stuart was best at. On this occasion, the Confederate cavalry commander with that responsibility was not Stuart, at least directly, but Fitzhugh Lee.

On the previous day, Fitz had been at Warrenton, near where most of Lee's infantry was concentrating, and moving toward Catlett's Station he encountered Lomax doing battle near Auburn with the Federal infantry that had gotten between him and Stuart's two brigades.

It apparently didn't occur to either Fitz or Lomax that their chief might be in trouble. Lee reported later that he found Lomax clashing with the enemy and "I engaged them only sufficient to ascertain their line of march, then withdrew my command and encamped on Warrenton road." Lomax wrote that he met the enemy at Auburn, held his position dismounted until Federal artillery began pouring canister into the woods where we was posted, and was then withdrawn by Fitz Lee, "but not before my men had been exposed to a heavy fire of artillery and had contended most gallantly with the enemy's infantry."[18]

The totality of Fitz Lee's report for the next day was, "On the 14th, I was ordered to move on the left flank of our army, and marched via New Baltimore and Gainesville to the vicinity of Bristoe Station, where I remained all night." He didn't mention that the purpose of moving to the left flank was to screen A.P. Hill's movements and that while attempting to do so he became engaged in a spirited skirmish near Gainesville with Federal cavalry under Judson Kilpatrick. Kilpatrick reported it, writing at 10 a.m. on the 14th that he was falling back on Gainesville and from there to Groveton with a heavy force of cavalry and artillery moving from the direction of Warrenton," and then at 5:50 p.m. that "I advanced with a strong force at 3.50 p.m. in the direction of Gainesville. We drove in the rebel pickets, and had a severe skirmish until dark. We succeeded in driving the enemy back on the road from New Market to Gainesville."[19]

A.P. Hill reported what happened as well. After leaving camp a mile from Warrenton at 5 a.m., with Richard Anderson's division in the lead, he marched along the Warrenton and Alexandria Turnpike to Broad Run Church, where information reached him "from various sources" that the enemy was moving by a road leading from Greenwich to the Warrenton and Alexandria Pike, and would come into it a mile below Buckland. Hearing wagons in the distance, Hill decided the reports must be true and directed Anderson to continue on the Pike toward Buckland and attack the enemy column while Hill moved with his other two divisions, commanded by Henry Heth and Cadmus Wilcox, and move toward the road leading from Greenwich, thereby squeezing the enemy column in a pincer's movement.

When Anderson came within sight of the enemy, however, it turned out to be cavalry instead of infantry, undoubtedly Kilpatrick's. By then Fitz Lee and his division were on the scene, and with Rosser in the lead, he began skirmishing with the blue riders. Thus Lee was diverted from serving as the eyes for Hill, who continued with Heth's division in pursuit of what he was certain was a fleeing enemy, picking up stragglers along the way. Coming to the crest of hills on the near side of Broad Run, Hill found the Union Third Corps and "determined that no time must be lost." He threw Heth's division into line of battle and advanced at an enemy who was "taken completely by surprise."[20]

Unfortunately for the Confederates, it soon became Hill's turn to be surprised. Movement—a Federal skirmish line—was observed on Heth's right and rear. Hill assumed it was the rear guard of the retreating corps to his front and did not change his plan of attack. In fact, the skirmishers were the advance elements of Warren's Second Corps. Syke's Fifth Corps was not far behind.

There followed the Battle of Bristoe Station. Rebel cavalry was not involved further. Jeb Stuart was miles away, but the infantry fight concerned him personally because his wife's brother, Brig. Gen. John R. Cooke, was at the center of the hottest part of the fight and was about to be wounded for the sixth out of seven times during the war.

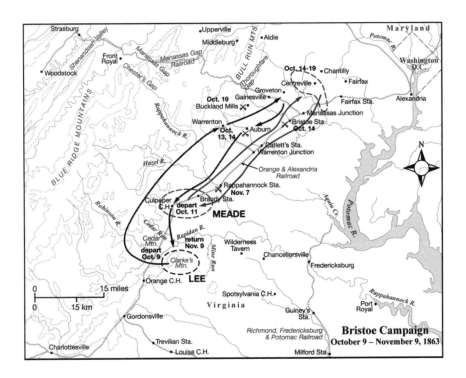

Bristoe Campaign
October 9 – November 9, 1863

When Heth was ordered forward, he sent a message to Cooke and to Brig. Gen.William Kirkland to take the lead. Cooke was already aware of what was happening on his right, where Federal infantry soldiers were not only appearing in large numbers, but were taking position behind a railroad embankment from where they could deliver enfilading fire on the two Rebel brigades with impunity.

Before that message arrived Cooke sent a courier back to Heth to alert him that his right flank was exposed, and no sooner did that messenger leave than one of General Lee's staff officers arrived and was made aware of the situation. He promptly left to warn Hill of the threat, but then the messenger arrived with Heth's orders for Cooke to attack immediately. Cooke did so, his men surging into an open field with no cover. The Federal troops "had only to lie down on the slope, rest their muskets on the track of the railroad and sweep the open field." Cooke was shot from his horse almost immediately, his shinbone shattered, and his brigade was "almost swept . . . out of existence."

A blow-by-blow account of the engagement reads like a rather pitiful sacrifice of human flesh and blood. Hill had dived into a boiling cauldron of Federal infantry in overwhelming numbers, and Heth's division was mauled. The conclusion of Hill's report, followed by Lee's endorsement, followed by President Davis's comment, sum up the battle quite succinctly:

Hill: "The (enemy's) position was an exceedingly strong one, and covered by the direct and enfilading fire of batteries on the rising ground in rear. . . . In conclusion, I am convinced that I made the attack too hastily, and at the same time that a delay of half an hour, and there would have been no enemy to attack. In that event I believe I should equally have blamed myself for not attacking at once."

Lee: "General Hill explains how, in his haste to attack the Third Army Corps of the enemy, he overlooked the presence of the Second, which was the cause of the disaster that ensued."

Davis: "There was a want of vigilance . . ."

Confederate losses were 933 killed and wounded and another 445 captured or missing. Total Union losses were just over 500. Instead of rekindling the glory of his Light Division miracle march days, A.P. Hill had seriously eroded his reputation as an effective corps commander.

Despite having thoroughly trounced Hill and brought Lee's plans to naught, Meade continued to fall back on Manassas, Centerville, and even Alexandria, believing that Lee was preparing to bring his entire army against the Federal right flank and rear. Jeb Stuart kept busy, putting Fitz Lee near Manassas to repulse any cavalry advance on October 16, and taking Hampton's Division and four pieces of the Horse Artillery toward Groveton, hoping to cross Bull Run above Sudley Ford and get in the rear of Meade's army at Centreville. There was intermittent skirmishing but it had been raining, the roads were extremely muddy and Bull Run was nearly out of its banks.

Jeb got across anyway and spent the night near Stone Castle. On the 17th he passed Gum Strings and went to Frying Pan Church, where he encountered a regiment of infantry from the enemy's Sixth Corps and skirmished with them for a couple of hours before determining that the entire Corps was entrenching a line on the other side of the Little River Turnpike perpendicular to it and slightly west of Chantilly.

That being the kind of information he was looking for, Stuart withdrew at sundown and returned the way he had come. He had just received a message from Lee's Chief of Staff, Colonel Robert Chilton, dated the 17th telling Jeb to report to General Lee, which he did at Gainesville the next morning, after spending the night near the Little River Turnpike.

Lee had determined to fall back, now that the Army of Potomac had withdrawn behind its fortified lines, and directed Stuart to screen the Confederate infantry as the army did so. That night Jeb took Hampton's division above Hay Market for forage and supplies, and encamped on the road. After dark a messenger arrived with news that Kilpatrick's division and six artillery pieces, in advance of a column of infantry, had left Fairfax Courthouse on the 17th and had attacked and driven in the Confederate pickets at Gainesville just at dark on the 18th. Kilpatrick had boasted that the Confederates were withdrawing and declared that he would catch Stuart before he was able to reach Warrenton. It was the kind of arrogant boast that made what followed particularly satisfying.

It was raining hard, but Stuart ordered Young's brigade to saddle up. He led them toward Gainesville, where he found that the Rebels were still in possession of the town. Accordingly, he moved on toward Buckland to continue screening the Confederate withdrawal. The Federal cavalry followed and Stuart thought he saw an opportunity. He sent word for Fitz Lee, who had been at Bristoe since the 16th, to join him on his right.

Stuart dug in along Broad Run the evening of the 18th to await Fitz's division. He had theorized that Kilpatrick was detached from the main body of the Federal army and that, if so, he "could inflict upon him severe injury."[21]

The morning of the 19th the Federal Cavalry attempted to force passage of Broad Run, in Stuart's front, but were repulsed and appeared to be about to attempt to move around his flanks. Just then a message arrived from Fitz—he was in position near Auburn and able to support Jeb, and suggested that Stuart fall back with Hampton's division in the hope that Kilpatrick would follow, giving Lee the opportunity to hit him in the flank and rear.

Stuart replied that he would fall back slowly in the direction of Warrenton until he heard Lee's guns. Kilpatrick took the bait, crossed Broad Run and followed. About two miles from Warrenton, at a place called Chestnut Hill, Stuart halted and allowed Kilpatrick to approach. Then he heard the sound of artillery from the direction of Buckland Mills, where Fitz had launched his attack, and, with Gordon in the center and Young and Rosser on his flanks, he attacked the enemy's front.

What followed turned out to be Jeb Stuart's last great cavalry victory. There would be additional clashes, but nothing of such magnitude or such satisfying conclusiveness.

Lee's attack on Kilpatrick's rear was made with Wickham's brigade in the front under the command of Colonel Thomas H. Owen, 3rd Virginia Cavalry, who hit them with dismounted sharpshooters and Breathed's battery of Horse Artillery. The rest of Lee's division then attacked at Buckland while Stuart and Hampton's division hit them in their front. Initially the Federals resisted stubbornly, with George Custer's brigade confronting Fitz Lee and that of Henry Davies confronting Stuart. Then suddenly the blue horsemen broke.

Davies was routed first, and what started as a retreat became a rout. As they came stampeding back on Custer, his men had little choice but to withdraw too, and soon everyone was running. As Colonel Owen described it, they fled "pell-mell, in great disorder and confusion, to save themselves the best way they could; but a great many were captured, killed, and drowned."[22] Stuart recounted that Kilpatrick's "whole division [was] dispersed in a manner graphically." They did not stop running at top speed for more than three miles, when they reached the safety of their own infantry, although the whooping Confederate pursuit didn't stop there and numerous infantrymen were taken prisoner as well. Custer's headquarters baggage and official papers were captured, along with 250 prisoners, eight wagons and ambulances, and abundant arms, horses, and equipment.[23] A Federal writer was quoted in Stuart's report as describing "the deplorable spectacle of 7,000 cavalry dashing riderless, hatless, and panic-stricken through the ranks of their infantry."

Certainly there were examples of Federal gallantry and effectiveness, particularly on Custer's part of the field. The commander of a section of Breathed's battery, P.P. Johnston, wrote, "The battle was of the most obstinate character, Fitz Lee exerting himself to the utmost to push the enemy and Custer seeming to have no thought of retreating."[24]

Otherwise, in the fine tradition common to both Confederate and Federal commanders alike of describing battles as they wanted them to have occurred rather than how they did occur, the post-battle reports would cause a reader to conclude that the two sides were occupying alternate universes. Colonel J.H. Kidd, of the 6th Michigan in Custer's Brigade, recorded that "Fitzhugh Lee was completely foiled in his effort to get in Custer's rear, or to break up his flanks.[25] Custer's report did not mention the rout, and that filed by Brig. Gen. Davies's seemed to describe what sounds like a completely different incident. Therein he "sent forward my wagons, artillery, and the rest of my column to the left . . . and then, with the First West Virginia Cavalry and the Second New York, attacked and drove back the rebel cavalry that were charging my rear. This done, . . . I struck the pike from Gainesville, through Thoroughfare Gap, about a mile below Hay Market . . . just in time to check Lee's cavalry, which were coming down through the Gap to cut off my brigade.[26]

As one historian wrote, quite kindly, of this report: "Davies wrote of this galloping retreat in words that do not convey the severity of the situation and illustrate to the historian that the official reports, written long after the firing has stopped, do not always tell the fullest of stories."[27]

Stuart concluded his report on the Bristoe campaign by noting that the matter of greatest concern during the "short and eventful campaign" was the shortage of forage for the horses "in a country worn out in peace, but now more desolate in war." He noted that on the 20th his command leisurely followed the retrograde movement of the army, "unannoyed by the enemy, whose blatant braggadocio a few days previous had threatened so much." He also observed with satisfaction—his report having been penned three months after the event—that "It is remarkable that Kilpatrick's division seemed to disappear from the field of operations for more than a month, that time being necessary, no doubt, to collect the panic-stricken fugitives."[28]

In his report Stuart also paid tribute to various members of his command who had done remarkable service, beginning with Fitz Lee for "severely chastising their favorite cavalry leader, Kilpatrick." Several others were mentioned, including Rosser and Blackford, but perhaps most notable was his inclusion of a man who was not only absent from the campaign, but who had been out of commission for four months before it began and for seven months by the time Jeb wrote his report—Heros Von Borcke, who was "I regret to state, absent, disabled by his wounds received at Middleburg in June." Jeb was loyal to his friends, and one suspects he included him in the hope that it would boost the wounded Prussian's spirits when he read the report.

NOTES

1 *Journal of the Military Service Institution of the United States*, Vol. 49, July-August 1911, page 142.

2 General James Longstreet, *From Manassas to Appomattox*, p. 331 (Philadelphia: J.B. Lippincott Co. 1896).

3 Longstreet did not merely suggest to Wigfall that sending him west might be beneficial, but that failure to do so would be disastrous, writing "If I remain here I fear we shall go, little at a time, till all will be lost. I hope that I can get west in time to save what there is left of us . . . . " (http://www.cincinnaticwrt.org/data/ccwrt_history/talks _text/smith_longstreet_chickamauga.html)

4 ORs, Volume XXIX, Part 2, p. 158.

5 *Ibid.*

6 Testimony of Wesley Norris (1866); reprinted in *Slave Testimony: Two Centuries of Letters, Speeches, and Interviews, and Autobiographies*," edited by John W. Blassingame; Baton Rouge: Louisiana State University Press).

7 ORs, Volume XXIX, Part 2, p. 390.

8 In his report, which he submitted on February 13, 1864, Stuart seems to have reversed the movements of Gordon's and Funsten's brigades, stating that Funsten moved down the pike and that Gordon was sent toward Stone House Mountain, which was

not consistent with either Gordon's or Funsten's reports, each of which were filed two months earlier than Jeb's, in December, 1863.

9 ORs, Vol. XXIX, Part 1, p. 375.

10 While battling the Confederate troopers for the ford Buford reported that he received ". . . instructions, of old date, for me not to cross the Rapidan at all, but to return and recross the Rappahannock at the station, or Kelly's." With those orders in hand and no sign of anticipated infantry support, Buford abandoned the fight and began recrossing the river, at which point the operation became a race, as Fitzhugh Lee crossed the river upstream at Raccoon Ford with Wickham's brigade, commanded by Col H.T. Owen, intent upon cutting off the Federal escape route.

11 *War Years with Jeb Stuart* at 239

12 Blackford recorded that five men were selected, but Stuart, despite not discussing the incident in the main body of his report noted at its end that " The 6 privates who volunteered to pass through the enemy's column were: Robert W. Goode, Company, First Virginia Cavalry; Sergts. Ashton Chichester and Shurley, McGregors battery, horse artillery; Privates Crockett Eddins and Richard Baylor, Company B, Twelfth Virginia Cavalry." Theodore Garnett essentially confirmed that these were those who carried news of Stuart's situation to Lee by recording that Chichester was the first to volunteer. *Riding With Stuart* at 14.

13 Blackford was probably guilty of exaggeration for the sake of an extraordinary story. Other sources put the distance at about 800 yards.

14 Quoted in Dan O'Connell, *TOCWOC: A Civil War Blog* http://www.brettschulte.net/CWBlog/2012/03/25/the-marching-campaign-bristoe-part-3/ (March 29, 2012).

15 Blackford said there were seven guns; other sources say six.

16 *War Years with Jeb Stuart* at 240.

17 ORs, Vol. XXIX, Part 1, p 417.

18 ORs, Vol. XXIX, Part 1, p. 466.

19 ORs, Vol. XXIX, Part 1, p. 376.

20 ORs, Vol. XXIX, Part 1, p. 426.

21 ORs, Vol. XXIX, Part 1, p. 451.

22 ORs, Vol. XXIX, Part 1, p. 423.

23 ORs, Vol. XXIX, Part 1, p. 452.

24 *I Rode with Jeb Stuart* at 394.

25 J.H. Kidd, *Personal Recollections of a Cavalryman with Custer's Michigan Cavalry Brigade in the Civil War*, p.223 (Ionia, Michigan, Sentinel Printing Company, 1908).

26 ORs, Vol. XXIX, Part 1, p. 387.

27 Vincent L. Burns, *The Fifth New York Cavalry in the Civil War*, p. 143 (Jefferson, N.C.: McFarland & Co. 2014).

28 ORs, Vol. XXIX, Part 1, p. 452.

CHAPTER 7

CAMP WIGWAM AND THE MINE RUN CAMPAIGN
October 23–November 30, 1863

Last night as I toasted
my wet feet and roasted
my small bit of beef by a similar blaze,
while nought but the wheezings,
the snorings, and sneezings
of comrades grouping in Dreamland's haze . . .
　—A Soldier's Dream (anonymous)

OLLOWING THE BRISTOE Campaign the Confederate army returned to Culpeper County and went into camp along both sides of the Orange and Alexandria Railroad, holding the line of the Rappahannock. On October 23, Stuart turned his attention to the absence of Brig. Gen. W.H.F. "Rooney" Lee, Robert E. Lee's son and a brigade commander in Stuart's cavalry corps.

Rooney had been severely wounded in the leg at the battle of Brandy Station on June 9, 1863, and on June 26 his younger brother, Robert Jr., delivered him to Hickory Hill, the home of another of Stuart's officers, Williams Wickham, the brother of Rooney's wife, Charlotte. It was there that Stuart and Rooney had visited both a wounded Wickham and Charlotte the year previously on the night of June 12, 1862, at the beginning of the first "Ride Around McClellan." About two weeks after Rooney arrived, in June 1863, a different type of visitor came calling.

Federals learned of his presence at Hickory Hill and sent a party to capture him. They arrived in the morning, just as Robert E. Lee, Jr. and Mrs. Wickham stepped out on the front veranda following breakfast. Hearing shots near the gate and thinking it was boys shooting for sport, Mrs. Wickham asked Robert to ride down and ask them to stop. Before he reached the gate Robert saw the raiders approaching, wheeled his horse about and raced back to attempt to remove and rescue his older brother.

Rooney protested, saying that he had always paroled wounded prisoners and felt certain the Yankees would do the same. Robert, Jr., being neither wounded nor, considering his family ties, expectant of leniency, ran into the formal gardens behind the house and burrowed under some hedges to hide.

The Wickham's manservant, Scott, seeing what was happening, led the Lee brothers' horses away from the house and hid them, which turned out to be both fortunate and tragic. The Yankees, after taking Rooney Lee prisoner, looted the house, seized the family's wagon and, not finding the horses, concluded that they had been taken across the nearby Pamunkey River to North Wales, the home of Williams Carter, uncle to Williams Wickham. Accordingly, part of the raiding party went there and, not finding the horses, they beat 80-year-old Williams Carter to death.

Lee would be held in prison for nearly nine months, during which time his two children died of Scarlet Fever and his wife, Charlotte, died of what Robert E. Lee said was a broken heart.

The last of those tragic events still lay ahead on October 23, when Stuart wrote to General Samuel Cooper, the Confederacy's Adjutant and Inspector General, as well as senior ranking general, to bemoan the absence of Rooney, saying he needed to be exchanged and promoted. "No officer of my command more richly deserves it than he," Jeb wrote, "and none would bring more zeal and patriotism to such a post than himself." In the meantime, however, Jeb needed a brigade commander for Rooney's troops, and he requested that Colonel John R. Chambliss, commander of the 13th Virginia Cavalry, be appointed brigadier and placed in command until Rooney Lee returned, at which time Chambliss could be assigned elsewhere.[1]

In a second letter to Cooper, dated the same day, Stuart requested that the 8th and 14th Virginia Cavalry regiments be ordered to join his command.[2] Both regiments were operating in Western Virginia, and while technically a part of the Army of Northern Virginia they were not then serving under Stuart's direct command.

On October 26, Jeb wrote to Flora, mostly to inquire about their new daughter, who was born October 9 but who would not be named Virginia

Pelham, Stuart's choice, until after November 2, 1863. The content of the letter contained gossip of both a family and military nature, and makes apparent that one or more letters Jeb wrote between then and October 6, the date of the previous one in time still existing today, have been lost. In addition to reporting that William Blackford had a new son, ten days old and also named Pelham, he made a rather mysterious comment.

After telling her that Colonel Boteler, the former congressman then serving as a voluntary aide-de-camp had returned and was a true friend, he wrote that "I have always believed that the slanders circulated against me were traceable to some individual, and I am informed it is Rob Swan—would you have believed it? The less notice we take of it the better, as he is a contemptible puppy & my friends have been so thoroughly aroused they will put him down. No man in the Confederacy stands lower than Bob."[3]

Swan was a Marylander born in 1827. He had been a lieutenant in the Mexican War who served with distinction at Chapultepec. He left the army in 1848 and was charged and tried for murder, but acquitted, after which he moved to California for three years. He joined the 1st Virginia Cavalry as its Major in July, 1861, but left the regiment in April 1862 after failing to be reelected. He served as a volunteer at Seven Pines in an unknown capacity and then became a volunteer aide-de-camp and adjutant for Brig. Gen. James J. Archer, with whom he'd served in Mexico.

In his next letter to Flora, dated November 2, 1863, Jeb shed a little more light on the subject:

> There seems to be quite a revulsion in favor of my command as well as myself everywhere. I have traced much of the vilification to Bob Swan, who boasted to a friend of mine that he had been moving heaven and earth to injure me & would leave no stone unturned to hurt me. You know he is a low life puppy, & mad because I did not recommend him for promotion which he did not deserve. "Truth crushed to earth will rise again"—make that your motto. People's opinion has changed but I have not, neither has my command.[4]

Jeb's quote about truth came from a poem entitled *The Battlefield*, by William Cullen Bryant, who lived from 1794 to 1878.[5]

Although nothing more on the subject surfaces in Stuart's letters, a theory can be pieced together to explain Swan's antipathy. The 1st Virginia was Stuart's first command in the war, having been formed in July 1861, meaning that he was its first colonel and Swan its first major. On September 11, 1861, the regiment, plus a pair of guns from the Washington Artillery, was engaged with Federal troops with the result that two regiments of the enemy were driven off and Jeb was recommended by Gen. Joseph Johnston, on September 14, for command of a newly formed brigade of cavalry. Generals Longstreet and Beauregard joined in the recommendation, and ten days later Jeb was promoted to Brigadier General.

In the same letter, Johnston said that the 1st Virginia "is so far exclusively Virginian. By all means keep it so where it can be done without prejudice in other respects. State pride excites a general emulation in the army, which is of inappreciable value in its effects on the spirit of the troops." He then recommended that its new colonel be Captain William E. "Grumble" Jones, and its Lt. Colonel be Fitz Lee, both of whom who were then company commanders in the regiment. Not only was Swan passed over for either command, but Johnston went on to say:

> I do not recommend Major Swan of that regiment for promotion because, though personally known to me to be a capable and gallant officer, yet his service and experience in the army heretofore have been in the infantry. I am informed that he would prefer that branch of the service. I therefore recommend his transfer to it. Being a Marylander, it would be preferable to put him in a Maryland regiment. He would be likely thus to serve our cause most effectively.

Considering that Stuart once described General Johnston as "as good a friend as I have in the Confederate States Army,"[6] the fact that Swan's prior infantry experience in the army was fourteen years previously, in the Mexican War, and that Johnston had been "informed" that Swan preferred that branch, it doesn't take much imagination to conclude that Jeb suggested to Johnston that Swan not only not be promoted but that he be transferred to a Maryland infantry regiment. Nor does it take much imagination to conclude that Swan was fully aware of those facts. When the 1st Virginia endorsed Stuart's analysis of Swan by refusing to re-elect him regimental major eight months later, it completed what was by then a considerable amount of loathing on Swan's part for his former commander. Swan never achieved higher rank during the war than he held when he enlisted, but the fact that he treasured the status that military grade and position represented can be assumed from the fact that the first and foremost word on his headstone, in Hollywood Cemetery in Richmond, is "Major."[7]

Other than that and some post-war Federal reports of Swan being "obnoxious" to loyal citizens in Maryland in May 1865, and in danger of being shot by similar citizens in Cumberland, West Virginia a year later, and that he moved to Alabama and died there in 1872, not much more is known about Swan.[8] The exact nature of the slanders he circulated about Stuart or other reasons he stood lower in Jeb's eyes than any other man in the Confederate States of America are not known.

On November 2, Jeb lost another of the "old guard" on his staff, although Chiswell Dabney was certainly not old. At 19, he had been the staff's youngest member, but he'd served with Stuart since December 20, 1861, making him one of its longest tenured. On that day he was promoted to captain, and became Adjutant and Assistant Inspector General for Brig. Gen. James B. Gordon, who commanded the North Carolina Brigade in Hampton's Division.

The man who would eventually replace Dabney, Theodore Garnett, was then serving as a private and courier for Stuart. Garnett had apparently been with Stuart since May, had participated in the Gettysburg and Bristoe Station campaigns, but was either wounded or became ill at some point, as he recorded after the war that he "was sufficiently recovered to return to camp" about the 3rd of November. By then Stuart had established his headquarters near Orange Court House at "Camp Wigwam," which Jeb sometimes called "Wigwam Comfort," sometimes "Wigwam Independence," and sometimes "Wigwam Contemplation." Garnett described the place in great detail.

It is fitting that this particular camp received particular attention and description because, other than The Bower, it was probably the most notable of Stuart's headquarters. He occupied it from about November 1, 1863 until May 4, 1864, meaning that it was his longest single place of residence during the war, and, as it turned out, his last. It may also have been one of his smallest headquarters camps due to the fact that several of Stuart's staff, as well as a large part of his command, were at home or on furlough during much of the winter.

The camp was laid out by Lt. Henry Hagen, remembered for his "grotesque fierceness of expression . . . abnormal tendency to develop hair" and a "voice . . . as hoarse as distant thunder."[9] It lay about a mile and a half northeast of Orange Court House, in a narrow valley covered with pine and cedar trees on one side and oak on the other. Tents were pitched "in regular order," which Garnett said was "a feature seldom found in any of the Corps, Division, or Brigade Headquarters of the Army of Northern Virginia." By this he probably meant that the order in which the tents were pitched was unusual because, whereas it was normal for a camp to be arranged with company streets and a specific command structure, Camp Wigwam was laid out differently.

Entering the valley from the direction of Orange Court House, a road wound through open, rolling fields that belonged to the estate of a Mr. Scott. The first tents, on the left, were those of Stuart's escort of couriers, commanded by Lt. Hagen. Near these were the tents of Sergeant Ben Weller, who was next in command of the couriers after Hagen, and of Forage Sergeant Buckner, which was recognizable by two large stacks of hay and piles of corn located nearby.

Before the war Weller had owned a large, curly-haired horse that he sold in 1847 to P.T. Barnum, who exhibited it as "the Woolly-Horse: the Horse with its Head Where its Tail Should Be," which Barnum accomplished simply by reversing the animal in its stall. Barnum falsely advertised the animal as a new breed of horse that had been discovered by Charles Fremont on his expedition through the Rocky Mountains, a claim over which Fremont sued Barnum. The lawsuit gave Barnum more publicity than grief, and led to Fremont being nicknamed "the Woolly Horse" when he ran for president in 1856.[10] Weller was one of Stuart's best couriers as well as an excellent judge of horses, and he provided Stuart with the horse he was riding when he was mortally wounded at Yellow Tavern, a large gray named "General."

Another hundred yards along the road from Buckner's and Weller's tents was that of Major Henry B. McClellan, Stuart's Chief of Staff. Next to it about thirty feet further was the tent of Major A.R. Venable, Stuart's Assistant Adjutant and Inspector General. In another thirty feet was Stuart's tent, "a splendid piece of canvas, beautifully pitched near an immense pine tree, having a brick chimney, a plank floor, and a frame-door swing on hinges." A sawdust walk ran in front of these three tents and ended at the door of a log hut that was occupied by Major McClellan's clerks. Behind the tents, about 20 yards up the slope of the side of the valley were three more tents pitched at thirty-foot intervals and connected by sawdust walks to the walk below. These were occupied by Captain Charles Gratton, the Ordinance Officer, Captain John Esten Cooke, Stuart's cousin-in-law and Assistant Adjutant General, and Dr. John B. Fontaine, Medical Director. By itself to the left and in front of Stuart's tent, almost in the bottom of the valley, was the headquarters mess table, which was built of pine boards raised about three feet off the ground, covered with a tent fly, and set off with benches constructed of chestnut logs split in two and smoothed down. Still further down the valley was the tent of the idiosyncratic Lt. Col. St. Leger Grenfell, who served briefly as Inspector General of the Cavalry until he disappeared around Christmas of 1863 in order to go to Chicago and get involved in the conspiracy to liberate Camp Douglass.

Of Stuart's tent, Garnett wrote:

> This was a large and commodious hospital tent, near the entrance of which Hagan had built a real brick chimney—none of your wooden affairs with barrel tops—which was supplied throughout the whole winter with cords of the finest hickory wood. The inside was furnished with a plank floor, and rough pineboard bedstead, on which the General's blankets and buffalo robe was spread, making a resting place scarcely less comfortable than the feather couches of luxury & ease.[11]

The tent also contained a writing desk in one corner, a couch, a table, and several chairs for visitors.

Of the other tents, Garnett said they had wooden chimneys daubed with "the red mud of Orange" with wall tents pitched in front of them. He also mentioned the camp having "waste places," or latrines, but did not specify their location.

On November 5, Stuart held a review of his corps and the Horse Artillery near Brandy Station. Like the second of those held in June, it was attended by General Lee, as well as Governor Letcher of Virginia and most of the well known generals of the Army of Northern Virginia. Again, as they'd done five months earlier, the horsemen walked by, trotted by, and then thundered by in a mock charge. The fact that the horses were bonier and many of the troopers more ragged did not diminish the drama. Spectators were charmed, and Jeb was in his glory. It would be his last review.

Jeb's thoughts returned to plans for a home. In his letter of November 2 to Flora he reported that he had enough money to purchase "the Madison place," which was the house on the Rapidan he'd written her about on September 17, but that he had not done so. He decided he preferred something near Scottsville if a suitable place could be found, but he could not make any arrangements without her, and at the end of the typical stream of consciousness missive he switched locations again, asking her if she might "fancy the suburbs of Lynchburg for a home or not." Flora was then staying in Lynchburg and he urged her to look for "some little cottage we could buy which would charm you."[12]

He was also intent upon finding a place for Flora to stay in or near Orange CH, and on November 21 he wrote to say he'd found a "large spacious home with two old people and no children." It had taken a great deal of diplomacy to get it, he claimed, saying that "Old Mrs. Scott" refused about five times but finally surrendered. It was raining as he wrote, a Saturday, and he wished he could be with her in a "snug little room at Mrs. Scott's with somebody in my lap & somebody's head on my bosom & *somebody's* hands—but never mind, it won't be long I hope." He also reminded her to bring her riding habit. On more than one occasion he'd mentioned that one of his horses, Lilly of the Valley, was perfect, or "in fine plight" for her.[13]

His plans and longing for his wife and a home did not interfere with his continuing a flirtatious correspondence with Nannie Price. On November 13, he revealed that he was guilty of horse infidelity by writing her to say he wished she were there, "gaily cavorting on my horse, Lilly of the Valley." Of her letters, he said he never showed them to anyone, but "read and re-read them till they are nearly worn out."

As intimate and semi-adulterous as Stuart's letters to Nannie often sounded, historians generally accept the adamant claim of Major W.W. Blackford that Stuart was absolutely faithful to his wife and that if it had been otherwise he would have known it. In that same letter Stuart asked "who rejoices in the honor of being Miss Nannie's beaux?" and stated that "He must be a monstrous clever fellow or he will never get *my* consent."

Nannie Price once claimed that she had stolen the hearts of all of Stuart's staff officers, and she may not have exaggerated much. She was obviously an exceptionally charming young lady, as well as Jeb's cousin, and whether or not they ever did more in a physical sense than flirt, she was plainly one of his closest personal confidants. A touch of that confidence was reflected in a November 13th letter when Jeb wrote of his "anxiety" to see his new daughter. Flora had sent him a lock of the baby's hair, and Jeb wrote that his son, Jimmie "is so demonstrative towards his sister, that one of his squeezes very nearly finishes her." More to the point he wrote that "she is said to be like Little Flora. I hope she is."

At the end of November came the Mine Run Campaign. It was not a mirror image of the Bristoe Station campaign, but it shared some elements. Whereas Lee, in October, had endeavored to take advantage of Meade's reduced numbers and go on the offensive, Meade concluded to do the same beginning November 24. Just as Lee had attempted to maneuver and attack Meade's right flank near Bristoe Station, Meade attempted to approach Lee's right flank south of the Rapidan from the direction of the Wilderness and Spotsylvania.

After Bristoe Station and prior to commencing the new campaign, the Army of the Potomac left the safety of its entrenchments around Alexandria and Centreville and advanced to the Rappahannock. On November 7 the Federals overran and took possession of two passages over the river, at Rappahannock Station and Kelly's Ford, causing Lee to fall back on and dig into a strong defensive line along the Rapidan. Left to his own devices, George Meade might have decided that was a good place to call it quits for the season and go into winter quarters, but the Lincoln Administration was still urging an offensive, at least when it was not prioritizing the defense of Washington.

So, when Meade learned in the third week of November that three crossings of the Rapidan—Jacob's, Germanna, and Culpeper Mine Ford—were virtually undefended, he decided there existed a potential avenue directly into Lee's rear. This was a rare and unexpected opportunity, and for once Meade did not hesitate. On November 23 he briefed his corps commanders and on the 24th the wheels were put in motion to deliver a smashing blow against the Army of Northern Virginia. Three strong columns, one for each of the three fords, would snake through the Wilderness, past Spotsylvania, and into glory.

At which point the heavens opened up and, for two days dumped tons of rain on the Army of the Potomac and, more particularly, the roads over which Meade intended to deliver his blitzkrieg. Streams and rivers swelled, Meade was forced to delay his advance, and Lee was afforded time to figure out what was happening.

On the 26th the weather allowed a resumption of the Federal advance and the three Federal columns each moved toward the fords again. Those approaching Germanna (Warren's Second Corps) and Culpeper Mine Fords (Sykes Fifth and Newton's First Corps) were in place and prepared to cross the river by 11:00 a.m. The one bound for Jacob's Ford, however, with Maj. Gen. William French's Third Corps in the lead and Maj. Gen. John Sedgwick's Sixth Corps following, was going nowhere. To Sedgwick's great amazement and utter chagrin, he commenced the march when everyone else did only to find French's men still asleep and their wagons unpacked. An hour was lost getting the juggernaut to begin. French arrived at the river a little after noon.

Then French's lead division detected movement on the other side of the river and, rather than cross and drive forward, French deployed a regiment of infantry and two batteries of artillery to see what it might be. Jacob's Ford was the highest on the river, and Meade decided he couldn't risk sending the other two columns across and into Confederate territory without making the crossing at Jacob's Ford as well, for fear that the two lower columns would be cut off on the far side of the river with no support on their right. Accordingly, in response to French's caution he stopped everyone at the river, posted batteries, cut new roads through the forests near the crossings and generally broadcast their position and intentions to any Rebel who happened to be in the vicinity.

Brig. Gen. Tom Rosser and his brigade of cavalry from Hampton's division were near the Culpeper Mine Ford and saw what was happening. He reported up the line of command and Lee responded immediately. Meade was in position to do one of two things—dash on Richmond or attack Lee's right flank. Either way it meant that Confederate infantry needed to be put in motion to head east along the Orange Turnpike and the Orange Plank Road to meet either threat.

Meanwhile matters went from frustrating to silly and possibly to surreal at Jacob's Ford. The pontoon bridge that was needed to establish the crossing turned out to be one boat short of enough. Federal engineers decided to build a trestle to span the gap, but when it was completed the steepness of the far bank proved to be too severe to allow either wagons or artillery to pass. After pondering his options, French ordered the wagons and cannons to go to Germanna Ford to cross while the infantry came up and made use of the makeshift pontoon bridge. Then, however, a wide ditch on the south side of the river was discovered that had to be bridged, causing further delay, and to add a ludicrous touch to the affair, French's infantry managed to get lost. By the time it had counter-marched and arrived at where it was supposed to be, it was almost dark and French ordered his men into bivouac.

Meade, stunned at French's bumbling,[14] issued fresh orders for November 27, that the army should move west on the Orange Turnpike and the Orange Plank Road, putting it on a collision course with Lee.

The collision, such as it was, occurred near Robertson's Tavern on the Turnpike when Confederates of Maj. Gen. Robert Rodes' Division of Ewell's Second Corps (Jubal A. Early commanding) met the oncoming Federals of Col. Samuel Carroll's 1st Brigade of the 3rd Division of Warren's Second Corps. Rather than a head-on smash-up, however, the contact barely bent fenders. Both sides slowed, sent out skirmishers, exchanged shots, and decided to wait for support. The affair at Robertson's Tavern was not a battle, but it established the battle lines for the opposing armies. A creek in the vicinity named Mine Run, along which the Confederates dug in, gave the campaign its moniker.

A larger and more deadly clash took place nearby at Payne's Farm on the 27th, when Brig. Gen. Henry Prince, commanding the 2nd Division of French's Third Corps came in contact with Maj. Gen. Edward Johnson's Division of Ewell's Corps. Prince was moving forward steadily, and might have driven Johnson handily, but when he came to a crossroads and didn't know which one to take, he made the mistake of seeking guidance from French. The corps commander's response was unintelligible, and when Prince asked for clarification he was ordered down the right hand fork even though the left fork appeared to be the better choice. Prince then received another order from French telling him he was on the wrong road and to "cease all operations." Prince rode to French's headquarters and after two hours of debate they decided to stay on the right hand fork.

This led Prince to Johnson and a battle ensued, complete with charges and counterattacks and a serious engagement on the part of the Stonewall Brigade, which lost a regimental commander to wounds and whose commander, Brig. Gen. James A. Walker, seized one of his regiment's colors when it faltered at one point, leaped his horse over a fence and rallied the brigade within eighty yards of the enemy under heavy fire, escaping unhurt. Ultimately the Rebels were driven back, but Johnson's 5,000 had delayed approximately five times that number of Federals for hours and prevented Meade from accomplishing anything of note.

The third and final clash of the Mine Run Campaign occurred at New Hope Church, and there the Confederate commander was Stuart.

When the advance of Meade's army was positively detected on November 26, Stuart was at Camp Wigwam. He immediately sent orders to his brigade and division commanders. Rosser's brigade was farthest away, near Fredericksburg, and he was contacted by telegram. Hampton, now back in the saddle, was near Twyman's Store in Spotsylvania County with his other two brigades, Young's and Gordon's. Fitz Lee was in Madison County. Hampton and his three brigades were summoned to the Plank Road while Fitz was ordered to hold the Rapidan line with one brigade west of Clarks Mountain and to relieve Ewell's corps with one brigade each at Morton's Ford and Raccoon Ford in order that the infantry could move to meet the threat. Lee and his division remained in those positions until December 3.

Stuart moved to meet Hampton on the night of the 26th, but his subordinate failed to appear until 9:00 a.m. on the 27th, and then only with Gordon's brigade, by which time the Yankees were getting close.

While General French had been confounding Meade and all concerned at Jacob's Ford and beyond on November 26, Maj. Gen. Sykes had performed flawlessly at Culpeper Mine Ford. His corps began its march at the appointed hour, 6 a.m., arrived at the ford by 10:30 a.m., and was across the river by noon. Then all progress ground to a halt while French got things raveled and then unraveled. The next morning, in response to Meade's new orders, Sykes set off down the Orange Plank Road with the cavalry division of Brig. Gen. David Gregg leading the way.

The two bodies of horsemen met near New Hope Church, with numbers greatly favoring Gregg. Not only was Young's brigade not yet up, but the Confederates were short of ammunition for the carbines and rifles the horsemen carried. They also had no choice but to fight on foot in what

Stuart called "peculiar undergrowth," all of which added up to "a very unequal contest."[15] After skirmishing and falling back, Hampton's dismounted horsemen were relieved by the arrival of Heth's division of infantry from Hill's Corps at about 3 p.m. Young's brigade also arrived and was deployed on foot as skirmishers for Heth's veterans. A battalion of Heth's artillery found an ideal position from which to bombard Gregg and Sykes, and as night fell the Confederate position was well stabilized and both sides dug in. After dark Young's brigade was ordered to take the place of portions of Heth's division along Mine Run.

The next day, the 28th, saw only skirmishing between the opposing forces, but that night General Lee sent orders to Stuart to move on the enemy's left and rear and report the enemy's strength. Stuart communicated this to Hampton, directing him to be prepared to move at an early hour, and then retired for the night at Verdiersville, affectionately known as "My dears ville," where fifteen months and a lifetime ago Jeb had lost his plumed hat, as well as some pride, to an unexpected body of Federal cavalry at first light.

At this subsequent first light Jeb rode to Hampton's position on the Catharpin road near Grasty's and Allmans and found his division but no General Hampton. The mission, as Jeb reported, "was not admitting of delay," so he set off down the Catharpin Road with Rosser's brigade, figuring that Hampton would catch up at any moment. When Hampton arrived at the camp of Gordon's and Young's brigades, not knowing that Jeb had intended for him to keep one brigade on the flank, he moved off with both.

After a few miles Stuart obtained the information General Lee had wanted him to acquire and sent a courier to Lee's headquarters to report it. A little further along the Catharpin Road was Parker's Store, as well as a brigade of Gregg's Federal cavalry. Rosser attacked, catching them by surprise, drove them several miles and captured the brigade's camp equipage and all its wagons except one, which the Yankees set afire.

Union reinforcements arrived and the two sides began battling from opposite sides of a railroad cut, neither able to unseat the other, but with Rosser becoming more and more overwhelmed and disorganized in his contest with superior numbers. Then Hampton arrived with his two brigades and a section of Horse Artillery from Hart's Washington South Carolina Battery. This was what was needed, and soon the Federal cavalry were retreating again with gray horsemen in pursuit, Young's brigade in the lead. The chase continued until it was learned that Federal infantry were ahead, also on the Catharpin Road. Young continued until he came within range of the enemy's artillery, at which point Stuart halted to study the situation.

A prisoner revealed to Hampton that Warren's Second Corps of the Army of the Potomac was ahead on the road. The gray cavalry were actually in their rear, although not in a position to do significant damage. Accordingly Stuart detoured to the left to Antioch Church, where he went into camp for the night.

Losses had been light, but they included two officers of Gordon's North Carolina Brigade as well as one of the six men who had volunteered to sneak through the enemy's lines to report Stuart's predicament the night of October 13, during the Bristoe Campaign—Private Richard Baylor of Company B, 12th Virginia Cavalry.

On the 30th, Stuart and Hampton's division were placed on the right of the Confederate infantry in a line that stretched across Terry's Creek in front of Jacob's Mill, running at a right angle to the cavalry's position the night before at Antioch Church. They held this position all day, dismounted, with Horse Artillery in place in case the enemy should advance. Other than skirmishing, patrolling, and reconnoitering, nothing of importance occurred, even though scouting parties were sent as far out as Spotsylvania and Chancellorsville. December 1 passed with even less excitement, although "a very reliable scout" named Michler brought in a report that the enemy would attack early on December 2. Reliable or not, no attack came and investigation revealed that the Federal army had withdrawn.

Although additional maneuvering occurred, the Mine Run Campaign was thus at an end. Stuart had been active and generally successful, but the cavalry's role was relatively insignificant compared to other campaigns. Nevertheless, at least one historical commentator described his actions as "another clear display of Southern leadership acting on their own initiative to confound Union efforts," including Hampton, in this case, for bringing along his two brigades when firing was heard at Parker's Store, arriving in time to bail out Rosser and inflict four times the casualties on the Federals, 106 to 25, than were inflicted on the Southerners.[16]

NOTES

1 Mitchell Letters at 351.
2 *Ibid.* at 352.
3 Whitehorse letters, Oct. 26, 1863.
4 *Ibid.*
5 It isn't difficult to imagine that *The Battlefield* was a favorite of Stuart's:

> ONCE this soft turf, this rivulet's sands,
> Were trampled by a hurrying crowd,
> And fiery hearts and armèd hands
> Encountered in the battle-cloud.
>
> Ah! never shall the land forget
> How gushed the life-blood of her brave—
> Gushed, warm with hope and courage yet,
> Upon the soil they fought to save.
>
> Now all is calm, and fresh, and still;
> Alone the chirp of flitting bird,
> And talk of children on the hill,
> And bell of wandering kine, are heard.
>
> No solemn host goes trailing by
> The black-mouthed gun and staggering wain;
> Men start not at the battle-cry,—
> O, be it never heard again!
>
> Soon rested those who fought; but thou
> Who minglest in the harder strife
> For truths which men receive not now,
> Thy warfare only ends with life.
>
> A friendless warfare! lingering long
> Through weary day and weary year;
> A wild and many-weaponed throng
> Hang on thy front, and flank, and rear.
>
> Yet nerve thy spirit to the proof,
> And blench not at thy chosen lot,
> The timid good may stand aloof,
> The sage may frown—yet faint thou not.
>
> Nor heed the shaft too surely cast,
> The foul and hissing bolt of scorn;

For with thy side shall dwell, at last,
The victory of endurance born.

Truth, crushed to earth, shall rise again;
The eternal years of God are hers;
But Error, wounded, writhes in pain,
And dies among his worshippers.

Yea, though thou lie upon the dust,
When they who helped thee flee in fear,
Die full of hope and manly trust,
Like those who fell in battle here.

Another hand thy sword shall wield,
Another hand the standard wave,
Till from the trumpet's mouth is pealed
The blast of triumph o'er thy grave.

6 Mitchell letters at 234–36.

7 *Find a Grave*, http://www.findagrave.com/cgi-bin/fg.cgi?page=gr&GRid=8754439.

8 See *Friends of Gettysburg*, http://www.friendsofgettysburg.org/FriendsofGettysburg/
TheGreatTaskBeforeUs/TheGreatTaskBeforeUsDetails/tabid/99/ItemId/297/Sep-
tember-14th-2011-Robert-Swan.aspx.

9 *They Followed the Plume* at 162-63.

10 *In the Saddle with Stuart* at 29; Fran Lynghaug, *The Official Horse Breeds Standards Guide*,
p. 148 (MBI Publishing, 2009). Fremont was also referred to as the Wooley Horse
in the song *Richmond is a Hard Road to Travel*.

11 *They Followed the Plume* at 33.

12 Whitehorse letters, Nov. 2, 1863.

13 Whitehorse letters, Nov 21, 1863.

14 The Official Records contain an interesting note concerning Meade's appreciation
for French's actions. The January 7, 1864 issue of the *New York Tribune* reported that
the Reverend S. A. Hall of Dover, New Hampshire called on General Meade and
asked for an explanation of the Mine Run Campaign, to which Meade said "I went
over the river to fight, and if my orders had been obeyed, I am confident that Lee's
army might have been defeated. My plan was to cross at Germanna Ford, take the
road to Orange Court-House, and push on rapidly. . . . But one of my corps commanders failed me . . . we lost twenty-four hours, and that gave Lee notice and time
to concentrate his army, and take so strong a position that it could not be carried
without great loss and a risk of losing our army. . . . . The corps commander referred
to was General French, who was probably too drunk to know or do his duty."

French sent a copy of the article to Meade to "respectfully invite the attention
of the major-general commanding the army to request to be informed whether the
statement made by a Rev. Mr. Hall, set forth in the paragraph marked, particularly

that italicized, were furnished and sanctioned by him." ORs. Vol. XXIX, Part 1, p. 747.

15 *Ibid.* at 898.

16 http://civilwarwiki.net/wiki/Battle_of_Mine_Run.

CHAPTER 8

THE HARD WINTER OF 1863–64
December 1, 1863 to February 21, 1864

The poor brave soldier ne'er despise
nor treat him as a stranger
Remember he's his country's stay
in day and hour of danger.
—From *The Soldier's Return* (1793) by
    Robert Burns, copied by Stuart into his
    personal day book on January 28, 1864

STUART AND HIS STAFF returned to Camp Wigwam, and for a month a brigade of infantry from Hill's Corps camped on the hill in front of the cavalry headquarters on the face toward Orange Court House. The foot soldiers stayed long enough to consume all available firewood in the area and then moved, taking with them—stealing—a set of cooking utensils belonging to Stuart's couriers.[1]

Jeb's family, Flora, three-year-old Jimmie, and two-month-old Virginia came to Orange early in December and moved into the home belonging to "Old Mrs. Scott" he had secured for them. Jeb was finally able to hold his daughter, whom he'd not seen since her birth, having only received a lock of her hair in a letter from Flora.

On December 9, 1863, General Lee sent instructions to Stuart to find positions for the cavalry where the men and horses could forage without being too far away from the field of operations. During this time period, Stuart's Cavalry Corps was organized as follows:

HAMPTON'S DIVISION
Maj. Gen. Wade Hampton commanding

Rosser's Brigade: Brig. Gen. Thomas Rosser
    7th Va. under Col. R. H. Dulaney
    11th Va. under Col. O.R.Funsten
    12th Va. under Col. A.W. Harmon
    35th Bttn Va. Cav. under Lt. Col. E.V. White
Gordon's Brigade: Brig. Gen. J. B. Gordon
    1st N.C. Cav. under Col. W. H. Cheek
    2nd N.C. Cav. under Col. William G. Robinson
    4th N.C. Cav. under Col D. D. Ferebee
    5th N.C. Cav. under Lt. Col. Stephen Evans
Young's Brigade: Brig. Gen. Pierce M.Young
    Cobb's Ga. Legion, under Col G.H. Wright
    Phillips Ga. Legion, under Lt. Col. William. W. Rich
    Jeff Davis Legion, under Lt. Col. John F. Waring
    1st S.C.Cav. under Col. John L. Black
    2nd S.C. Cav. under Lt. Col. T.J. Lipscomb

FITZ LEE'S DIVISION
Maj. Gen. Fitzhugh Lee commanding
W.H.F. Lee's Brigade (commanded by Chambliss
    in Lee's absence as a prisoner)
    9th Va. Cav. under Col. Richard L.T. Beale
    10th Va. Cav. under Col. J. Lucius Davis
    13th Va. Cav. under Lt. Col. Jefferson T. Phillips (in
        Chambliss's absence)
Lomax's Brigade, Brig. Gen. Lunsford L. Lomax
    5th Va. Cav. under Lt. Col. H. Clay Pate
    6th Va. Cav. under Col. Julian Harrison
    1st Bttn Md. Cav. under Lt. Col. Ridgely Brown
    15th Va. Cav. under Col W.W.Ball
Wickham's Brigade, Brig. Gen. Wms. C.Wickham
    1st Va. Cav. under Col.R.W. Carter
    2nd Va. Cav. under Col. T. T. Munford
    3rd Va. Cav. under Col Thomas H. Owen
4th Va. Cav. under Lt. Col W. H. Payne

Jenkins and his brigade were in western Virginia and Imboden's brigade was in the Shenandoah Valley. While both were technically under Stuart's command each operated independently.

In compliance with the commanding general's direction. Stuart dispatched Fitz Lee that week with Wickham's and Chambliss's brigades, plus much of the Horse Artillery, to Albemarle County, while Lunsford Lomax's brigade remained along the Rapidan, picketing the fords. When Federal troops raided into western Virginia, Wickham and Chambliss were sent to the Shenandoah Valley, and ultimately Fitz had regiments on both sides of the Blue Ridge, with artillery wintering in Charlottesville. Before the winter was very old, Fitz allowed most of his regiments, both officers and men, to go home for the season and to secure horses.

Rosser's brigade of Hampton's division was sent to Augusta County, also in the Shenandoah, while the other two brigades, Gordon's and Young's, stayed with the main body of the army, largely for the purpose of picketing river fords. Many of the division's officers and men, however, were also sent home or south to find and secure horses and forage. Some companies and regiments were in serious danger of becoming infantry if fresh horses were not found.

The only cavalry that Stuart kept near his headquarters were some of Lomax's brigade, which camped near Barnett's Ford on the Rapidan.

On December 12, Jeb's Chief of Staff, Henry McClellan, requested and received a twenty-day leave, but not merely for the purpose of going home for the holidays. He'd met and fallen in love with a Virginia girl from Cumberland County named Catherine Macon Matthews. They would be married on December 31, 1863. The union would be long and happy, and would produce nine children.

On December 13, Jeb wrote to his brother Alick, in part to discuss the family salt business, in part to exchange gossip and pleasantries, but principally to return a check Alick had given him for the purpose of purchasing a home. He didn't say that it was the Madison place, although that was the one house he'd spoken about most seriously, and he explained to Alick that the owners had decided to postpone the sale until "spring after the war." He was also thinking about what would follow war's end, and declared that he wanted only to "devote my life to agricultural pursuits. . . . If I should survive this war." He'd been thinking about the "old homestead" at Patrick, where he spent most of his boyhood, and wondered if it could be bought.

On December 18 he wrote a cousin, Alexander H.H. Stuart, who lived in Augusta County. He had not communicated with him or his family in a long time and wanted to both renew the acquaintance, which had begun in 1854, and to thank him and his family for the kindnesses "so often shown me." It was from this cousin that Jeb had obtained the bay horse Chancellor, which had been shot beneath him at the battle of Chancellorsville. Jeb recounted that he'd had four horses shot so far in the war, but that he would "compromise to have all my horses shot, to escape myself." In a somewhat similar vein he wrote that he was gratified that "the mortality in my staff has been less for six months past than before." Six months took him back to the loss of Von Borcke, Channing Price, and others.[2]

In fact, Stuart's staff was greatly transformed from what it had been the previous spring. Chiswell Dabney and Walter "Honeybunn" Hullihen had been promoted and transferred. Channing Price and William Farley were dead. Channing's brother, Assistant Engineer Thomas Price, Voluntary Aide Harry Gilmor, Aide-de-Camp Thomas Turner, Aide-de-Camp James L. Clark, Aide-de-Camp Henry S. Farley, and Ass't Adjutant General Richard B. Kennon had been transferred. Inspector Heros Von Borcke and Aide-de-Camp Benjamin White were both wounded and disabled. Quartermaster Samuel Hairston, his brother, Ass't Adjutant General J.T.W. Hairston, Surgeon Talcott Ellison, and Inspector Frank Terrill had resigned, and Aide-de-Camp Robert Goldsborough had been captured.[3]

Still, there were good times to be had. A typical evening's entertainment, as described by one his staff, was to gather at the General's tent for a serenade by the "Amateur Glee Club," consisting of Sam Sweeney as leader of the band, on banjo, Sam's left-handed cousin, Bob, on violin, Private William Pegram of the 4th Virginia, one of Major McClellan's clerks, on flute, Captain Theodore Garnett on triangle and, occasionally, Major McClellan on guitar. All could sing, but Stuart, a baritone, McClellan, a tenor, and Private James Grant, 10th Virginia, a clerk and a bass, were particularly noteworthy. They would then "go through a mixed program of songs, jokes, back-stepping, and fun-making until the general, tired of our performances, would rise on his buffalo-robe and say 'Well, good evening to you all gentleman,' and in five minutes thereafter the camp would be hushed in sleep."[4] As picturesque and charming as such an evening must have been, it probably paled in Jeb's memories compared to evenings at The Bower, months earlier, when Heros Von Borcke and Tierman Brien performed their outrageous skits and the presence of John Pelham and Channing Price provided assurance that all was right with the world.

The days before Christmas were spent making the camp more weather-proof—cutting and hauling wood, mixing mud and daubing tent chimneys, and laying in such provisions as could be found. Never abundant, foodstuffs consisted particularly of bacon, beef, potatoes, hardtack, and "middlin" (pork). Despite there being a primary mess tent, most of the staff and couriers sorted themselves into individual groups, or messes, to share provisions, cook, and eat together. Garnett, who was then a courier and not yet an officer, messed with three clerks, Privates William Pegram, William Berkeley and James Grant. Private Berkely had a young black boy who could cook, though was apparently not heavily burdened by the demands of slavery, as Garnett wrote that he "sometimes cooked for us and sometimes *he didn't.*" He remembered that at times they nearly starved even when food was available simply because they were all too lazy to cook for themselves.[5]

On Christmas night a serenading party was assembled to go into town and "give the ladies some music." Stuart did not join them but once again Sam Sweeney was the maestro and Bob Sweeney was on violin. They went from house to house, and at one which appeared dark, they decided to awaken the residents, only to have the door thrown open to reveal an ongoing party. There was eggnog and there were ladies. The floor was cleared, the musicians took position, partners were selected and they "chased the golden hours with flying feet until the dawn of the day." Knowing they were due back in camp the soldiers insisted on first escorting each of the ladies to their respective homes.

Others felt little like celebrating the holiday season. The war had dragged on for nearly three years, they were away from their families, and they knew from two winters of experience that they had a long, cold, depressing six months or so to endure. Stuart's quartermaster, Major Phillip H. Powers, wrote his wife on December 26 to first wish his family a "*merry holiday,*" and then to immediately acknowledge that there could not be a holiday for "a poor woman with four children, a body full of ailments and pains, and a husband in the rebel army." He had not celebrated much. The previous day, Christmas, he had been promised a bowl of eggnog by friends in Orange, but the most important ingredient—"spirits"—did not arrive and he consequently "passed a quiet and sober day in his tent reading *Women in White*," a mystery novel written by Wilkie Collins in 1859.[6]

Stuart hosted a Christmas eve dinner at his headquarters in honor of two visiting Englishmen, Fitzgerald Ross and Frank Vizetelly.[7]

Vizetelly had visited Stuart's camp before, particularly in October and November 1862. He was a war correspondent and a talented sketch artist who drew many depictions of Civil War scenes and events for publication in the *London Illustrated News*. Ross was a soldier, or at least a veteran of the Austrian Huzzars, and was the man who had interviewed General Lee about the Gettysburg campaign on July 9, 1863.

The Englishmen took "the cars" from Richmond to Orange Court House on the 24th, which was a "bitterly cold day." They were met at the station by a mule-drawn ambulance driven by one of Stuart's couriers, Private John C. Pierson of the 4th Virginia who was destined to die at the Battle of Five Forks on April 1, 1865, eight days before Appomattox.[8] Ross recorded the trip to Camp Wigwam as being "over two miles of frozen road," but Private Pierson made the trip as short as possible, keeping the mules going as fast as they "could scamper." At one point along the way, in fact, they had a race with a mounted soldier and "beat him hollow."

They were given a hearty welcome at Stuart's large tent, ushered in and seated before a roaring fire. The two Sweeneys were playing on banjo and violin, and "a quartet of young fellows," no doubt the glee club, sang songs in which everyone joined. Ross noticed that Private Grant had "a magnificent voice."

One of the favorite songs sung was Blackford's *Cavalier Glee*, and Ross liked it so much that he wrote down all the words and included them in the book he published about his visit to the Confederacy, *Camps and Cities of the Confederate States*, which he completed in March 1865. Vizetelly, who had been an artist and correspondent in France, Austria, Italy, and the Mediterranean Islands, told "some of his best stories." Ross wrote that Stuart's camp was "always one of the jolliest," that Stuart was fond of music and singing, and "is always gay and in good spirits." He noticed that whenever Jeb laughed, which "frequently happens," that he "winds up with a shout that is very cheering to hear."

That night Jeb turned his tent and blankets over to the Englishmen and went into town to stay with Flora. The next morning they all visited her at the Scott house, and met Jeb's son, who at age three was calling himself "General Jimmy J.E.B. Stuart, Jr." Ross noted that Jimmy had a habit of "running about amongst the horses' legs," and opined that horses never seemed to kick in America but that the same couldn't be said about mules, and that Jimmy's lack of fear caused everyone some anxiety. After visiting Stuart, the two Englishman went to General Lee's headquarters.[9]

On New Year's Eve, Jeb and his family boarded the train in Orange and rode to Richmond, and went from there to Dundee.

One can imagine the scene, as well as imagine Flora's mind returning to it again and again over the next 59 years. The little family, husband and wife with boisterous three-year-old son and precious 11-week-old little girl, bundled against the cold, him in extravagant uniform, plumed hat, tall boots, probably with saber at his waist, being recognized everywhere they went, but together like a normal family on holiday. There would have been distractions—the rough ride, the uninsulated cars, the cold, the cinders from the engine, Jimmy unable to sit still, Virginia fussing, Jeb alternating between attention to her and the kids and responding to the attention of other passengers. There were reasons for worry and Flora rarely failed to locate them, but she must still have cherished the moments, the break with routine, the ever so rare opportunity to be with her General, to have him within arm's reach, to have his arm to hold, his confident voice and laugh to reassure her. Perhaps she thought how right the trip seemed. Perhaps she thought about how she longed for the day when they could be together like this daily, with the war behind them, living in a home of their own, enjoying those "agricultural pursuits" Jeb intended to pursue. Surely she expected nothing less.

It would be the only such trip of its kind.

Once the family was at Dundee with the Price family, Jeb mixed duty with pleasure, traveling to Fredericksburg and to Charlottesville to inspect scattered units of his corps, then returning to Dundee and to Richmond for parties and socializing. On or about January 15, he attended a party at the home of a Mrs. Randolph, who was frequently mentioned by Mary Chesnut in her diary, and who was probably Mary Adams Elizabeth Pope Randolph, the wife of Brigadier General and former Confederate Secretary of War, George Wythe Randolph. Mrs. Randolph hosted a charades party, and raided her friends' homes for props and costumes, it not being enough to merely act out a scene when a full theatrical performance could be staged.

The beautiful Richmond socialite, Hetty Cary, was there. She was described by an acquaintance as "the most beautiful woman of her day and generation," and "the handsomest woman in the Southland—with her classic face, her pure complexion, her auburn hair, her perfect figure and her carriage, altogether the most beautiful woman I ever saw in any land."[10] It should surprise no one, then, that Jeb noticed her. He was, Mrs. Chesnut observed, "devoted" to her and Cary did not dissuade his attention in any manner. Her cousin, Constance Cary, and Mary Chesnut watched him flirting with her and Constance pointed to Jeb's collar insignia and remarked "Hetty likes them that way, you know—gilt-edged and with stars."[11]

Heros von Borcke was finally recovering from his throat wound, and was up and about, although he could still barely speak. He'd attended a party on Christmas day at the home of Brig. Gen. John S. Preston, Superintendent of Conscription for the Confederacy and a member of the Richmond elite, and on January 8 he accompanied Lt. Preston Hampton, son and aide of Wade Hampton, to a gathering at Cary Hetty's home. The day before, January 7, the Confederate Congress had adopted a resolution thanking Von Borcke for his service to the Confederacy, and the ladies in attendance asked him about it. Mary Chesnut wrote that he was "as modest as a girl—in spite of his huge proportions," and also wrote down Von's response when Hetty declared "that is a compliment indeed!"

> Yes, I saw it, and the proudest day of my life when I read it. It was at the hotel breakfast table. I try to hide my face with the newspaper I grow so red. But my friend, he has his newspaper too, and he sees the same thing. So he looks my way, he says, pointing to me "Why does he grow so red? He has got something there!" Then he laughs. Then I try to read aloud the so kind compliments of the Congress but he—you—I cannot. . . ."

At that Von put his hand to his throat. Mrs. Chesnut recorded in her diary that night that "His broken English and the difficulty of enunciation with that wound in his windpipe makes it all very touching—and very hard to understand."[12]

Stuart was back at Camp Wigwam by the 18th, and he rode into Orange with Captain John Esten Cooke and Major McClellan, where they visited the lovely Mrs. Grinnan, wife of Dr. Grinnan. Cooke was busy writing, his real life occupation, and had just finished a chapter in his life of Stonewall Jackson entitled "Manassas." Furthermore he'd received a letter from *The Magnolia Weekly*, a magazine published in Richmond that had begun publishing in 1863 and billed itself as "a home journal of literature general news." It offered Cooke eight columns of print per issue, which he thought he would fill with his recollections of the war "in natural humorous tone— no affectations of 'humorous sadness.'"[13]

On the 19th Jeb piled on the Von Borcke bandwagon by sending a letter to General Cooper after hearing that the recommendation that Von Borcke be appointed Brigadier General and sent to Europe as an envoy was deemed by Cooper as "impracticable." Jeb disagreed and renewed his advocacy that Von be made a brigadier, citing as precedent the promotion of Camille Armand Juiles Marie, Prince de Polignac, a French officer who offered his services to the Confederacy in 1861 and was subsequently promoted to Brigadier in January 1863 (and in April 1864 to Major General), his service being principally in Louisiana. Compromising, he argued that if it really was impracticable to make Von a brigadier, then "I presume it will not be impracticable to confer upon him the rank of Colonel." This latter plea would be partially granted, for Von would be promoted to Lt. Colonel and would be sent by President Davis on a diplomatic mission to England. Jeb would not see it, however, as he would be seven months dead by the time it happened.

Mrs. Chesnut recorded seeing Von Borcke one more time, on February 5 at the home of the Prestons. She and her husband arrived and heard Von telling the guests the proper pronunciation of his name and describing the various ways Southerners had butchered it. At that point one of the guests, seeing a chance for sport, threw open a door and shouted "A gentleman has called for Major Bandbox." Von Borcke later agreed that that was the worst pronunciation he'd heard yet.[14]

The same day that Jeb wrote General Cooper about Von Borcke, he wrote his brother Alick. A letter containing a draft for $1,000 mailed by Alick some days earlier had not arrived, and Jeb urged him to stop payment on it. Along with some gossip about mutual friends he lamented the army's suffering for lack of shoes, blankets, and rations, but declared that he had "never been cast down," and that "if Congress & the people will hold up our hands we will fight the enemies of our cause & country—and God will bless with victory our arms." The cause was blessed, he believed, and the people need only "reach forth our united arms in one grand effort" and independence would be theirs.

Two depressing, if not shattering, events occurred within Stuart's close circle about then. The first and worst was the death of Sam Sweeney. The talented banjo player and provider of Stuart's musical score since at least November 1862 died at an Orange Court House hospital on January 13, 1864. When Stuart wrote to Flora about "poor Sweeney's death" on January 30, he reported the cause as smallpox, as did John Esten Cooke in his journal on January 28. By pure coincidence, another great musician of the period, Stephen Foster, died the same day in New York City.

Sweeney had played a thousand tunes at hundreds of evening campfires, formal balls, informal parties, military missions, and visitations by dignitaries, and those who loved his music as well as the man agonized over his passing. Cooke wrote that it was "a great loss," and "what shall we do without him?" He added that Sweeney was a gentleman in character and manners, knew his place everywhere, was ever modest, obliging, respectful, and "had the *savoir faire* which makes a man graceful in the hut or the palace."[15]

There is some doubt about the cause of Sweeney's death due to the fact that there is no record of an outbreak of smallpox in the area at that time. There has even been speculation that he died of other causes but that Stuart was told it was smallpox in the hope that he would not direct that Sweeney be disinterred and given a full military funeral. In fact, Sweeney's grave was either unmarked or, more likely, the marker was lost with the passage of time. Nevertheless, in 2010 local Orange historians determined that the location of burial for all Confederate soldiers who died in either of the two hospitals located at Orange Court House in 1864, was a five acre plot that is now a part of the Graham Cemetery on the western edge of the town. On June 6, 2010, they formally dedicated a Confederate headstone at the edge of the plot and had a ceremony in the presence of about 100 people who remembered and cared. The headstone reads "Pvt. Samson D. Sweeney, Co. H, CSA, 1832, Jan. 13, 1864."

The other sad change was less final and certainly less sorrowful, but it represented additional erosion of the underlying foundation of Stuart's glory—W.W. Blackford left his staff.

Blackford had been under Jeb's command since the beginning of the war and on his staff since June 24, 1862. Other than Von Borcke, Pelham, and perhaps Channing Price, he was the closest and most intimate staff officer to serve him, and he could not be replaced. At least the change was an advancement for the engineer, for he was notified on January 25 that he was to be promoted from Captain to Major and transferred to the newly established First Regiment of Engineers. By April he became a Lt. Colonel.

On the 23rd, knowing that transfer orders were on the way, Blackford wrote his father to give him the news and to lament leaving the General. "I have been with him for almost three years and our relations have always been friendly, without a single exception. We have been together in almost every engagement fought by the Army of Northern Va., besides his numerous cavalry engagements and raids. I leave only two of the old staff behind me.[16] Since the second battle of Manassas five have been killed, three wounded, and two taken prisoner."[17]

Stuart was not at headquarters the day Blackford left, but this was to Blackford's liking, in part because he was able to avoid a painful parting scene but in larger part because it meant Stuart wrote him a letter of farewell, which was one of Blackford's most prized possessions for the rest of his life.[18]

The reason Stuart was not at Camp Wigwam when Blackford departed is probably because he was in Charlottesville with some of his staff officers, where, as John E. Cooke recorded, "they 'inspected' and frolicked, at balls, etc." At one such event an elderly lady cautioned her younger companions "not to dance round dances or let Gen. Stuart kiss them." Jeb thought the story humorous and recounted it to those who had not been with him.[19]

On January 27, Stuart wrote letters, one to a Mrs. Howard B. Shackleford in Charlottesville, asking her to make the city as agreeable as possible for Jeb's old friend, Surgeon Carey, with whom he had served in the west before the war, and who would be visiting there. Another was to General Cooper, discussed below, and a third was to Flora, who had stayed at Dundee when Jeb returned to Camp Wigwam on the 19th. In the latter he continued to discuss the question of where they should buy a permanent home. He'd recently decided that Charlottesville might be ideal, and had looked at a couple of houses there. The society was excellent, an Episcopal Church was nearby, and he urged her to go see them. The house in Orange belonging to Mr. and Mrs. Scott was then rented to someone else, but Jeb had arranged to have it for Flora again on and after February 15.

On the night of January 27, Private Theodore Garnett was asleep in Major McClellan's tent when a heavy hand fell on his shoulder. He turned over and looked up to see Major A.R. Venable, Stuart's Assistant Adjutant and Inspector General, standing over him.

"Get up, the General wants to see you in his tent," Venable informed him. Garnett hastily pulled on his boots and jacket and "groped" his way to Stuart's tent. He knocked on its hinged door and heard "Come in." He entered and found Stuart stretched out on his couch with Venable sitting nearby. It was not the type of arrangement that might accompany a late summoning, and Garnett immediately suspected that "some trick or joke was about to be played on me by my fun-loving chief," particularly because Venable seemed to be trying to hide a grin.

Stuart pointed to his open desk, on top of which his private letter book was sitting, surrounded by pen, ink, and paper. "Sit down there, Garnett, and copy that letter for me." Jeb ordered. Garnett obeyed, picked up a pen and wrote:

> Headquarters, Cavalry Corps
> Army of Nor'n Va
> January 27, 1864
> Gen. S. Cooper, A&I Genl.
> Richmond
> General,
> I have the honor to recommend Private Theodore S. Garnett, Jr., of Co. "F," 9th Va Cav. for appointment as 1st Lieut. and Aide-de-Camp to be assigned to duty on my Staff, vice Lieut Chiswell Dabney, promoted.

The next morning Garnett joined the rest of the staff for breakfast. Garnett's assignment and promotion would be dated effective November 3, 1863, the day that Dabney transferred from Stuart's to John B. Gordon's staff.[20]

Stuart became poetic on January 28—literally—by copying several poems that he liked into a notebook now in the collection of the Virginia

Historical Society, by penning an original poem for his sister-in-law, Elmira "Ellen" Spiller Brown Stuart, Alick's second wife, and by re-writing an old standby poem for her that he'd liked for at least a decade and sent to at least three other women.

Alick married Ellen Brown in 1862 after the death of his first wife, Mary Taylor Carter, that same year, and Stuart's poem to her was of six stanzas entitled "Dedication." The other, old standby, was one he'd written to other women since 1854, the recipients being "the one I love" that year, "Miss Belle Hart," on December 5, 1862, and Robert E. Lee's daughter, Agnes, in 1863. On this occasion, Jeb entitled it "Lines to Georrge (sic)" the meaning of which is not apparent.

The old standby poem consisted of three stanzas that begged its recipient to think of him under several different circumstances—when genius, wealth, and fashion bowed at her feet: when music delighted her ear, when zephyrs whispered that love is near, and even when friends proved false. The first line of the last stanza was supposed to be "But when misfortune frowns upon that lovely dimpled face," but that January 28 Jeb changed it to "But when misfortune frowns upon my dearest Ellen's George face," whatever that means.[21] One suspects it was a private joke based on Stuart having compared Ellen to someone named George.

The "Dedication" poem was more bellicose, and paid homage to "sweet woman in angelic guise," "the maid of Saragossa," Joan of Arc, and, apparently the spirit of southern womanhood, for whom the war was being fought and whom peace would crown with rainbow splendor." However freely and emotionally it may have flowed from Jeb's heart, soul, and pen that cold winter day, it is so stilted and stylized that it is difficult to read without exciting a slight gag reflex a century and a half later.[22]

On January 30, Jeb wrote Flora again. He'd not heard from her since leaving Dundee and was feeling anxious. He had purchased 48 pounds of butter at $4.75 a pound and the total of $228 had nearly "strapped" him. He'd sent a scarf to Von Borcke which he thought would be "so becoming." He mentioned the poem, "Dedication," saying it had received many compliments, asked about Jimmie and Virginia, worried more about the site of their future home, and reported on letters he had received from Shepherdstown, Urbana, and The Bower, as well as an embroidered French merino shirt made for him by "willing hands and loving hearts" at the Bower.

He also wrote brother Alick that day, mostly to report military news—Garnett's joining his staff, a new young private named Charles D. Lownes who had come by way of Alick and enlisted in the 4th Virginia when he was unable to join Mosby (and who would serve as a headquarters courier until the day Stuart was mortally wounded), and other recent events. Apparently Alick was considering joining the army, and Jeb told him to keep him informed of what he decided, and that he would give him a strong recommendation. He was certain that the campaign of the following spring would be the one to watch—"A gigantic struggle is before us. God grant we win the victory."[23]

On February 2, Stuart received a letter from his close friend, Maj. Gen. G.W. "Custis" Lee, one of Robert E. Lee's sons and an influential member of President Davis's staff. He opened it "Dear Beaut," and signed it "Growls"—West Point nicknames. He'd received a note from Jeb dated the 29th, and the content was almost certainly about Jeb's desire for promotion, which Custis said he'd thought over a good deal, and which he promised to "bring up at a fitting time." Apparently Jeb had also suggested swapping Wade Hampton, with whom he had a cordial but not close relationship, for Stephen Dill Lee, another old friend. Custis had already mentioned this to Secretary of War Seddon, who thought it agreeable for all concerned and who said he would take it up with the president, but suggested that Hampton himself apply for the change, which apparently did not happen.

A few days later Stuart sent Garnett to General Lee's headquarters for what Garnett characterized as the only leave-of-absence ever requested by Jeb. It was approved and Garnett accompanied his commander to Richmond via the railroad from Orange Court House. They changed cars in Gordonsville, and Garnett discovered a lady friend from Winchester who had boarded the train with her brother at Staunton. The brother surrendered his seat next to the lady, whom Garnett identified only as "Miss J.C." and they talked for about half an hour, at which point Garnett proposed introducing her to General Stuart. To his surprise, she declined, and when he asked why she revealed that she had heard that General Stuart never failed to kiss every young lady he encountered, which was an honor she, like the elderly lady in Charlottesville, thought it only proper to avoid.

Garnett assured her that such a report was "slanderously exaggerated," and that he was certain he could obtain "exemption papers" for her. He did admit to seeing the General surrounded by a "bevy of beautiful young ladies" in one Virginia village who had "submitted most gracefully, nay even cheerfully to the trying ordeal of a kiss from General Stuart," but that had been just after a battle, when the smoke and din had scarcely subsided. He had never, he promised, known the General to demand any unwilling tribute "in cold blood" when there was no firing going on.

By now Stuart had noticed both the young lady and the way that Garnett was earnestly talking to her, glancing over at him, then looking away. Stuart caught Garnett's eye more than once, and conveyed the message that he expected to be introduced, but Miss J.C. stood her ground and would not allow the introduction to occur. Stuart chided Garnett about the matter later, and still later. Garnett at first declined to reveal the reason for his impolite failure to make the introduction until finally "on one occasion when he was running me about it," he revealed the horrible truth.

One wonders about the manner in which Miss J.C. recounted the story later, with pride one may assume, and whether her listeners felt admiration for her purity or amazement at her naiveté.

In Richmond, Garnett and Stuart were bombarded with invitations to "starvation parties," which Garnett said were falsely named, but at which "the youth and beauty of Richmond's fairest and best were wont to assemble." The city was filled with strangers, but it seemed especially cheerful, such that "even in the midst of war . . . (were) . . . scenes of peace."

Garnett outfitted himself as befitted a staff officer, making numerous changes in his wardrobe, but most critically he arranged to get a new horse. He had previously lost two horses in Maryland and had since been riding a "miserable Yankee 'cob'." Now Jeb not only instructed him to "go get another horse and keep well-mounted," but he supplied just the horse that Garnett needed—none other than Lilly of the Valley.

One wonders about the sales pitch Stuart made to Garnett. Lilly was the horse he designated specifically for the ladies, writing in at least three different letters to Flora and to Nannie Price that she was the ideal horse for them to come ride and "cavort" on. Yet the way Garnett heard it, Lilly had "too much life and spirit at that time for cavalry service," and even though she had carried Jeb "on many a long march," she was not one of his favorites. Garnett paid $1,500 for her, at least $1,200 of which was in "New Issue Confederate Notes."

Stuart's other horses at that time were Virginia, a large bay mare, Maryland My Maryland, a smaller, more compact bay, and Star of the East, a sorrel with light mane and tail. Garnett referred to Maryland and Star as "horses," meaning males or "horse colts," which probably meant they were young stud horses rather than geldings.[24]

All three would die at Camp Wigwam that winter from "Glanders," an infectious, bacteria-borne horse disease that often entered the body through a cut or scratch and was followed by ulcerations, swollen lymph nodes, mucous in the eyes, nose, and respiratory tract, sensitivity to light, and infection of the lungs. Unless treated properly death usually followed within seven to ten days. Accounts of the disease go back to Ancient Greece, and whereas antibiotics usually cure the animal today, treatment during the Civil War was confined to quarantine and a wide range of experimental, rarely successful fumigations, opening of nasal cavities, and injections or insertions of mercury, iodine, phenol, or creosote oil.[25]

The exact date of the death of his three animals is not recorded, but in a postscript to a letter dated February 8, Stuart told Flora to "kiss my little Virginia and tell Jeb Pa's horse Maryland is getting well." Because Flora and the family returned to Orange on February 15, so that no other letters mentioned the condition of the horses, mid to late February is an educated guess for when they succumbed to the disease. After the three died, Stuart purchased the gray "General" from Sergeant Ben Weller. Other than the gray Jeb had only one other horse, a young one he called "the Pony," and it would be with only those two that he prepared for the Spring Campaign.[26]

At one point, probably a few days before January 28, Stuart's Chief of Staff, Major McClellan, summoned the sergeant of couriers, Ben Weller, and Private DeWitt Clinton Gallher, a courier from the 1st Virginia, to accompany him on an unusual trip. John Esten Cooke recorded in his journal that he accompanied McClellan on the same or a similar trip, and the nature of it causes one to believe that such expeditions could not have been frequent, but Private Gallaher wrote after the war that there were only three of them and did not mention Cooke. It was called, according to Cooke, "running the machine," or crossing into enemy lines under a flag of truce for a particular purpose.

In this case the purpose was so that Henry McClellan could visit his brother, who was then serving on the staff of a Federal Major General.

Henry had four brothers and all served in the Union army. The name of the brother he visited on this occasion is not positively recorded, but it was probably Carswell McClellan.[27] Their sister had recently died in Philadelphia, and Henry decided he needed to talk to a member of his estranged family, learn more details, and deliver his condolences and regrets.

Such a journey into enemy lines was no walk in the park, particularly during a cold, wet winter. They first stopped and explained their mission to North Carolinian pickets, who were on a bleak hill and forbidden from lighting fires so that they were, in Gallaher's recollection, nearly frozen. Beyond them several miles were mounted outpost pickets who were required to stay mounted at all times to avoid being surprised. After explaining again and obtaining as much information about what lay ahead as they could, they ventured into "no man's land," carrying a white handkerchief tied to a saber.

Toward evening they came upon two Federal pickets who ordered them to stop and explain themselves, which they did. One of the Yankees hurried to the rear and returned at a gallop with a captain, to whom they again explained the purpose of their visit before they were escorted another couple of miles to the Federal "reserve," where soldiers were allowed to both dismount and to build a fire, around which everyone was huddled.

A courier was sent from there ten miles to Culpeper to summon Captain McClellan, while the three, or possibly four, Confederates chatted with their Federal counterparts, all of whom Gallaher described as boys. The Rebels shared all the tobacco they had with them and the Federals produced and passed around a bottle of brandy, of which Gallaher wrote years later, "I have taken several drinks of alcoholic nature in my life but if I live a century I should never forget that brandy! We were nearly frozen and that brandy seemed like a nectar of the Gods to us." The Yankees seemed to have the same attitude toward the Southern tobacco.

Just before midnight horses were heard approaching at a gallop. One of the riders pulled up, dismounted in a hurry, and the two brothers rushed into each other's arms, both weeping. They went a little ways away, huddled together and talked for several hours, during which Henry's brother told him that he did not blame him for taking the side where his conviction lay, but that the war would end next summer, and not with a Confederate victory. They then rose and "bid each other goodbye, and this was scarcely less emotional and pathetic than their meeting there," after which the Rebels rode back to their lines, arriving about sunrise.[28]

The winter dragged on. Members of the staff established friendships in Orange and most weeks saw the arrangement of a dance at one of their homes. Stuart rarely joined them, but would go to the home of Dr. Andrew Grinnan, "Brampton," where he'd headquartered previously. Prior to Sweeney's death Jeb arranged an occasional "moonlight serenade," by approaching the large home with all or most of his staff and the two Sweeneys playing their stringed instruments from the rear. There they would socialize—Dr. Grinnan's wife was young and attractive—and most would join in a game they called the "Prussian Ambuscade," the rules to which have been lost but which probably had elements similar to Hide and Seek, Kick the Can, and Capture the Flag.

Brampton was outside the Confederate picket lines, so that risk accompanied the visits, and a tale passed down through the Grinnan family held that the house was approached one evening while Stuart was present by a squadron of Federal cavalry intent upon his capture. Supposedly Jeb escaped by exiting out a second story window and climbing down a large pine tree.[29] If the incident did occur, neither Stuart nor any of his staff made mention of it in their letters or diaries.

Winter was the time for Stuart to catch up on his post-campaign reports, and John Esten Cooke was his scrivener. Jeb spent most of February 4 dictating his recollections of the Sharpsburg campaign and Crampton's Gap to Cooke. On the 5th they tackled and nearly finished the Dumfries raid. Anyone who reads the detail of Stuart's reports and considers that they were recalled and recorded a year to eighteen months after the event cannot help but marvel at the man's memory as well as understand why there were occasional errors.

Visitors of a military nature came and went, with John S. Mosby the most noteworthy, but including scouts from behind enemy lines such as the sons of the late Redmond Burke, John and Matthew, Private Charles Curtis, and Ben Stringfellow of the 4th Virginia, and Private Washington Toler of the 6th Virginia.[30] Each brought intelligence about the enemy as well as entertaining tales about their particular adventures.

Another flavor of semi-military visitors were deserters and prisoners. These were questioned until they offered no new revelations and were then usually put on a train to Libby Prison in Richmond. Some were said to be sent to another, more secret place. Whether it actually existed is anyone's guess, but the accepted rumor was that it was intended for "first-class deserters who desired to return to private life in their Northern homes by means of the underground railroad." It was so surrounded by mystery that no Confederate soldier knew or discovered if it really existed, but its purpose was broadcast to the Federals across the river by propaganda notices printed in English, German, and French, and distributed along the picket lines. It was intended to convince any of the enemy who deserted that they would be safely and swiftly transported to their homes and safety. Most soldiers in the field thought it was "a consummate humbug."[31]

On one occasion a rather unique sort of deserter showed up at Camp Wigwam. He was a young Yankee accompanied by a younger Virginia girl, each on horseback. They were accompanied by a single rider from the picket line and were delivered to Stuart, who first asked the soldier the nature of his "Yankee pedigree," to which the deserter answered that he "was of Irish *consent*." The story the couple then recounted was that they were lovers and that the girl had promised to marry him on the condition that he desert and join her in the Confederacy. The young man barely hesitated, and compounded his disloyalty by stealing two horses from his regiment for their escape. Now that they had reached bona fide Confederate territory, they wanted to find a preacher as quickly as possible in order to consummate the arrangement.

Amused, Stuart sent them to the Court House so that they could get the ceremony performed. Although nobody recorded anything about their physical characteristics, one of Stuart's couriers remarked as they were ushered out of camp that "That gal must ha' wanted a husband the very worst sort."[32]

Lack of promotion was still eating at certain folks in Camp Wigwam. Captain John Esten Cooke had written to Maj. Gen. Custis Lee about being appointed a major, and on January 30 received a letter back "with a long string of whys and wherefores explaining everything but their refusal to promote me." Others had been promoted, and Cooke swore on his honor that he did not begrudge those from captain to major of George Freaner, Benjamin S. White, and Garland M Ryals, all of whom were "bully boys, lads of mettle," personal friends, "and good luck to 'em." He was toying with the idea of making another application for reconsideration at the War Office.[33] It is entirely possible that the refusal to promote Cooke was due to some of his writings in Confederate newspapers in which he criticized certain governmental officials.

Another one with promotion on his mind was, of course, Jeb Stuart, and it was probably no secret to anyone at headquarters that he was feeling overlooked. Cooke, in closing his small tirade to himself about not being made a major, wrote of Jeb that "I like him as well as if he was Captain-General which he ought to be!"—there being no such rank of course but the implication being that it was one superior to all others.

Jeb's tirade was not to himself, nor to Flora, but to someone who might have a say in the matter—Senator and Colonel Alexander R. Boteler.

Boteler occupied some interesting roles in the annals of the Confederacy. Prior to the war he was a farmer and a politician. He was elected to the House of Representatives in 1859, but resigned when Virginia seceded and was first elected to the Virginia legislature in 1861 and to the Confederate Congress a few weeks later. What proved particularly useful, however, was his friendship with an obscure officer named Thomas J. Jackson who, after winning fame at First Manassas, became embroiled in a brewha, in February 1862, near Romney, Virginia involving Jackson, Brig. Gen. William W. Loring, Secretary Judah P. Benjamin, Governor of Virginia John Letcher, and President Davis. Eleven of Loring's officers had petitioned to have Jackson's command withdrawn to Winchester, which inspired Jackson to submit his resignation. Letcher, with Benjamin's approval, sent Boteler with a letter asking Jackson to reconsider. He proved to be the man for the job, as Jackson did agree, under certain conditions, to remain in the army.

Thereafter, beginning at the end of May 1862, Boteler served as a voluntary aide-de-camp on Jackson's staff, with the rank of colonel, and following Stonewall's death he returned to the Confederate Congress, where he was instrumental in designing the "Great Seal of the Confederate States of America." In August he became a voluntary Aide-de-Camp for Stuart and on February 6, 1864, Stuart penned a letter to President Davis recommending that Boteler be made presiding judge of a military court authorized by Congress, a pet project of Stuart's.

The same day, which happened to be his 31st birthday, Stuart wrote Boteler to discuss the latter's upcoming departure from Congress and the hope that he would be appointed to the military court. The larger purpose of the letter, however, was to fuss about the lack of attention and the promotion being denied him, certainly the thing he most wanted for a birthday present:

> I send you a slip showing the thanks of Congress to various individuals. Don't you think the curious will wonder that the Chickahominy, the 1st Pennsylvania and Catlett's Station Expeditions were not worth thanks by the side of some of those in this list; to say nothing of the victory at Fleetwood 9th of June—at Chancellorsville 3rd of May, etc. I hear Hood is Lieutenant General. I have all along been his senior, and while it is but a compliment to him well deserved, I don't' see what command they can give him. For my part, *I yield to no man in the Confederacy in quantity and quality of service.* I know that General Lee would not have another in my place. I command two *Divisions of Cavalry*, one division of which is analogous in point of importance to two divisions of infantry, besides a battalion of Horse Artillery. Withholding the rank of Lieutenant General seems to me a mere quibble, for a Corps is two or more divisions by accepted military definition. While rank should be *no* patriot's *motive*, it is nevertheless the acknowledged evidence of appreciation, and when withheld from one occupying a position corresponding to higher rank the inference is against the officer and prejudicial to him. These, my dear Colonel, are a few grumbling reflections which you must excuse as they are intended entre nous [between us], but for such action as you may deem discreet and proper. Custis Lee says he will bring the matter up if occasion offers, but you may have a chance in your own way to have something done for a growling old soldier like myself.[34]

The tranquility of camp life was interrupted that same February 6 when the enemy made a demonstration at Morton's Ford. Like many military stratagems, it was intended to be much more dramatic and effective than it proved to be. Maj. Gen. Ben Butler had received a report on February 2 from a subordinate in North Carolina, Brig. Gen. Innis Parmer, saying that he'd been attacked by 15,000 men from Pickett's Division and Hoke's

Brigade. Butler put two and two together and decided that Lee had dispatched so many troops from the Army of Northern Virginia to North Carolina that the Confederates must be stretched thin. Accordingly he proposed, and Halleck and Stanton endorsed, a plan for the Army of the Potomac to move against Lee in order to distract him while Butler made a dash from the south and captured Richmond.

John Sedgwick was temporarily in command of the Army of Potomac while Meade was absent on leave, and he didn't think there had really been much of a reduction in Lee's forces, but orders being what they were, he dispatched the First and Second Corps, as well as Kilpatrick's division of cavalry, to threaten Lee at Morton's, Barnett's, and Raccoon Fords.

The plot thickened when Butler received a "cipher letter" revealing that Federal prisoners in Richmond were about to be transferred to Georgia, so that, in his words, it was "now or never . . . the time to strike . . . [and] rescue our friends."

Yet that was still not enough drama. A Union private in the 1st New York Mounted Rifles named William Boyle had been convicted of murdering one of his officers and was awaiting execution, but Lincoln had temporarily suspended all executions in Butler's department, and while that temporary reprieve was in effect, Boyle managed to befriend and convince a guard to let him escape. Not only did he gain freedom, but he made his way to Richmond and informed authorities there that large numbers of cavalry and infantry were being consolidated by Butler for the purpose of taking Richmond. He was believed and the Confederates reinforced and strengthened their defenses in Butler's direction so significantly that his forces called off their attack when they made contact with those defenses.

Meanwhile Sedgwick's Federals, led by a division commanded by Brig. Gen. Alexander Hays, crossed at Morton's Ford. To round out the "bad fiction" nature of the script for the day, Hays was drunk, having "added two or three extra fingers to his morning dram," as one of his officers described it. As his soldiers waded into the frigid river, Hays followed on his horse swinging an ax over his head, trying to chop at some tree branches and shouting, "We will cast them down as I do this brush!" The Rebels on the other side of the ford were a part of Ewell's Corps, including a battery of the Richmond Howitzers, who opened fire and did their own casting down. Not only were they dug in, with artillery, but they outnumbered the

Federals, so that Ewell was amazed that they would dare attack.

Soon the Federal advance halted, the men of Hays division took cover, and what had been intended as an offensive took on the characteristics of a siege, the attackers being the ones besieged. The affair at the ford ended when Ewell launched a counterattack, which one Federal officer imaginatively described as the "enemy retreating toward us," and drove Hays back to where he'd started. Kilpatrick was able to obtain some intelligence of the Confederate cavalry of an obvious nature—that Hampton's division was woefully short of horses and other supplies—but it cost the Federals 11 dead, 204 wounded and 40 missing, whereas Ewell reported only four killed and 20 wounded.[35]

Stuart and Lomax's Brigade rode to Barnett's Ford, the most southerly of the three places where the demonstration was staged and the farthest away from the heaviest fighting. It was Lt. Garnett's first brush with battle as a staff officer, and he recalled that as soon as word came that Yankee cavalry were moving toward the Confederate left, Stuart took the only two couriers whose horses were saddled and rode toward the ford, telling his staff to follow. When Garnett caught up, Stuart was with Brig. Gen. Lomax on a hill, directing the positioning of a battery and watching Federal cavalry emerge from the woods on the opposite side of the river. Two brigades from Hill's Corps were in rifle pits along the Confederate side of the Rapidan, and Garnett recorded the dramatic yet anticlimactic scene that followed.

A squadron of blue horsemen, sun glinting off their sabers, led off in beautiful order, and accelerated to a gallop, preparing to attack Hill's entrenched infantry. Garnett watched with admiration, but wondered "what fool could have ordered a charge, across a swollen stream, at a rocky ford, and in the face of two brigades of infantry lying within fifty feet of the water's edge." On they came, and when about 200 yards from the river they disappeared from view behind the opposite bank. The Confederates waited, knowing that they would quickly appear again, silhouetted against the sky, within deadly range and destined for destruction.

The leading files of the enemy, six men, appeared and "with one impulse and with a noise like an explosion of a powder magazine, every musket is discharged at these half dozen horsemen." Every shot missed. The Confederates aimed too high, and the Yankees wheeled about and disappeared again, leaving the Confederates indignant and disappointed.

Some skirmishing followed, but after an hour the enemy withdrew and Stuart led his men five miles upriver to a covered bridge at Liberty Mills, where the cavalry crossed in the company of Brig. Gen. Samuel McGowan's brigade of infantry, hoping to fall on the flank of the retreating enemy but having to content themselves with driving off the rear guard from some recently constructed earthworks.[36] When Jeb wrote about the affair to Flora on the 8th, his principal complaint was that the enemy's "bold demonstration" had prevented a "Divine Service" scheduled for Saturday the 7th.

In the same letter, Jeb reported that John Mosby had visited and brought him a superb pair of heavy gauntlets, which may be the pair now on display at the Museum of the Confederacy with Stuart's hat, saber, saddle, boots, fieldglasses, and carbine. He also defended himself against what must have been a recent scolding by Flora for his flirtatious ways and how it was affecting her, saying:

> As to being laughed at about your husband's fondness for society and the ladies, all I can say is that you are better off in that than you would be if I were fonder of some other things that excite no remark in others. *The society of ladies will never injure your husband,* and ought to receive your encouragement. My correspondence with the ladies is the kind of correspondence which pertains to the position I hold, and which never could obtain with me were I a subordinate officer, such no doubt as you hear insinuations from. Such men have not sense enough to understand it but I am thankful to say I have—and I hoped that my wife could not for one moment be made a prey to any twinge or unpleasant feeling at anything of the kind.

Nice try Jeb. Yes, were you an alcoholic, a notorious gambler, drug addict or some "other thing" that might cause injury, as opposed to merely a battlefield target of neon dimension, Flora might have cause for concern. Instead, simply because your reputation is such that mothers warn their daughters not to dance with you and young ladies on trains decline your introduction for fear of your kissing them (probably only a misdemeanor assault), your short-sighted wife is unable to see that you are only doing your duty. A man in your position really has no choice in the matter, after all, even though many do not have sense enough to understand it the way you do and the way you hoped your wife must. Poor unencouraged man.

This is, perhaps, an appropriate place to discuss a sideline to the study of Stuart during the last eleven months of his life, being a graphological analysis of his handwriting and what it reveals about his personality.

Graphology enjoys a reputation only slightly higher on the credulity scale than palm reading and astrology, yet it has a greater basis for confidence. Nearly everyone's handwriting, and personality, is different, and writing often changes as a person ages, experiences an illness or injury, or simply experiences a change in moods. Some aspects of handwriting reveal common sense characteristics. A person, for example, who leaves small margins on the sides, top. and bottom of a page, and whose lines of cursive are close together, is a frugal person who is subconsciously seeking to use most of the page. A writer's signature and the capital letter "I" are self-images on paper, such that a large fancy signature is often the reflection of a confident or egotistical individual. Yet should one's signature be markedly different from his or her handwriting, it suggests a façade—a desire to project an image to the world that the writer doesn't believe. Graphology is employed in criminal forensics and even in medicine, as certain personality traits and even diseases manifest themselves in how a person forms their letters, words, and sentences.

Still, the purpose of including an amateur analysis of Stuart's handwriting herein is not intended for any purpose other than fun, on the off-chance that it might reveal something telling or surprising about the man.

If one puts any stock in graphology, Stuart was, above all else, a man who hated procrastination. He did not leave jobs unfinished. He was true to his duty to the end, and never started something he did not complete. He was confident and pleased with himself but not nearly as egotistical as one might suspect. What you saw in Jeb Stuart was exactly what he was. He did not pretend to be a flashy, attention-getting dandy. He *was* a flashy, attention-getting dandy. He loved the limelight and he loved society. He was also extremely generous with his friends, outgoing, loyal, and devoted to those for whom he cared. He was detail-oriented but willing to take short cuts when they were offered. He was very comfortable in his religious beliefs but was neither overbearing, proselytizing, nor judgmental in regard to the beliefs of others. He was athletic and somewhat artistic. Always optimistic, he did not, however, make firm, long-range plans for the future. He was very satisfied with his career and his daily life, and was balanced between head and heart, ideals and the mundane.

If there was one failing, one shortcoming in Jeb's personality, it may be the very same one that was bothering Flora Stuart in February 1864—Jeb Stuart was sexually unfulfilled.

The word "unfulfilled" can be interpreted many ways and, indeed, the characteristic of Stuart's handwriting to which this trait might be attributed was not constant. Suffice it to say that according to some graphological theory, one's sexual proclivities manifest themselves in handwriting via the lower loops—the y's, j's, g's, and f's that extend below the line. A sexually satisfied person makes those loops much in the way he or she learned when first taught how to write—with a complete but not exaggerated loop, neither too large, too narrow, non-existent, nor failing to close. Jeb's y's, g's, j's, and f's sometimes have only a small loop, sometimes no more than a straight line, and yet are sometimes large and exaggerated. Perhaps it explains some of his behavior; perhaps it is silly speculation.

A final word on the subject is that, whereas loops below the line reflect one's attitude toward the mundane aspects of life—sex and money particularly—the opposite is true of letters that extend above the line, such as most capital letters and lower case b's, f's, and l's. Such letters supposedly reveal one's attitude toward religion, honesty, and ideals, so that the more "standard" the letter and its upper loop or upper case character, the more "normal" the person's attitude toward religion and idealism are likely to be. This, in turn, makes the lower case "f" one of the most singularly significant letters for graphological analysis because it, of all the alphabet, has one loop that extends above and one that extends below the line. A person more interested in sex and money than in going to church might have no upper loop at all in his or her "f" but quite a healthy lower loop, or vice versa for a religious celibate. The loops of Jeb Stuart's lower case f's, no matter what the condition of his y's, g's and j's, were almost a mirror image of each other, indicating a well-balanced man.[37]

The letter of February 8 was one of Stuart's longer ones. Jimmy had a toy wheelbarrow that needed repair and which he'd left behind at Mrs. Scott's so that when Jeb sent for it to have it fixed it set off a rumor that the army was about to move and he needed the wheelbarrow to haul equipment. Richmond, which Flora would soon be visiting, was "a queer place with a *few* queer people in it," and if anyone there spoke to her of subjugation, it was because of a total lack of ignorance about the armies. Returning to the only topic that rivaled his concern about not being promoted, he discussed yet another house that they were considering purchasing, probably in Charlottesville, and which Alex (Alick) had looked at as an investment. Jeb was afraid it had some objectionable neighbors because some similar homes had been pointed out to him as "gambler's dens."

On February 10, Stuart wrote Boteler again. Congressman John Allen Wilcox, an ally of Boteler's, had died three days earlier and Jeb empathized with the loss before returning to the subject of his own promotion, theorizing that one reason he'd not been promoted was because he had not been wounded. Certainly the promotion of John Bell Hood to Lt. General, which was effective February 1, would seem to have been some compensation for his loss of one leg and one arm.

February 12 was another quiet day in camp, with weather that was sunny, warm, balmy, and spring-like. Stuart had been heard recently singing in his tent, and on that day Private William Pegram, a courier, and Major McClellan formed a duet to sing "Jine the Cavalry" and "Bingo," the latter folk song about a dog having been around since at least the 1780s. A Dr. Caney visited, and entertained everyone with his account of witnessing the "Veteran Homeguard" responding to an alarm in Richmond. One of its members, a "big fat fellow with equipments on and musket at hand" was seen "blubbering" at the door as he bade his wife farewell. For supper there was ice cream and custard.

On the 21st a large envelope arrived postmarked Oglethorpe, Georgia and addressed to "John Esten Cooke, care of Gen. J.E.B. Stuart, Army of Virginia." He opened it and found it filled with pressed flowers and a note honoring John Pelham, or more precisely John Esten Cooke's sketch of Pelham published in newspapers following Pelham's death —"an unknown Georgian sends you a small cluster of young spring flowers. You loved the 'Gallant Pelham' and your words of love and sympathy are 'immortelles' in the hearts that loved him . . . I may never meet you but you have a true friend in me . . . my friendship for him was pure as a sister's love . . . I had never heard his voice. . . . Your name is ever in my prayers!" Heady words for any writer to receive.[38] Cooke wondered who might have sent them and whether they would ever meet. If that happened it was not recorded.

NOTES

1 *In the Saddle with Stuart* at 30.

2 Whitehorse letters, December 13, 1863.

3 Robert J. Trout, *With Pen & Saber: The Letters and Diaries of J.E.B.Stuart's Staff Officers*, p. 219 (Mechanicsburg, PA: Stackpole Books, 1993), cited hereinafter as *With Pen & Saber.*

4 *In the Saddle with Stuart* at 30 and n. 20.

5 *Ibid.*

6 *They Followed the Plume* at 218.

7 Jeffrey Wert wrote that Frank Lawley also attended, and while all three were apparently invited, Ross recorded that Lawley "was prevented." William Stanley Hoole's account of Lawley's time in the Confederacy confirms this, saying that Lawley "remained in Richmond as the house guest of Mr. and Mrs. Gustavas A. Myers. (It is worth noting that Lawley frequently visited the ailing Heros Von Borcke, who was also in Richmond, about this time). Hoole's book about Vizetelly mentions that "shortly before Christmas he bade his many Virginia friends adieu and was off again, this time for Wilmington," but that trip must have occurred after Christmas instead of before. Wert, at 326; F. Ross, *A Visit to the Cities and Camps of the Confederate States*, pp. 204-05 (Edinburgh & London: William Blackford & Sons, 1865), cited hereinafter as Ross.; W. Hoole, *Lawley Covers the Confederacy*, p. 79 (Tuscaloosa: Confederate Publishing Co., Inc., 1964);W. Hoole, *Vizetelly Covers the Confederacy,* p. 129 (Tuscaloosa: Confederate Publishing Co., Inc., 1957).

8 Ross at 204; *They Followed the Plume* at 318.

9 Ross at 204-207.

10 Douglas, Henry Kyd, *I Rode With Stonewall, The War Experiences of the Youngest Member of Jackson's Staff,* 271, 375: (Chapel Hill: University of North Carolina Press, 1968).

11 Chestnut, Mary, *A Diary from Dixie,* 275 (New York: Appleton & Co. 1906).

12 *Ibid.* at 272-73.

13 *With Pen & Saber* at 222.

14 *Ibid.* at 285.

15 *With Pen & Saber* at 223.

16 Blackford was referring to John Esten Cooke and William Fitzhugh, although he thereby failed to give credit to Henry Hagen, who had joined the staff in May 1862. Henry B. McClellan, certainly a foundation member of Stuart's staff, had only been in that role since May 1863.

17 *With Pen & Saber* at 222.

18 *War Years with Jeb Stuart* at 249.

19 *With Pen & Saber* at 223.

20 Robert E. L. Krick, *Staff Officers in Gray: A Biographical Register of the Staff Officers in the Army of Northern Virginia*, 108 (Chapel Hill: University of North Carolina Press, 2003), cited hereinafter as *Staff Officers in Gray*; *They Followed the Plume* at 94-95; *Riding With Stuart* at 31-32.

21 The complete poem may be found at Whitehorse letters, Jan. 19, 1864, or at Monte Akers, *Year of Glory*, 351, n. 19 (Havertown, PA: Casemate Publishing, 2012).

22 The entire poem read as follows:

DEDICATION
Wigwam
January 28, 1864
Within this consecrated shrine,
Let gems of pure affection shine,
The old, the young, the sad, the gay,
Their off'rings, and their homage pay.

While Mars with his stentorian voice,
Chimes in his dire discordant noise,
Sweet women n angelic guise,
Gives hope, and bids us fear despise.

The maid of Saragossa still,
Breathes in our cause her dauntless will,
Beyond Potomac's rock-bound shore,
Her touch bade southern cannon roar.

Joan of Arc with fierce intent,
Has oft o'er southern saddle bent,
To guide the hero o'er the plain,
And help to Victory with her rein.

But softer than the chimes of even,
Gentler than the dews of heaven,
See her' o'er the wounded bending,
All her soothing power lending.

Soon may peace with rainbow splendor,
Crown the heroine-defender,
Through life her deeds shine forth in story,
In death receive the crown of glory.—J.E.B. Stuart

23 Whitehorse letters, Jan. 30, 1864.

24 *In the Saddle with Stuart* at 32-36.

25 J. Blancou, *Early Methods for the Surveillance and Control of Glanders in Europe*, http://www.oie.int/doc/ged/D8902.PDF.

26 *In the Saddle with Stuart* at 36.

27 Gallaher and Cooke recorded that Henry's brother was a captain on Meade's staff, whereas Carswell served on the staff of Maj. Gen. A.A. Humphreys. At Gettysburg on July 2, Carswell McClellan came across mortally wounded Confederate Brig. Gen. William Barksdale while searching the battlefield for a wounded comrade, and became the last man to assist and speak to him. After the war he wrote a book about the military campaigns of Grant and another about those of Sheridan.

28 *They Followed the Plume* at 197-200; *With Pen & Saber* at 223.

29 Cooke, Helen Grinnan, *Notes of Times at Brampton, Shackleford Family Papers (1980)*; National Registry of Historic Places Nomination application for Brampton, (May 1983), http://www.dhr.virginia.gov/registers/Counties/Madison/056-0001_Brampton_1985_Final_Nomination.pdf

30 *In the Saddle with Stuart* at 38; *They Followed the Plume* at 302, 303, 305, 322, & 323.

31 *In the Saddle with Stuart* at 37.

32 *Ibid.* at 38.

33 *With Pen & Saber* at 223-24.

34 Mitchell letters at 367-68.

35 ORs, Vol. XXXIII, p. 141; Clark B. Hall, "A Curious Affair:" The Battle of Morton's Ford, February 6, 1864," http://www.brandystationfoundation.com/cse-columns-pdf/mortons-ford.pdf.

36 *In the Saddle with Stuart* at 39-40.

37 It is hoped the reader will forgive the author's side trip into graphology, a minor but entertaining hobby. Handwritten historical documents often reveal a backstory about a character or an event. A favorite is the famous letter of February 24, 1836 by William B. Travis from the Alamo to "the people of Texas and all Americans in the world." Travis began boldly and with confidence, informing the letter's recipients that despite being besieged by a thousand or more Mexicans he had answered their demand for surrender with a cannon shot, that he would never surrender or retreat, and that he called in the name of Liberty for reinforcements to come to their aid "with all dispatch." Then, perhaps after having been interrupted by the news, he wrote that "the enemy is receiving reinforcements daily and will perhaps increase to three or four thousand in four or five days." Between the writing of "all dispatch" and "the enemy is receiving reinforcements" Travis suffered a complete loss of confidence. The nature of his writing demonstrated that his feelings switched from great confidence almost to despair. A couple of sentences later his handwriting reveals that he rallied, regained his confidence, and promised to die like a soldier.

38 *With Pen & Saber* at 228-29.

James Ewell Brown ("Jeb") Stuart (1833–1864), who commanded the cavalry of the Army of Northern Virginia until his death in battle.

Stuart's personal battle flag, sewn by his wife, Flora in 1862. It accompanied most of his early campaigns but accidentally fell into a fire at Stuart's headquarters and was damaged. Sent home for repair, it was still in Flora's possession when Stuart was mortally wounded. She displayed it at the Virginia Female Institute in Staunton (now Stuart Hall) while she was principal there after the war, and it was donated to Stuart Hall by the family in the 1960s. In 2006 it sold for $956,000. *Photo courtesy of Heritage Auctions, Dallas, Texas, and the Texas Civil War Museum, Fort Worth, Texas*

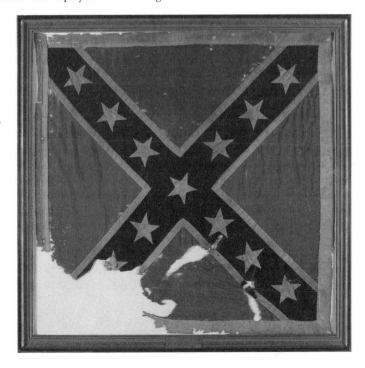

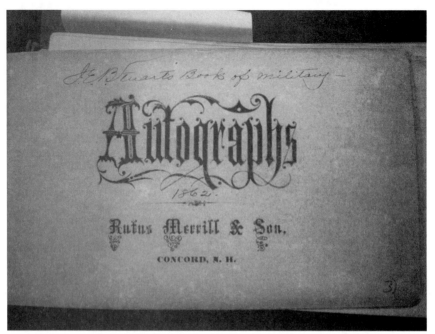

Cover page of Stuart's book of military autographs, in which he collected the signatures of 28 well-known Confederate officers, including Lee, Jackson, Longstreet, Ewell, Hood, and A.P. Hill, as well as seven foreign visitors, an assistant secretary of war, and two of Stuart's staff officers, in 1862–1864.
—*Courtesy of the Virginia Historical Society*

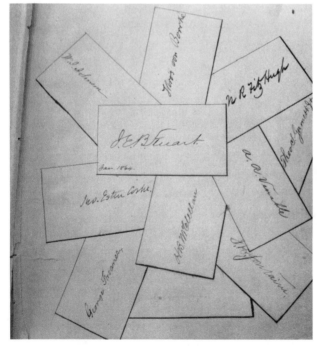

Inside front page of Stuart's "Keepsake Album," in which he collected poems and other writings, containing Jeb's signature and those of nine of his staff officers.—*Courtesy of the Virginia Historical Society*

The Rector House, near Atoka, Virginia, where Stuart was headquartered on June 23, 1863, prior to beginning what would become the Gettysburg campaign.

"The Bower," where Stuart and his cavalry returned following the Gettysburg campaign and camped for two weeks. Previously occupied by Stuart and his staff for what has been described as "25 perfect days" during the Autumn of 1862, Stuart's second period of time there was much less perfect due to the intervening deaths of staff members and exhaustion following the invasion of Pennsylvania.

The Brandy Station battlefield. Here the horsemen of both sides met in June 1863 for the largest cavalry battle in North American history, and then again in October 1863, as the struggle continued after Gettysburg.

The author at Sam Sweeney's grave marker, Graham Cemetery, Orange, Virginia. Sweeney was Stuart's well-known banjo player and band leader. He died at an Orange hospital on January 13, 1864, reportedly of smallpox. Sweeney's grave was either unmarked or, more likely, the marker was lost with the passage of time, but in 2010, local Orange historians determined the location of burial for all Confederate soldiers who died at Orange Court House in 1864, and on June 6, 2010, formally dedicated a Confederate headstone at the cemetery.

The .36 caliber Whitney revolver Stuart carried at Yellow Tavern and fired until empty in the seconds before he was mortally wounded. Often depicted as carrying the LeMat revolver now in the collection of the Museum of the Confederacy, Stuart found the Whitney, which is said to have been designed based on the best qualities of Colt and Remington revolvers, to be lighter and less cumbersome. Its use by Stuart at Yellow Tavern was confirmed by the Stuart

family when the revolver was donated to the Virginia Historical Society (Battle Abbey) where it is now on display.—*Courtesy of the Virginia Historical Society*

One of at least four uniforms owned and worn by Stuart during the war, and noteworthy for the "battle jacket" design he preferred that was more compatible with mounted service than an officer's frock coat. This uniform was not the one worn by Stuart at Yellow Tavern (in which he was probably buried) but insect damage on the right side above the waist has occasionally been misidentified as a bullet hole that caused his mortal wound.—*Courtesy of the Virginia Historical Society*

Jeb Stuart's wife, Flora. Nearly the opposite of Stuart in disposition—worrisome and pessimistic—Jeb's letters to her are filled with attempts to reassure her and bolster her spirits. Despite his well-known admiration for and flirtations with other women, Stuart remained absolutely loyal to Flora, and his fondest wish at the end was that she would arrive before he died. She did not.

"Stuart Hall," in Staunton, Virginia, formerly Staunton's Virginia Female Institute, an Episcopal school for girls chartered in 1844, and named in 1907 for Stuart's wife, Flora, who served as principal of the Institute from 1880 until 1899.

Right: Frank Smith Robertson, a member of Stuart's staff for the last year of the general's life. Robertson's memoirs of Stuart were not published until fifty years after his death in 1926, and he was buried with his most prized possession—a letter to him from Stuart praising Robertson's bravery under fire.

Left: John Esten Cooke, Old South novelist, cousin by marriage to Stuart, and staff member from March 1862 through Yellow Tavern. A man who rubbed shoulders with and chronicled the lives of some of the Confederacy's greatest leaders, his idolization of Stuart was, for the most part, not reciprocated.

Albert Jenkins: Although technically a member of Stuart's cavalry corps, Jenkins usually operated independently, with great effect, and is a candidate for having the longest beard of the Civil War.

Russell A. Alger: Colonel commanding the 5th Michigan Cavalry at Yellow Tavern and postwar Senator from Michigan, Alger brought Flora Stuart to tears in a visit after the war by informing her that he had instructed one of his troopers to kill her husband.

George Custer, who forged his early reputation in swirling battles against Stuart's equally dashing cavalry. Custer's Wolverines charged repeatedly against Stuart's men at Gettysburg, and it was Custer's division in the lead when Sheridan's juggernaut met Stuart for the final time, at Yellow Tavern.

Heros von Borcke in 1884, on his single return to the United States since his departure to Europe in 1865, and after having gained approximately 150 pounds.

Ulric Dahlgren: The son of Rear Admiral Dahlgren and inventor of the Dahlgren Gun, the young, recently-minted Colonel participated in a raid on Richmond, in which he was killed. Papers were found on his body in which he proposed killing Jefferson Davis, and the Confederate cabinet set off a controversy that has not been settled to this day; the game of hide and seek with his body reads like a macabre Agatha Christie mystery.

William Henry Fitzhugh ("Rooney") Lee, son of Robert E. Lee and younger brother of Curtis. He commanded a division in Stuart's Cavalry Corps in 1864, after being disgracefully abducted by enemy cavalry while recovering from a wound; he was held in Union prisons for nine months.

Henry B. McClellan: Pennsylvania born, first cousin to Maj. Gen. George McClellan, with four brothers who served as Federal officers, McClellan nevertheless threw in his lot with the Confederacy and served on Stuart's staff for the last year of Stuart's life. His book, *I Rode with Jeb Stuart*, is a detailed account of that year as well as the rest of McClellan's wartime experiences.

Williams Wickham: Grandson of a signer of the Declaration of Independence, brother-in-law to Rooney Lee and member of the FFVs (Finest Families of Virginia), Wickham commanded a brigade under Fitz Lee and fought at Yellow Tavern, where Stuart's final order before being mortally wounded was, "Order Wickham to dismount his brigade and attack."

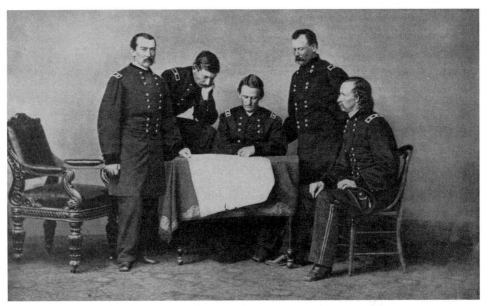

Philip Sheridan with his immediate subordinates: Forsyth, Merritt, Devin and Custer. President Lincoln valued Little Phil's battlefield dynamism, while he also observed: ". . . not enough neck to hang him, and such long arms that if his ankles itch, he can scratch them without stooping."

Judson Kilpatrick, center, in Stevensburg, Va. with staff members and others. Nicknamed "Kill-cavalry," he was Stuart's self-appointed nemesis, and a favorite opponent of the Rebels. Never able to live up to his boasts, his bungling of the Dahlgren Raid on Richmond ended his welcome in the Eastern Theatre of the war and he was transferred to Sherman's army.

Men of the 3rd Pennsylvania Cavalry, who vied with Jeb Stuart's men repeatedly, including at Brandy Station (where this photo was taken in early 1864) and on East Cavalry Field at Gettysburg.

A plumed hat, sabre, gauntlets and pistol that had belonged to Jeb Stuart, now on display at the Museum of the Confederacy in Richmond.

John Mosby (center) and some of his men, most of whom, like
the Grey Ghost himself, had also ridden with Stuart's cavalry.

Wade Hampton commanded a brigade, then a division under Stuart, and after Jeb's death commanded the cavalry corps, receiving the promotion to lieutenant general that was always denied to Stuart.

Thomas L. Rosser, a dashing commander under Stuart and later under Early in the Shenendoah.

Fitzhugh Lee, nephew of Robert E. Lee, and a talented division commander under Jeb Stuart.

A section of the Orange and Alexandria Railroad and telegraph wires destroyed by Stuart's men in October 1863 as Lee's army withdrew from Bristoe Station to the Rappahannock. The wooden ties were piled together and set on fire, whereupon they would heat the rails and allow them to be rendered unusable.

An early photo of Stuart's grave in Hollywood Cemetery, Richmond VA.

Jeb Stuart's statue on
Monument Avenue
in Richmond, VA.

CHAPTER 9

THE DAHLGREN AFFAIR AND THE FEDERAL ARMY COILS

February 22 to April 30, 1864

*Colonel Dahlgren was a gallant and dashing soldier,
a man of polish and education, but of unbounded
ambition, which induced him to undertake the
desperate adventure he was on. He treated me and
the other prisoners with all proper courtesy and
consideration, shared his rations with us, and
conversed quite freely.*

—Henry Blair, formerly 1st Lt., Salem
Artillery, captured by Dahlgren on Feb.
29, 1864, writing about the affair on
August 22, 1874, at Salem, Virginia

AT THE END OF February and the beginning of March there occurred one of the more unusual, and controversial, incidents of the war—the Dahlgren affair.

Lt. Col. Ulric Dahlgren was the son of Rear Admiral John A. Dahlgren, designer of the Dahlgren Gun and the "father of American naval ordnance." Commissioned a captain in 1861 at age 19, Ulric became a member of Maj. Gen. Joe Hooker's staff, and participated in the fighting at Brandy Station on June 9, 1863. During the Gettysburg campaign he was given a small command of ten men and four scouts who disguised themselves in civilian clothing and attempted to get in the rear of Lee's army to gather intelligence. Following the battle, on July 6, 1863, he was wounded in the right leg during a clash at Hagerstown, and on July 12 the leg was amputated below the knee.

On February 23, 1864, wearing a prosthetic leg and using a crutch,

Dahlgren, now a colonel, met with Brig. Gen. Judson Kilpatrick to hear Kilpatrick's proposal for a raid on Richmond. Kilpatrick had secured permission from President Lincoln and Secretary of War Stanton to make the expedition which, in Kilpatrick's opinion, had the potential of freeing the Union prisoners of war at Libby Prison, Castle Thunder, and Belle Isle, destroying Confederate rail lines and canals, and wreaking general havoc in the capital city of the Confederacy, which Kilpatrick believed was weakly defended by Home Guard troops. Dahlgren was intrigued, and wrote his father that the raid would be "the grandest thing on record." Kilpatrick bet his commanding officer, Maj. Gen. Alfred Pleasonton, five thousand dollars that he would be able to enter Richmond.

The raid was comprised of three elements—the main raiding body comprised of Dahlgren's and Kilpatrick's cavalry, which planned to penetrate the City's defenses; a feint by the Army of the Potomac intended to distract Lee's attention, and another raid, under Custer with 1,500 horsemen, further west in the vicinity of Charlottesville.

The expedition set out from Stevensburg, near Culpeper Court House, the night of February 28, 1864, at 7 p.m. Dahlgren commanded a little more than 400 men, comprised of troopers from the First Maine, First Vermont, Second New York, Fifth New York, and Fifth Michigan cavalry regiments. Kilpatrick followed with another 3,500 men, but the two columns did not travel together, and while Kilpatrick intended to attack the Rebel capital, the real work and accomplishment of the raid was to be carried out by Dahlgren.

Dahlgren proceeded to Ely's Ford on the Rapidan, where his men captured a commissioned officer and thirteen men who were guarding the ford. From that point on they were inside Confederate lines, and they took the road to Chancellorsville and Spotsylvania Courthouse, with their first target being Fredericks Hall Station on the Virginia Central Railroad, where a Confederate artillery park contained 68 guns guarded only by lightly armed artillerymen.

About two miles from the station Dahlgren came upon a "contraband" who informed him that additional troops had been sent to protect the station, and he decided not to risk a fight that might prevent him from getting into Richmond.

The next day, February 29, Kilpatrick and his troops reached Beaver Dam Station, where they tore up rails and destroyed Confederate supplies.

However, they failed to stop a train that came through on its way to Richmond which then spread the word that Federal cavalry were on the move inside Confederate lines. The Home Guard turned out and on March 1st a citizen got word to Brig. Gen. Pierce Young, commanding Butler's brigade of Hampton's division, that Federals were heading for Richmond. Gordon then telegraphed Generals Hampton and Stuart, and ordered the 320 men who comprised the brigade to be ready to pursue.

The same day, in order to steer around Fredericks Hall Station, Dahlgren enlisted the aid of another black man, named Martin Robinson, who was described by a Southerner who knew him as "a burly, black negro man," belonging to a Mr. David Meems, of Goochland. Martin said he could take them on a road about two miles south of the station and then to the railroad tracks. They followed him there, cut the telegraph lines, tore up the tracks, and rode into Goochland County. It began to rain but they plodded on.

Along the way the raiders captured a wagon and seven men who were gathering wood, and then came to a log cabin with several horses tied outside that appeared to belong to soldiers. Inside a court martial was in progress and Dahlgren took everyone prisoner, including Colonel Hilary P. Jones, Captain David Watson, a Captain Dement of Maryland, Lt. Henry E. Blair, four other Confederate officers including two majors, and a handful of privates. The prisoners were put on horses and taken along but that night everyone except Captain Dement and Lt. Blair escaped.[1] About 2 a.m. on March 1 they halted at a country store, fed their horses, cooked some rations, and caught a few hours' sleep.

The next morning they stopped at a house belonging to Arthur Morson and relieved the household of some wine and silver wine goblets, then proceeded to Dover Mill, which they burned.

The farm of Confederate Secretary of War John Seddon was located nearby, and Dahlgren was then in a position to do damage to some notable Confederates, had he contented himself to terminate the raid at that point. Seddon's home was named Sabot Hill. Half a mile distant was Eastwood, the home of Plumer Hobson, whose wife was the daughter of the former Governor of Virginia, Henry A. Wise, who was then a brigadier general. Unbeknownst to Dahlgren, General Wise had arrived at Eastwood just the night before, being on furlough from Charleston. Federals remembered Wise as the governor responsible for the hanging of John Brown, or at least the governor who didn't pardon him, and his capture—in his daughter's house deep within Confederate lines—would have been enough of an accomplishment to make the raid a resounding success.

Dahlgren was then within 20 miles of Richmond, and he planned to assault the city that night at about 8 p.m. According to his signal officer, Lt. R. Bartley, the plan was to ride to the outskirts of Richmond and wait for Kilpatrick to attack the city in the vicinity of the Brooke turnpike, at which point Dahlgren's party would split and launch the most critical part of the raid. One portion of the command was to go to the Appomattox Bridge, where the Richmond & Danville Railroad crossed, destroy it, enter Richmond, secure the bridge to Belle Isle, and release the prisoners held there. The other column was to enter Richmond and release the prisoners at Libby Prison and Castle Thunder, after which the two columns and their prisoners would unite and return to Federal lines.[2]

First, however, Dahlgren went to Sabot Hill and pounded on the door. He was answered by Mrs. Seddon. Although surprised to find a Yankee officer on her threshold, she maintained her composure, and when Dahlgren introduced himself, she asked if he was any relation to Admiral Dahlgren. Upon being told that he was the admiral's son, she responded, "Your father was an old beau of mine in my girlhood days when I was a schoolmate of your mother's in Philadelphia."

That statement was later proclaimed to have "saved Richmond," for Dahlgren not only removed his hat and promised Mrs. Seddon she would not be harmed, but he accepted her invitation to come inside and visit. Mrs. Seddon asked the family butler, "Uncle Charles," to go to the cellar and bring up some blackberry wine, vintage 1844, and the young officer and the Southern lady discussed his family and her recollections. While that was going on, a soldier who had accompanied General Wise from Charleston discovered the Federal camp and informed the General who, along with his son-in-law, dashed to Richmond to spread the alarm. The city's defenses in the direction from which Dahlgren was expected were immediately reinforced.[3]

Once Dahlgren returned to his command and the plans for the evening attack were finalized, they followed Martin to the ford, only to discover in the hardest way possible—by the drowning of at least one of Dahlgren's men—that the river could not be crossed there. Instead, the place to which

Martin had brought them was a ferry site, except that the steam-powered ferry was then on the other side of the river with no plans to cross and assist the Federals.

It is not known whether Martin intentionally deceived the Federals or, more likely, that he simply did not know that the river crossing was not a ford. Another version of the story is that there was a ford near the point to which Martin conducted Dahlgren's column, but that winter rains had swollen the James so that it was then too deep to cross.

It made no difference to Dahlgren, who ordered that the man be hanged and then saw that the execution was carried out.[4] Confederate Lt. Blair, who was present, said that "For some reason they supposed he [Martin] was attempting to play them false and get them entrapped, and they hung him with a leather strap to a tree on the road side until he was dead, cut him down and left him dead in the road."[5] Either Blair was mistaken about the body being cut down or someone hanged it again if a more colorful, postwar account written by a man who was a young boy living nearby at the time is to be believed:

> . . . his body [was] left swinging from a limb over the roadside. The neighbors allowed this coal-black corpse to hang there for a week as an object lesson to impress the slaves of the vicinage with a new idea of Northern feeling toward the blacks. I shall never forget when a seven-year-old boy, and passing along the road one evening at twilight, how the cold chills ran over me when this gruesome spectacle met my horrified vision—the neck of the darky thrice its ordinary length and his immense pedal extremities suspended scarcely three feet above the ground.[6]

Unable to cross the James, Dahlgren decided to move down the side he was on and attack the upper portion of the city. Doing so would actually shorten the distance they needed to travel, but would not place them in a favorable position to reach Belle Isle and free the prisoners.

On they went, and when within about three miles of the city they captured three pickets guarding the road, after which they concealed themselves in the brush and woods nearby. About 4 p.m. they heard cannon fire from the direction of the Brooke Turnpike, which they interpreted to be Kilpatrick attacking, even though it was four hours before the agreed upon time. This seemed incomprehensible, as Dahlgren's force was too small to attempt the raid in the daytime, and the plan had not been for either of them to try to penetrate Richmond's main defenses until after dark. After a while the firing seemed to be moving farther off, which Dahlgren suspected meant that Kilpatrick was being repulsed. However, thinking perhaps Kilpatrick would renew the attack after dark, Dahlgren told his signal officer, Lt. Bartley, and his other staff officer, Captain Gloskoski, to be prepared to fire signal rockets as soon as it was dark, which was a pre-arranged signal intended to bring all the Federal forces together in the event of defeat.

Dahlgren waited until dark, formed his men and attacked. They drove Confederate pickets back to the inner line of earthworks, at which point Rebel reinforcements, including some of Hampton's cavalry, arrived and it became obvious they would not be able to drive through at that point. Leaving about 40 men in place to keep the Rebels occupied, Dahlgren took the rest of his men, turned east, crossed the railroad at Hungary Station, and from there rode to the Brooke Turnpike, picking up various contrabands along the way. There a citizen informed them that Kilpatrick was retreating down the Peninsula, and it became clear that the raid was not going to be a success. Accordingly, he determined to attempt to reach Butler's lines at Gloucester Point by cutting through King William and King and Queen counties.

In fact, Kilpatrick had not retreated down the Peninsula. He had attacked the Richmond defenses earlier than Dahlgren anticipated, but remained engaged, or at least on hand, until dark when, not having heard from Dahlgren, he withdrew and went into camp near Atlee's Station. There he was attacked by Hampton and Gordon's little brigade of just over 300 men, supported by artillery. They drove Kilpatrick away and captured 87 prisoners and 133 horses.[7]

Dahlgren's retreating raiders crossed the Pamunkey River at Hanovertown Ferry and Mattaponi Creek at Dabney's Ferry, where they were fired upon. Things were getting worse. Hampton was in his rear and many of Dahlgren's men had become separated from the command. Although nearly all of those men eventually reached Kilpatrick and safety, Dahlgren only knew that they were lost. By daybreak on March 2, his command consisted of his officers, 75 men, about 50 contrabands, and a small herd of extra horses.

From Dabney's Ferry they headed toward Stevensville, but on a hill between the ferry and Aseamancock Creek they found a company of infantry in the road. Dahlgren ordered a charge and managed to drive them into the woods before he hurried on. About dark they reached the creek, crossed and paused to rest and feed the horses for half an hour. Shortly after they started again they discovered Confederate cavalry on the road ahead.

Dahlgren, Major Cook, and Lt. Bartley rode ahead, verified that the enemy was there in force, and sent an order back for the rest of the column to come up. Bravely, or foolishly, Dahlgren then rode forward alone with his pistol in his hand and called out to the horsemen in the road to surrender. Predictably the Confederate response was that the Federals should surrender, at which point Dahlgren raised his revolver to shoot the officer in command of the Rebels. His weapon misfired—only the cap exploded—and Confederates in hiding behind brush along the road, not more than twenty feet away, fired a volley, killing Dahlgren and Major Cook's horse and sending the rest of the Federals scampering back a hundred yards. It was then about 11:30 p.m. on March 2, 1864.

The remaining Federals held a panicky council of war and decided to abandon their horses and try to escape on foot, which they did and which succeeded for some of them for almost 24 hours. Others surrendered to their Confederate officer prisoners, many were captured nearby, and all of them had been taken prisoner by the following night, some flushed out of hiding by bloodhounds.

That might have been the end of it, and the whole affair might have been chalked up as just another botched raid. Of the three elements of Kilpatrick's raid, only that part commanded by Custer was worthwhile, as he was able to threaten Charlottesville and capture 50 prisoners and 500 badly needed Confederate cavalry horses. The real excitement, however, was just beginning.

The Confederate horsemen who blocked Dahlgren's escape were members of Co. H, 9th Virginia Cavalry, of Rooney Lee's brigade, commanded by a Lt. James Pollard, plus 28 men of Co. E, 5th Virginia, of Lomax's brigade, commanded by Captain E. C. Fox. Both regiments were in Fitz Lee's division. The men concealed in the brush who fired the fatal volley were mostly home guard troops, plus some infantry from the 42nd Virginia Battalion.

It was one of the home guard soldiers, 13-year-old William Littlepage, who found the papers. He was looking for a watch, but searched the dead officer's inner pockets (Dahlgren's watch was in the Colonel's overcoat and was recovered by a Lt. Hart) and came away with a memorandum box and a cigar case.

To say that Littlepage was a member of the home guard is a slight stretch. He was a pupil of a teacher named William W. Halbach, who was exempted from military service due to his health and because he was a teacher with the "requisite" number of students. Halbach nevertheless formed a company out of his students between the ages of 13 and 17, because, as he later said, "I felt it my duty to do what I could to encounter the raids of the enemy."[8]

According to Halbach, his company was accepted by the president, and on this particular occasion, Halbach and Littlepage were at Stevensville when Confederate cavalry "rangers" passed through on their way to intercept Dahlgren. Wanting to be part of the action, the two set out on foot, followed, and reached the point at which the ambush of Dahlgren was being set up about dark. A few hours later the Federals approached and were fired upon, after which Littlepage was the first to reach Dahlgren's body. In addition to retrieving the dead man's papers and cigars, the boy figured out that there was a wooden leg to be had, and tried unsuccessfully to tug it off.

The soldiers of the 5th, 9th, and 42nd Virginia units departed in order to chase down the fleeing Federals or to accompany those already captured into Richmond. Halbach, Littlepage, some local citizens and an unnamed man Halbach described as a lieutenant who claimed to have been a prisoner of the Federals—almost certainly Lt. Henry E. Blair of the court martial—but who nobody knew whether to believe, were left behind.

Not knowing but that other Federal raiding parties were on the road, the party decided to go into some nearby woods to spend the night, and as they were spreading their blankets, Littlepage approached Halbach and said "Mr. Halbach, will you have a segar?" Questioned about where he'd obtained cigars, Littlepage described his search of the dead man, including his attempt to pull off the wooden leg. This caused Lt. Hart to tell them the identity of the dead officer, and to warn Littlepage that if more Yankees came along and caught him with anything belonging to Dahlgren that they would almost certainly "hang us all from the nearest tree." Accordingly, Halbach took the papers from Littlepage but allowed him to keep the cigar case.

The next morning when it was light, Halbach read the papers and was stunned by what they contained.

There were four documents—a draft of an address Dahlgren intended to make to his troops, a set of "Special Orders and Instructions," a small memorandum book, and a letter addressed to Dahlgren. The contents of these four items were subsequently printed in the Richmond newspapers and were actually photographed—possibly one of the first instances of photocopying—in order that they could be delivered to General Meade to prove the depth of Dahlgren and all of Yankeedom's depravity. The papers were, in a word, sensational.

After 150 years and all that the world has witnessed in the way of military cruelty and depravity, the Dahlgren papers seem rather mild today. That was not the case in 1864. Assuming the papers were valid—and there have been plenty of claims that they were not—the smoking gun statements boil down to one paragraph each from the address and from the special orders.

The address is a page in length and might have taken two minutes to read aloud. The survivors of Dahlgren's command all agreed that he never delivered it to them, and one can imagine that if Dahlgren wrote it, he did so before the raid began, back when he was anticipating that it would be "the grandest thing on record." It contained a requisite amount of bravado: "You have been selected from brigades and regiments as a picked command to attempt a desperate undertaking, an undertaking which, if successful, will write your names on the hearts of your countrymen in letters that can never be erased, and which will cause the prayers of our fellow-soldiers now confined in loathsome prisons to follow you and yours wherever you may go," and then got down to the Plaintiff's Exhibit Number One:

> We hope to release the prisoners from Belle Island first, and having seen them fairly started, we will cross the James River into Richmond, destroying the bridges after us and exhorting the released prisoners to destroy and burn the hateful city; and do not allow the rebel leader Davis and his traitorous crew to escape.[9]

The special orders were aimed at guides, pioneers, the signal officer, quartermaster, commissary, scouts, pickets and men in Rebel uniform (which, if there were any, were not seen by the Confederates), and detailed the Colonel's plans to burn mills, destroy canals, and particularly for the two columns to move in concert and for one not to get ahead of the other before segueing into Plaintiff's Exhibit Number 2:

> The bridges once secured, and the prisoners loose and over the river, the bridges will be secured and the city destroyed. The men must keep together and well in hand, and once in the city it must be destroyed and Jeff. Davis and cabinet killed. Pioneers will go along with combustible material. The officer must use his discretion about the time of assisting us. Horses and cattle which we do not need immediately must be shot rather than left. Everything on the canal and elsewhere of service to the rebels must be destroyed.[10]

The memorandum book contained the "Programme of the Route and Work," written in lead pencil and detailing Dahlgren's planned route of march and proposed accomplishments.[11]

The letter read as follows:

> Colonel DAHLGREN, etc.:
> Dear Colonel: At the last moment I have found the man you want; well acquainted with the James River from Richmond up. I send him to you mounted on my own private horse. You will have to furnish him a horse. Question him five minutes, and you will find him the very man you want.
>
> Respectfully and truly, yours,
> John C. Babcock.

On the margin of the letter was written "He crossed at Rapidan last night, and has late information."

Southern indignity sizzled, and the story circulated nationwide as proof that Yankees were scoundrels. Federals did a good deal of denying and distancing themselves, as well as accusing the Confederates of having forged the documents. General Lee's letter to General Meade closed with the polite demand "I beg leave respectfully to inquire whether the designs and instructions of Colonel Dahlgren, as set forth in these papers, particularly those contained in the above extracts, were authorized by the United States Government or by his superior officers, and also whether they have the sanction and approval of those authorities."[12] One can only guess what the Confederacy would have done if the Federals had confessed to having approved the papers—declare war?

Kilpatrick was called upon to explain the papers, and he responded on April 16 by saying he had carefully interviewed the officers and men who accompanied Dahlgren (many of whom were then in a Confederate prison) and that:

> All testify that he published no address whatever to his command, nor did he give any instructions, much less of the character as set forth in the photographic copies of two papers alleged to have been found upon the person of Colonel Dahlgren and forwarded by General Robert E. Lee, commanding Army of Northern Virginia. Colonel Dahlgren, one hour before we separated at my headquarters, handed me an address that he intended to read to his command. That paper was indorsed in red ink, "Approved," over my official signature. The photographic papers referred to are true copies of the papers approved by me, save so far as they speak of "exhorting the prisoners to destroy and burn the hateful city and kill the traitor Davis and his cabinet," and in this, that they do not contain the indorsement referred to as having been placed by me on Colonel Dahlgren's papers. Colonel Dahlgren received no orders from me to pillage, burn, or kill, nor were any such instructions given me by my superiors.[13]

Perhaps only a lawyer would notice that the sentence around which Kilpatrick placed quotation marks and which he said was not indorsed by him was not the precise sentence contained in the papers allegedly retrieved from Dahlgren's body. The comparison is Kilpatrick's "exhorting the prisoners to destroy and burn the hateful city and kill the traitor Davis and his cabinet," versus Dahlgren's "exhorting the released prisoners to destroy and burn the hateful city; and do not allow the rebel leader Davis and his traitorous crew to escape." The differences are only slight, and perhaps were unintentional on Kilpatrick's part. Yet in order to quote the sentence he had to have had it available, and perhaps by changing it he could cleverly and honestly deny seeing and endorsing it.

Yet it may be the letter from John C. Babcock, who was an agent in the United States Bureau of Military Information, that is the most curious. It purports to say that he supplied "the very man" Dahlgren needed to guide him into Richmond. Yet could the man secured as a guide for Dahlgren by Babcock have truly been Martin Robinson, a black slave known to the people of Goochland County, the property of a Mr. David Meems? If so wouldn't the fact that he showed up one day riding Babcock's horse have been noticed, even though he was somehow supposed to return that horse and get another from Dahlgren? Is it possible that poor Martin Robinson ambled into Dahlgren's gunsights completely by accident, was mistaken for the guide promised by Babcock, was questioned for the recommended five minutes and found to be acquainted with the James River from Richmond up, after which he innocently became a cruelly treated pawn of history?[14]

Dahlgren's body and its parts enjoyed a historic expedition all their own. The first piece of the man to become wayward, the lower right leg amputated on July 12, 1863, was placed in a lead and wooden box and installed in the cornerstone of a new foundry—Building 28—then being constructed by Admiral Dahlgren at the Washington Naval Yard. A metal plaque was installed on the wall above its resting place that read "Within this wall is deposited the leg of Col. Ulric Dahlgren, U.S.V. wounded July 6, 1863 While skirmishing in the Streets of Hagerstown with rebels after the battle of Gettysburgh."

In 1915, Building 28 was partially demolished and replaced by a metal fabrication shop, but the original wall and the plaque remained. That building was then demolished in 1942, but the leg was not found. Nevertheless the plaque was reinstalled at a higher location in the new wall. In 1998 the building was demolished yet again and replaced with what is now the Naval Sea Systems Command ("NavSea") parking garage but the plaque remains at its approximate original location, which would have been the southwest corner of Admiral Dahlgren's foundry.

There are two theories about what became of the leg, the first being that Confederate sympathizers stole it, and more likely, that it was removed and buried with the rest of Dahlgren's body when it was finally interred in the family plot in Philadelphia in November 1865.

The rest of the body, except for the leg, was missing a finger by daylight on March 3. Some accounts saying it was a ring finger and others a pinkie. Considering that men commonly wore rings on the little finger to avoid getting a hand snagged during manual labor (West Point graduation rings were then pinkie rings), it could have been either. The ring, which contained diamonds, was taken by Cornelius Martin of Company H of the 9th Virginia, who cut off but apparently did not retain Dahlgren's finger. In October 1865, F.W.E. Lohmann, a Federal agent who was a grocer in Richmond and who served as one of Elizabeth Van Lew's contacts during the war, tracked Martin down and forced him to reveal the location of the ring, which was in the possession of a Dr. Saunders, who produced it under duress. Lohmann was also able to track down and obtain Dahlgren's pocket watch and overcoat, the latter having been pierced by four bullets on the left side.[15]

Dahlgren's wooden leg was removed and taken to Richmond, where it was put on display in a Richmond shop window, after which it was returned to Lt. James Pollard, who was considered to have been the man responsible for setting up the fatal ambush. Ironically, a few months after the affair, Pollard also lost a leg, and endeavored to use Dahlgren's but it was too short for his needs. Nevertheless, one of Mosby's Rangers, John Ballard, developed a similar need and wound up wearing Dahlgren's leg for the last ten months of the war.[16]

Initially Dahlgren's body was buried, without a coffin, near where it fell by Halbach, Littlepage, and the other home guard types who stayed behind. Then, "in compliance with a promise made to a scout by the name of Hogan," the men agreed to construct a coffin and Halbach fashioned a wooden grave marker with the Colonel's name on it. However, as they were taking the body out of the ground to place in the coffin, a messenger from President Davis arrived to retrieve the body. The nature of the scout's promise was not revealed, but perhaps it was that the men would receive due credit for their appropriate handling of the controversial dead man.

Dahlgren's body was carried to the office of Maj. Gen. Arnold Elzey, who commanded the Department of Richmond. It was either already or was then placed in a common pine coffin and taken to Oakwood Cemetery, a mile west of the city, in a four-mule street wagon escorted by a Confederate officer and two soldiers. Oakwood was where soldiers who died at Chimborazo, Howard's Grove and other Richmond hospitals were buried, so there were various attendants and grave diggers, most of them slaves, at the place. These were ordered to leave in order that the location of Dahlgren's grave would not be known, out of concern that Union sympathizers would retrieve it.[17]

However, one of the black grave diggers hid and watched the burial of Dahlgren, and later told Martin Meredith Lipscomb, the man who was responsible for the burial of all Union prisoners who died in Richmond. Accordingly, when the grocer/agent F.W.E. Lohman came around a month later asking if anyone knew the location of Dahlgren's grave, Meredith introduced him to the black grave digger, who became alarmed, frightened, and protested that he knew nothing about the matter. He was finally persuaded, with the aid of a hundred dollar note, to reveal the location of the grave by walking past and tossing a stone on it.

At 9 p.m. on April 6, 1864, Lohman, his brother, John, and Lipscomb drove to the cemetery in a mule-drawn cart, where they met three black grave diggers, and proceeded to Dahlgren's grave. The mule became excited, supposedly at the smell of the dead, but it was calmed and after about 20 minutes of digging the pine coffin was uncovered. When they removed it from the grave, however, it fell apart. The body "had not decomposed in any perceptible degree," so Lohman wrapped it in a blanket, paid the grave diggers $1500 and departed. Again the mule became difficult to manage "as animals frequently are when drawing a dead body for the first time," and it took longer than expected to haul the body to the home of a Union man named William S. Rowlett, who lived on Chelsea Hill, a half mile northeast of the city.

The body was rather brazenly hauled through Richmond, down Broad Street to Seventeenth Street, up Seventeenth to its northern terminus, and thence up the hill to Mr. Rowlett's, arriving at 2 o'clock on the morning of April 7. Lohman went in search of a metal coffin, which he obtained. Along his way, Lohman notified other Union sympathizers, including several ladies, who flocked to Rowlett's to have a look. That afternoon the metal coffin containing the body was disguised by covering it with young fruit trees, and it was driven to the farm of another Union man, Robert Orricks, who lived in Henrico. About 4 p.m. they buried it beneath an apple tree in a field.[18]

A few months later, Orricks passed through Confederate lines and was able to get word to Admiral Dahlgren of the location of his son's body, and in June 1865, following the fall of Richmond, it was removed from its hidden grave and taken to Washington, D.C., where the admiral identified the body as that of his son but determined that the weather was too hot to transfer it to the family plot in Philadelphia. Accordingly he waited until October 30, at which time a full ceremony with complete military pomp and circumstance was conducted in the nation's capital. The metal coffin was covered with an American flag, on top of which was Dahlgren's commission as colonel from Secretary Stanton. Pall bearers included two generals and six colonels, the funeral was attended by President Andrew Johnson and most of his cabinet, and the presiding minister was Henry Ward Beecher. As part of the eulogy Beecher declared "Dahlgren! As long as our history lasts, Dahlgren shall mean truth, honor, bravery and heroic sacrifice."

The casket then traveled to Philadelphia, where it lay in state in Independence Hall, the first to do so since Lincoln's the previous April, after which it was interred in the Dahlgren family plot in North Hill Cemetery. Absent from the ceremony was Judson Kilpatrick. After the failure of the Dahlgren raid and the succeeding furor, his star descended, at least in the Army of the Potomac, and he was sent to the western theatre, where he served under Sherman.

Stuart's involvement in the Dahlgren affair began on March 1, when word of Custer's raid on Charlottesville reached Camp Wigwam. Most of his cavalry were home on "horse detail" to procure badly needed mounts, or in the Valley. Stuart had only Wickham's small brigade, which had recently relieved that of Lomax, less than 300 men, to lead against Custer's 1,500. There was no hesitation. Stuart ordered Wickham to bring "his whole available force," which turned out to be only the 2nd Virginia and Co. K of the 1st Virginia, and they jangled off to chase the man who would later become known as "Yellow Hair" and "Son of the Morning Star."

At 10 p.m. word came in that Breathed and McGregor's batteries of Horse Artillery had repulsed Custer, and that the enemy column was in retreat toward Standardsville. Stuart counter-marched a short distance and then struck off cross-country with a local guide in an attempt to catch or cut off the Federals. They rode for about four hours and went into camp, and about daybreak a small scouting party from the 2nd Virginia came in to report that they'd encountered a squadron of the enemy who were "showing fight."

The Confederates moved out at a brisk trot and in less than a mile came upon the enemy who did, indeed, show fight. In the following skirmish, Stuart and Captain Charles Gratton, his staff Ordnance Officer, came nearly face to face with about 12 Federals, being separated only by a fence that bordered the lane Stuart and Gratton were riding along. Instead of retreating, Stuart continued cantering along the lane "rather too leisurely," occasionally turning to Gratton and saying, "Shoot that fellow Gratton!, Shoot him!" pointing to a Yankee who was then "plugging away at them both." Instead, Gratton's horse was shot in the hind quarters, which caused it to limp badly as Stuart and Gratton galloped away.[19]

General Lee dispatched nearly all of A.P. Hill's Corps toward the scene of Custer's raid, which was exactly what Kilpatrick had hoped for. It began to snow, and after Stuart conferred with General Lee and they agreed there was nothing more for the cavalry to do, he found an old cabin in which he and his staff spent the night of March 1–2, and they started back to Camp Wigwam the next morning.

Passing a long column of infantry going the other way, Stuart and his men arrived at Camp Wigwam about 1 p.m. and had what Lt. Garnett described as "two meals in one by having an early dinner." Stuart, who loved coffee and drank it at least three times a day, emptied and replenished several times the silver cup he always used, and everyone expected to be able to get some welcome rest. No sooner had they finished eating, however, then a courier brought word that Kilpatrick was raiding against Richmond on the far right of the Confederate line. Stuart and the few staff officers who had fresh mounts to which they could transfer their saddles were soon on the way to Richmond to counter the new threat.

Jeb spent the night of March 2 at Verdiersville, and then rode to Chancellorsville, where he found General Ewell's Corps on the march in the same direction, again fulfilling Kilpatrick's plan. Stuart's staff, once everyone caught up, consisted of Major McClellan, Captain Gratton, Lt. Garnett, Lt. Hagen, and half a dozen of Hagen's couriers, as well as General Lee's son, Robert E. Lee, Jr., then a lieutenant. It was learned that Hampton was on the way to meet Kilpatrick and that Rosser's brigade was on its way from Gordonsville, and Jeb decided to wait for Rosser's arrival in case a sizeable force was needed to further confront Kilpatrick.

There is no record of what Stuart directed Lt. Hagen to do until a couple of days later, and one wonders if the "scout by the name of Hogan" who appeared at the first grave of Dahlgren and asked the men who were there to dig up the body and place it in a coffin, was Hagen.

Stuart took his staff to the home of a family he knew near Catherine's Furnace. Everyone crowded in and the host set out a decanter of apple brandy that most of the officers accepted happily. Garnett, in deference to Stuart's abstinence, didn't partake, and wrote later that he never "forgot the loss of that drink."[20]

Stuart spent only about 15 minutes at the warm house, and then pushed on toward Hanover Junction, which was 40 miles away. They stopped for a few hours at the home of Dr. Flippo, on the Telegraph Road, arriving there about 3 a.m. on March 4, not having eaten or slept for 24 hours, and with some of the staff having ridden for 75 miles. At times the troopers dozed in their saddles, and Stuart did so with Lt. Garnett on one side and Lt. Lee on the other, each holding one of the General's sleeves to keep him from listing to port or starboard.

At Dr. Flippo's they fell asleep on the floor, in chairs, "anywhere," and Stuart, as was his habit concerning staff officers, used Garnett, who was leaning against the dining table, as a pillow. He only did so for half an hour, however, and then shook everyone awake and continued the long ride.

They arrived at Hanover Junction about 7 a.m. Along the way they caught up with a few stragglers from Rosser's brigade, which had gotten ahead of them. They also ran into the distinct odor of a skunk, which persisted for two or three miles, and when they reached the junction they discovered the reason—one of Rosser's staff had been sprayed. The odor was so strong that some of Stuart's staff became nauseous, and the unfortunate target of the skunk was given a week's furlough to recover from his "wound."

At Hanover Junction word reached Stuart that Hampton had attacked Kilpatrick at Atlee's Station and that the Federals were retreating toward the lower Chickahominy. This news was accompanied by a rumor that Colonel Dahlgren had been killed by a scouting party of the 9th Virginia under Lt. James Pollard.

It was decided that the threat was over, and Stuart and his staff accepted the invitation of Lt. Garnett to ride to his home at Cedar Hill where they had breakfast and rested for the remainder of the day. The next morning Stuart and his staff left their horses in the charge of Lt. Hagen and took the train back to Orange Court House, arriving in the evening and Hagan the next day.

Although Stuart was not present at the scene of Dahlgren's killing, it was his cavalry that brought the raiders to bay, and it was to him that all of the campaign reports were directed, including those of Lt. Pollard and Captain Fox. These latter sparked a small controversy as to which of those junior officers most deserved credit for the ambush, and Jeb solicited extra reports from each before determining that Pollard deserved the credit. Pollard's report then ascended the chain of command with glowing endorsements: "Lieutenant Pollard deserves great credit for his gallantry," from Stuart; "heartily concurring in the commendation of General Stuart," from Robert E. Lee; and "a gallant exploit, and one which exhibits what a few resolute men may do to punish the enemy on their marauding raids," from Secretary Seddon.[21]

It was heady stuff for a young lieutenant.

There followed some relaxation and recreation. A.P. Hill's corps organized a "Grand Tournament and Ball," which was held in an open field next to the Orange & Alexandria Railroad near the home of a Major John H. Lee. Cavalrymen were not allowed to participate, only watch, because the contest was for "knights," all of whom were infantry officers.

The contest was to see who could decapitate or spear three Yankees and one wooden ring in the shortest time with a saber while galloping at full speed on horseback. The "Yankees" were stuffed cloth "heads" mounted on poles about 20 yards apart along a 150-yard course. The first head was five feet high, and was to be taken with a "right cut." Next was a ring suspended from a tree that was to be taken at "tierce point" (saber point extended with wrist turned so that the sharp side of the blade points upward). Third was a head only one foot off the ground to be taken with another right cut, and finally was another head five feet from the ground that was supposed to be pierced at "carte point" (saber held out and to the side with sharp side of the blade down).

Some 30 knights turned out in their finest uniforms and on horses beautifully furnished, in order to compete "for that most alluring of all earthly prizes—a woman's smile." A regimental band provided martial music and a large crowd was on hand to watch. After the winners had been announced, a "Queen of Love and Beauty" crowned, and the crowd dispersed, several of Stuart's staff officers stayed behind to compete among themselves. They added the jump of a high fence to the field of competition, which caused more than one of them to receive "some memorable falls."[22]

Hill's corps' grand ball followed a few days later, and was held at a home known as the Marye House located a few miles north of the Court House. It had all the trappings of the various balls that Stuart, Von Borcke and others had sponsored or attended the previous year, but Jeb declined to go, saying he was too busy, and sent Venable, Fontaine, and Garnett of his staff instead. They, in turn had to make excuses for his absence to the ladies, some of whom claimed the only reason they attended was because they expected to see (and probably get kissed by) him.

On the way home after leaving "the banquet hall deserted," the trio heard someone crying out in pain from a deep gully near the road, "Atwell, Oh! Atwell!" Examination revealed it to be a Confederate general whom Garnett identified only as "General H___," but who was almost certainly Maj. Gen. Henry Heth of Hill's corps, who was the only Confederate general with a staff officer named Atwell in the entire army.[23]

Heth's horse, which was nearly unmanageable, had "pranced" off the road and into the ditch, inflicting several bruises which were less injurious than the humiliation of having it happen and then to have his staff ride unwittingly away. Stuart's staff helped pull Heth out and turned him over to members of his staff who had by then returned. The next morning the three officers were late to breakfast and were scolded by Stuart, but their reports about Heth, and particularly about the comments of the ladies who regretted not seeing him, mollified him.

Rumors about Stuart being replaced by John Bell Hood were still extant, and they surely worried Jeb. Why else would Hood be promoted to Lt. General but without a command while Stuart was not? A small bit of satisfaction came when it was learned that Federal Major General John Sedgwick, upon hearing the rumor, exclaimed, "I'm glad of it! Stuart is the best cavalry officer ever foaled in North America."[24]

On March 9, General Lee visited Stuart's camp and had dinner with Jeb, Mrs. Stuart, Brig. Gen. Williams Wickham, a Mrs. Berkely, Lt. Garnett, and Captain John Esten Cooke. Lee wore an old blue cape, and Flora took the opportunity to repeat one of Jeb's favorite stories about Cooke, who had fallen from his horse during the Battle of Gaines Mill when an enemy shell flew overhead and everyone ducked. When Stuart asked anxiously if Cooke was hit, John said, "No General, I only dodged a little too far," which became one of Jeb's favorite barbs to repeat around his cousin-in-law. General Lee, hearing the story, turned to Cooke and said kindly, "That's right—you dodge as many as you can, Captain."[25]

Cooke had just finished reading Victor Hugo's *Les Miserables,* which was published in 1862 and became wildly popular, but which was so well-written, in Cooke's opinion, that it made him feel inferior. He was still working on his book about the life of Stonewall Jackson, as well as various articles and magazine pieces, but he brooded into his journal, "Why should I try to write in the lifetime of my masters? I sit in my tent by the dying fire and consider myself nobody."[26]

On March 16, Jeb waxed poetic again, more or less. He penned a short bit of free verse addressed to "Coyota" in Mt. Holly, Pennsylvania, written on official Confederate Cavalry Corps stationary. It read:

> My sweet little pet
> *Coyota*
> who unites the gentleness of the
> Lamb
> to the courage of her species—
> forming a happy combination of
> excellence
> and
> beauty which
> once seen
> can never be forgotten—
> J.E.B. Stuart
> Major Gen'l

The identity of Coyota and Jeb's purpose in writing her is unknown. One assumes that he intended the name as a female coyote, although a coyota is also a Mexican sugar cookie that originated during the 19th Century.

April 1, 1864 arrived and with it some serious thoughts of the upcoming spring campaign. There was a general expectation that this would be the year when the war was decided. Everyone had had similar thoughts during each of the previous three years, of course, but now the South *needed* it to be decided. There were still those who believed that final, outright victory on the battlefield could be accomplished, but many were looking ahead to the presidential elections and thinking that just a few more Confederate victories, or just stubborn resistance, would turn Lincoln out of office and that the North would sue for peace.

Which was not to say that April Fool's Day was ignored. Rooney Lee had finally returned from being a prisoner and Dr. Fontaine thought it was a good joke to ask the thin John Esten Cooke to give the robust General Lee a pair of his underwear, as Rooney had none. Cooke and some others went to Orange and sent a telegram to Major Henry McClellan, supposedly from his wife, saying she had a headache and had decided not to come visit as she had recently planned. Jeb decided to have another one sent to Dr. Fontaine announcing the birth of a son in his family, but a letter from home arrived for the surgeon reporting the status of his wife's pregnancy—she would give birth to a daughter named Ellen Stuart Fontaine on April 27— and spoiled Jeb's plan.

Von Borcke came for a visit that day as well. Everyone was thrilled to see him, but he was very thin and frequently coughed in a way that was clearly painful. Stuart seized on the visit as an opportunity to renew his campaign to get Von Borcke promoted, this time by writing a letter to General Braxton Bragg, who was by then serving as President Davis's principal military advisor, proposing that Von be made a brigadier and given command of all cavalry in and near Richmond.

Jeb wrote several other letters, in addition to the one about Von Borcke, proposing promotions—for Rooney Lee to be made a Major General and given a new division consisting of Rosser's and Chambliss's brigades; for Captain James Breathed of the Horse Artillery to be made a major, and for Lt. Col. Dearing to be put in command of the Horse Artillery.

On April 5, Stuart wrote a short note to Flora on a "military dispatch" form and playfully filled in the blank for its number as "1,000,000." The message sounds like a lame scheme to bilk her out of her money. He asked her to send him all the five dollar notes she had so that he could change them for fifty cent notes, saying the latter would be much more convenient and "pretty soon of more value." Considering that inflation in the Confederacy was growing ever more rampant, his proposal sounds completely counterintuitive.

The same day he sent a note to General Lee saying that the bearer accompanying it was delivering "a Rock from the lower Rappahannock." Were it not for a reply note from General Lee the next day thanking Jeb for the watermelon and inviting him to come dine, historians might have pondered long and hard the significance of Stuart sending river rocks to the commanding general.

On April 9, having no possible knowledge that the Army of Northern Virginia had only one year left to exist, Stuart wrote another letter to Custis Lee. He had recently, on November 28 at the end of the Mine Run Campaign, ridden with his staff along the Orange Plank Road after dark past the men Hill's and Ewell's Corps who were settling down before fires to camp for the night. When the foot soldiers heard that Stuart was passing by, they rushed to the edge of the road and began cheering him, regiment after regiment, brigade after brigade, down the line like a wave at a modern football game. At one point Jeb stopped, removed his hat and sat motionless on his horse and watched the wild, impromptu ovation in his honor.

Colonel Boteler was present but rather than being behind Stuart he was in a position to see him and his staff riding into the view of the infantrymen. He was impressed, and wrote that Stuart looked "like an equestrian statue, both man and horse being as motionless as marble," and that "it was really a grand spectacle to see these gallant horsemen coming toward us out of the gloom of night into the glare of the fire, making their welkin ring with the wild war cries and the earth to tremble beneath their horses' hooves."[27]

Rather than be humbled by the experience, it reminded Jeb of how unfair it was that he still had not been promoted, which was why he wrote Custis again. "You will, I trust, pardon the egotism, when I allude also to the confidence my immediate command have in my leadership, and to the greeting with cheers by the Infantry Corps (which I have also commanded in battle). . . ." He wanted the promotion so badly that he was willing to go to the equivalent of Confederate Siberia in return for it. "If therefore his Excellency the President . . . believe[s] that my promotion with the view to assignment to the Transmississippi Dept. would be productive of more good to the interests of the Confederacy at large than the continuance in this army, I shall cheerfully accept it. . . ."

The Trans-Mississippi Department was that part of the Confederate States located west of the Mississippi, consisting of Texas, Arkansas, Missouri, the Indian Territory and western Louisiana. It was not merely the western theatre of the war, but the far reaches of Confederate influence which, since the fall of Vicksburg and loss of the Mississippi River, often seemed as distant from Richmond as the moon. It was also the place, as with John B. Magruder and Simon Boliver Buckner, where Confederate hopes for fame and glory went to die. Jeb was not merely demonstrating how anxious he was for promotion—to the extent of leaving his beloved Virginia—he was jockeying for what he believed was a possible opening in the overall command structure. Major Gen. Theophilus H. Holmes had been recently relieved of command of the Trans-Mississippi, and departmental command was typically filled by a lieutenant or full general. Sterling Price was rumored to be a favorite for the position, which would ultimately go to E. Kirby Smith, but Jeb at least threw his plumed hat into the ring.

In reality, as revealed in a "Confidential & Private" postscript to the letter, what Stuart was actually hoping for was that one of the Lt. Generals then commanding Lee's infantry corps, Longstreet, Ewell, or Hill, would be named to command the Trans-Mississippi and that he, Stuart, would replace whichever one it was. Jeb even went so far as to speculate and make recommendations about who should succeed him in command of Lee's cavalry corps. Hampton was "a gallant officer, a nice Gentleman, and has done meritorious service, but there you *must stop.*" He was not the man for the command. He would not fit General Lee, and he should be given command of the Department of the Mississippi "before my promotion," so that he could operate out there with cavalry and horse artillery against gunboats. The best choice to be his successor was either Stephen D. Lee or Fitz Lee.

The letter was quite revealing, not only about Stuart's ambitions and the manner in which he had been calculating the fate of others, but about Robert E. Lee as well. "Your father will never apply for Hampton's removal or transfer because his son [Rooney] and nephew [Fitz] are immediately affected by it." "He [General Lee] told me not long ago that he wished Hampton would go and stay—very emphatically." He added that if Lee would allow Hampton to succeed him, doing so would cause the commanding general's hair to become more whitened, adding that "he once said he owed many of his gray hairs to [Maj. Gen. Lafeyette] McLaws."

Jeb closed the remarkable letter by saying that prompt action was required, that he also wanted Rooney Lee—Custis's brother—to be promoted and given command of a division, and that Custis had best not neglect the contents of his confidential postscript, because it was "very important to the country."[28]

Days at Camp Wigwam were quickly drawing to an end, but that didn't mean they were not still boring. Garnett recalled that the only events worth recording were that members of the staff would receive boxes from home containing "old hams, turkies, vegetables, sweetmeats, and other good things" that were shared. Upon the arrival of one such box, Garnett's mess decided to invite Robert E. Lee to come dine with them and prepared a "royal" dinner for him, but he declined, sending three members of his staff instead. Otherwise, a majority of the members of his mess voted to restrict their grocery bill to $100 per man per month. Because Garnett received only $130 per month and gave $10 of that to his servant, he did not have "a very extensive margin for sundries to go upon."[29]

By April 10, John Esten Cooke was approaching the end of his epic biography of Stonewall Jackson, having just completed his description of Chancellorsville and Jackson's wounding. Two days later he finished it, a total of 1,182 pages, although he expected it to top out at 1,300 or 1,400 once it was converted to uniform-sized paper and text. No sooner had Cooke finished the manuscript than Stuart, on the 13th, informed him that his role on the staff had been converted to "Inspector of Horse Artillery." No promotion was involved and Cooke was obviously crestfallen, but he tried to sound like a good soldier in his diary, saying "Well—so be it. It is rather a hard thing to break the thousand ties for two years growing; but n'importe! . . . All is in the hands of God who doeth all things well. The rest is not important. Still, Esperance!"[30]

On April 24, Jeb wrote to Flora. He had recently been lecturing her again about the need to be more optimistic—"more than one half our ills in this life are imaginary"—and was delighted to hear she was more cheerful and that "the lessons" contained in a former letter were buoying up her "drooping spirits." Of particular interest in the letter was reference to the personal battle flag that she had sewn for him in 1862 and which had fallen from his tent into a campfire the following December and become damaged on one corner. He had sent it to her soon thereafter to be repaired but she had not been able to do so, possibly because she had been unable to secure any gold fringe for its border, which Jeb wanted and about which he wrote "you have no idea what an improvement it will be."[31]

On April 25 Stuart sent a long, scolding letter to Brig. Gen Rosser. He had failed, or refused, to send certain enlisted men from his brigade to Stuart's headquarters, apparently so that Stuart could put them to use as scouts and couriers. Rosser had sent some of the men but not all, writing in regard to one of them that the man was a valuable non-commissioned officer who could not be spared from his company, and remarking that once a soldier was detailed for special service he would never be returned to his company. To make matters worse for Rosser, he had written that because of the friendly relationship between Rosser, McClellan, and Stuart, Rosser expected that there would be no "animadversion" on Stuart's part because of his failure to follow orders. To the contrary, Jeb became quite "animadversive" and dressed Rosser down severely.

He wrote Flora again on April 28. A man named Carson had outraged Jeb by being a bore, spending a day at Dundee, and by telling Nannie Price to include in a letter to Flora that he, Carson, sent his love. This revealed that a certain shoe was now on somebody else's—Jeb's—foot, such that the green-eyed dragon of jealousy was nipping at him instead of Flora. "I want you to write Cousin Nannie that you have no use for a commodity such as Carson's love & please to restore it to him untouched. Carson is either the biggest liar or the biggest rascal in the Confederacy."

He also mentioned that Dabney Ball, Stuart's Chief of Commissary and chaplain, had a daughter he'd named Belle Stuart Ball, and that "our dog Beauty is a great pet & now quite intelligent." The identity of Beauty, like other pets that came and went in Stuart's life and family, is not known. He sent an "automation dancer" (a toy similar to a puppet mounted on a springboard that could be made to dance) for Jimmy. He also reminded her again about the flag, having enclosed a list of battles she should list on the flag, half on each side, and that she should try once more to secure fringe for its border.[32] This letter may not have been the last Jeb ever wrote to Flora, but it is the last to have survived.

The end of the month found John Esten Cooke performing his new duties as inspector of the Horse Artillery. He had also made arrangements to have his manuscript of the Jackson biography copied and forwarded to London for publication. He expected to be paid five hundred pounds for it, which he thought would buy from five to ten thousand dollars' worth of land.[33]

Other old friends came to visit. Governor Zebulon B. Vance of North Carolina came through, meeting with significant Confederate officers, making stump speeches to the troops and spinning yarns when in a social setting. Garnett and other staff officers made the rounds in Orange, visiting and revisiting lady friends, enjoying meals, singing and playing music; but a feeling of sad apprehension hung in the air. He wrote that "every visit to our fair friends was paid in sad anticipation that the hour of final farewell was drawing nigh, and each 'good-bye' was whispered as tho' it was our last."[34]

There was a sense of preparation, of spring cleaning, of last fond visits, and of "girding one's loins" for the upcoming battle. It was most certainly about to come.

NOTES

1 "Statement of Judge Henry E. Blair," *Southern Historical Society Papers*, Vol. 13 (1889), p. 540.

2 "Statement of Lieutenant Bartley, of the United States Signal Corps," *Southern Historical Society Papers,* Vol. 13 (1889), p. 522.

3 In the category of minor coincidences is the fact that the horse General Wise rode to Richmond had belonged to his son, Jennings Wise, who was killed at Roanoke Island in 1862 and who was the subject of a wartime sketch entitled Jennings Wise, Captain of the Blues by Stuart's staff officer, John Esten Cooke.

4 As with much of the story of the Dahlgren affair, there was another version of the story, supplied by Dahlgren's signal officer,. Lt R. Bartley, who recorded that:
This is the most mysterious case I ever heard of. This man (Martin Robinson) came down from Washington city, sent by Stanton, who was a personal friend of the Colonel. He made a bargain with Kilpatrick and Dahlgren to take them to a ford at Dover Mills and take them over, when his services would cease, and in case of any mistake or treachery on his part he was to be hanged, and if it came out all right he was to receive a large sum of money. He took charge on those terms, took us safe through and had plenty of chances to make his escape, but still kept on with us. When asked why he had misled us, he did not, or could not give a satisfactory answer. The Colonel then told him he would have to carry out his part of the contract, to

which the guide assented, and admitted that was the agreement and made no objection to his execution. He went along to the tree without any force and submitted to his fate without a murmur.

J. Wm. Jones "The Kilpatrick-Dahlgren Raid Against Richmond." *Southern Historical Society Papers,* Vol. 13 (1889), pp. 515-560.

5 "Statement of Judge Henry E. Blair," *Southern Historical Society Papers,* Vol. 13 (1889), p. 540.

6. Richard G. Crouch, M. D., "Woman Saved Richmond City: Thrilling Story of Dahlgren's Raid and Mrs. Seddon's Old Blackberry Wine. How Governor Wise Got Time to Give Warning," *News-Leader,* May 16, 1906. Another version of the story was that Martin was hanged with Dahlgren's bridle reins, which fails to explain how the Colonel steered his horse thereafter.

7 *I Rode with Jeb Stuart* at 403.

8 E. Pollard, *The Lost Cause: A New Southern History of the War of the Confederates: Comprising a Full and Authentic Account of the Rise and the Progress of the Late Southern Confederacy—the Campaigns, Battles, Incidents and Adventures of the Most Gigantic Struggle of the World's History, Drawn from Official Sources and Approved by the Most Distinguished Confederate Leaders,* p. 504 (New York: E.B. Treat & Co. 1867).

9 The entire address read as follows:

Headquarters Third Division, Cavalry Corps, 1864:

OFFICERS AND MEN:

You have been selected from brigades and regiments as a picked command to attempt a desperate undertaking an undertaking which, if successful, will write your names on the hearts of your countrymen in letters that can never be erased, and which will cause the prayers of our fellow-soldiers now confined in loathsome prisons to follow you and yours wherever you may go. We hope to release the prisoners from Belle Island first, and having seen them fairly started, we will cross the James River into Richmond, destroying the bridges after us and exhorting the released prisoners to destroy and burn the hateful city; and do not allow the rebel leader Davis and his traitorous crew to escape. The prisoners must render great assistance, as you cannot leave your ranks too far or become too much scattered, you will be lost. Do not allow any personal gain to lead you off, which would only bring you to an ignominious death at the hands of citizens. Keep well together and obey orders strictly and all will be well; but on no account scatter too far, for in union there is strength. With strict obedience to orders and fearlessness in the execution you will be sure to succeed. We will join the main force on the other side of the city, or perhaps meet them inside. Many of you may fall; but if there is any man here not willing to sacrifice his life in such a great and glorious undertaking, or who does not feel capable of meeting the enemy in such a desperate fight as will follow, let him step out, and he may go hence to the arms of his sweetheart and read of the braves who swept through the city of Richmond. We want no man who cannot feel sure of success in such a holy cause. We will have a desperate fight, but stand up to it when it does come, and all

will be well. Ask the blessing of the Almighty, and do not fear the enemy.
    U. DAHLGREN, Colonel, Commanding.
10 The compete orders were as follows:
SPECIAL ORDERS AND INSTRUCTIONS.
The following special orders were written on a similar sheet of
paper and on detached slips, the whole disclosing the diabolical plans
of the leaders of the expedition:

Guides, pioneers (with oakum, turpentine, and torpedoes), signal officer, quartermaster, commissary. Scouts and pickets. Men in rebel uniform. These will remain on the north bank and move down with the force on the south bank, not getting ahead of them, and if the communication can be kept up without giving an alarm it must be done; but everything depends upon a surprise, and no one must be allowed to pass ahead of the column. Information must be gathered in regard to the crossings of the river, so that should we be repulsed on the south side we will know where to recross at the nearest point. All mills must be burned and the canal destroyed, and also everything which can be used by the rebels must be destroyed, including the boats on the river. Should a ferry-boat be seized and can be worked, have it moved down. Keep the force on the south side posted of any important movement of the enemy, and in case of danger some of the scouts must swim the river and bring us information. As we approach the city the party must take great care that they do not get ahead of the other party on the south side, and must conceal themselves and watch our movements. We will try and secure the bridge to the city, a mile below Belle Isle, and release the prisoners at the same time. If we do not succeed they must then dash down, and we will try and carry the bridge from each side. When necessary, the men must be filed through the woods and along the river bank. The bridges once secured, and the prisoners loose and over the river, the bridges will be secured and the city destroyed. The men must keep together and well in hand, and once in the city it must be destroyed and Jeff. Davis and cabinet killed. Pioneers will go along with combustible material. The officer must use his discretion about the time of assisting us. Horses and cattle which we do not need immediately must be shot rather than left. Everything on the canal and elsewhere of service to the rebels must be destroyed. As General Custer may follow me, be careful not to give a false alarm.

Transcriptions of the originals, now lost, contained the following paragraphs, which were not included in the photographic copies forwarded by General Lee to General Meade:

The signal officer must be prepared to communicate at night by rockets, and in other things pertaining to his department.

The quartermasters and commissaries must be on the lookout for their departments, and see that there are no delays on their account.

The engineer officer will follow to survey the road as we pass over it, etc.

The pioneers must be prepared to construct a bridge or destroy one. They must have plenty of oakum and turpentine for burning, which will be rolled in soaked balls and given to the men to burn when we get in the city. Torpedoes will only be used by the pioneers for destroying the main bridges, etc. They must be prepared to destroy railroads. Men will branch off to the right with a few pioneers and destroy the bridges and railroads south of Richmond, and then join us at the city. They must be well prepared with torpedoes, & etc. The line of Falling Creek is probably the best to work along, or as they approach the city Goodes Creek, so that no re-enforcements can come up on any cars. No one must be allowed to pass ahead for fear of communicating news. Rejoin the command with all haste, and if cut off cross the river above Richmond and rejoin us. Men will stop at Bellona Arsenal and totally destroy it, and anything else but hospitals; then follow on and rejoin the command at Richmond with all haste, and if cut off cross the river and rejoin us. As General Custer may follow me, be careful not to give a false alarm.

11 Essentially a "To do" list, the memorandum book contained the following:
Saturday Leave camp at dark (6 p. in.). Cross Elys Ford at 10 p. m.
Twenty miles Cross North Anna at 4 a. m. Sunday. Feed and water one hour.
Three miles Frederick Hall Station 6 a. m. Destroy arts 8 a. m.
Twenty miles Near James River 2 p. m. Sunday. Feed and water one hour and a half.
Thirty miles to Richmond March toward Kilpatrick for one hour, and then as soon as dark cross the river, reaching Richmond early in the morning (Monday).
One squadron remains on north side and one squadron to cut the railroad bridge at Falling Creek, and join at Richmond; 83 miles.
General Kilpatrick Cross at 1 a. m. Sunday; 10 miles.
Pass river 5 a. m. Resistance.
Chilesburg Fourteen miles; 8 a. m.
Resistance at North Anna; 3 miles.
Railroad bridges at South Anna; 26 miles; 2 p. m. Destroy bridges, pass the South Anna, and feed until after dark; then signal each other. After dark move down to Richmond and be in front of the city at daybreak.
Return In Richmond during the day. Feed and water men outside.
Be over the Pamunkey at daybreak. Feed and water and then cross the Rappahannock at night (Tuesday night), when they must be on the lookout.
Spies should be sent on Friday morning early, and be ready to cut.

12 ORs, Vol. XXXIII, p. 178

13 *Ibid.*

14 As Stuart may have written, with affectation, *Nous ne le saurons jamais*—We'll never know.

15 D. Schultz, *The Dahlgren Affair: Terror and Conspiracy in the Civil War*, p. 259 (New York: W.W. Norton & Co., 1999). There always being volunteers for claiming credit for good deeds, Lt. R. Bartley, Dahlgren's signal officer, wrote after the war that he was the one to have tracked down and retrieved the ring, which he gave to Dahlgren's sister.

16 *Ibid.*

17 E. Pollard, *supra,* at 506.

18 "Col. Ulric Dahlgren.; Curious Story Regarding the Disposition of his Remains," *The Richmond Bulletin*, August 13, 1865.

19 *Riding with Stuart* at 42.

20 *Ibid.* at 46.

21 ORs. Vol. XXXIII, p. 209

22 *Riding with Stuart* at 47.

23 *Staff Officers in Gray* at 64.

24 John Esten Cooke's journal entry for March 8, 1864. *With Pen & Saber* at 231.

25 *Ibid.*, entry for March 9, 1864.

26 *Ibid.*, entry for March 13, 1864.

27 Wert at 337 citing Boteler's diary

28 Whitehorse letters, April 9, 1864.

29 *Riding With Stuart* at 48.

30 *With Pen and Saber* at 235.

31 For a color photo of the flag see Monte Akers, *Year of Glory*, photo section following p. 175.

32 Whitehorse letters, April 28, 1864.

33 *With Pen and Saber* at 237.

34 *Riding with Stuart* at 49.

GRANT LAUNCHES TOTAL WAR, FROM THE WILDERNESS TO YELLOW TAVERN

May 1–11, 1864

There is a Future! O, thank God!
Of life this is so small a part!
'Tis dust to dust beneath the sod;
But there, up there, 'tis heart to heart.
—*Lorena*, as sung by Jeb Stuart
  at Laurel Hill, May 8, 1864

ELIEVING THEY WOULD be ordered to break camp any day, Stuart's staff opened the month of May with plans for what they knew would be their last ball near Camp Wigwam, a "May Party." It was to be held May 2, a Monday, at Montpelier, the home of James Madison, only a few miles from Orange Court House.

Stuart said they could use the Headquarters ambulance, but again he declined to attend the party. Staff officers from Hill's corps were invited, as was the brass band of Brig. Gen. Ambrose Wright's brigade, as were, of course, the ladies of Orange and the surrounding area. Montpelier was then owned by a banker from Baltimore named Thomas Carson, and the old mansion was occupied by his brother, Frank Carson, and family.

Garnett and other members of the staff escorted two or three ambulance loads of ladies to the party, the band played, partners were chosen, and they danced from morning until dark, at which time the ladies were returned to their homes and the officers returned to camp.

The next evening, May 3, they received orders to march.

The Army of the Potomac was in motion, heading for the lower fords of the Rapidan in what would become known as the Overland, or Wilderness, Campaign, and Lee's army was mobilizing to meet them. Early on the 4th Stuart sent Garnett to Lee's headquarters with specific information about the enemy's movements and then followed personally, arriving just after Garnett had delivered his message. Stuart dismounted and conferred with the army commander, then mounted again and headed toward the Plank Road in the direction of Verdiersville. They camped that night at Parker's Store.

Except for Rosser's brigade, Stuart's cavalry was still scattered. Chambliss's brigade was still in Orange County with orders to wait until the enemy left its camps near Culpeper and to then destroy whatever supplies they left behind. Fitz Lee, with Lomax and Wickham's brigades, was in the neighborhood of Hamilton's Crossroads, and Hampton, with Young's and Gordon's brigades, was near Guiney Station. Stuart's orders to the different brigades were to come as rapidly as possible and take position on the army's right flank.

Rosser's brigade and some of the Horse Artillery were already on the army's right, on the Catharpin Road, and on the night of the 4th a Union prisoner was brought into the headquarters camp. Numerous questions were put to the man, who was plucky and not intimidated by his captors. One of the questions was, "Where's y'all's pontoon train?"

"We ain't got any," was the reply.

"Well then how do y'all plan to get back across the river?"

"Grant says that if we need to go back across the river, all the men left can go over on a log."[1]

Grant had crossed the Rapidan at Germanna, Ely's, and Culpeper Mine Fords on May 4 with nearly 120,000 men to confront Lee's 65,000. His plan was to travel light and move as rapidly as possible, camping the first night near Wilderness Tavern but getting past the thick underbrush of that area well before Lee could get in position to confront him. However light and rapidly he believed he could travel, his Army of the Potomac was almost 70 miles long, with 4,300 wagons, 835 ambulances, and a herd of cattle in its trail. Meade did not move as rapidly as Grant intended, and lost precious time waiting for the wagon train to catch up. Meade also failed to send out enough cavalry to track Lee's movements, in large part because he believed that Stuart was near Fredericksburg, and he ordered the bulk of his horsemen there. Finally, Grant underestimated how quickly Lee could respond and get in front of him.

From Lee's perspective, fighting in the Wilderness had advantages. The superior Federal artillery would be unable to easily deploy, and the Federals' inability to see the Confederates' movements and the confusion of fighting nearly blind significantly diminished their superiority in numbers. Accordingly he ordered his army to intercept the advancing Federals before they could get out of the Wilderness.

Ewell marched east on the Orange Court House Turnpike to Robertson's Tavern, where he bivouacked, unaware that he was only about four miles from Warren's Union Fifth Corps. Hill moved on a parallel route to his right, along the Orange Plank Road. Longstreet and his corps had returned from Tennessee that winter and camped at Gordonsville, over 20 miles away, but were given immediate orders to join the army once the Federal move was detected. If Ewell and Hill could keep Grant pinned in place for a day, it was hoped that Old Pete could approach from the southwest and fall on Grant's flank.

Stuart and General Lee were near the Brock Road on the morning of May 5 when the armies made contact and skirmishing began. Infantry on both sides moved up and threw out battle lines as well as they could in the nearly impenetrable undergrowth. Along the Plank Road, to its left, was a rare open field, which had once been an orchard, and it was there that Lee, General Pendleton, General Stuart and their staffs gathered. Lee was atop Traveller, studying a map, but several of the others were dismounted, holding their horses' reins, chatting, and essentially ignoring the battle that was growing in intensity nearby.

The field sloped away about 200 yards and disappeared into blackjacks, willow oaks, stunted pine, and thickets, but nobody was paying particular attention until a skirmish line of Federal infantry materialized out of the woods at the lower edge of the field, less than 200 yards away and within easy rifle range. Lee did not notice them and continued talking with the officers who were around him. Others stared in disbelief and began to move in slow motion, as if quick action and panic would cause the enemy to react and fire a volley that could wreak irretrievable damage to the Confederate cause. Dismounted staff officers began to mount, staring at the unexpected visitors. Lee continued to talk, and suddenly the Federals did an about face and disappeared back into the woods.

A Confederate battle line was immediately run up and out toward the point where the enemy had been seen but they were gone.

A courier soon arrived from Rosser. His brigade was engaged with Brig. Gen. James Wilson's Federal cavalry on the extreme right, along the Catharpin Road, and Stuart rode to the scene, arriving just in time to see Rosser driving Wilson in disorder in the direction of Todd's Tavern.

Stuart returned to the Plank Road and consulted with General Lee again. The Third Corps divisions of Henry Heth and Cadmus Wilcox had become hotly engaged, the full weight of Hancock's Union Second Corps, reinforced by other units, bearing down upon them. Lee was just behind the front line, exposed to fire, riding among some stragglers saying, "Go back now. Go back boys. We need you in the front now." Colonels Taylor and Venable of Lee's staff tried to persuade him to remove himself from danger but he insisted on staying until he was certain the line was secure. The infantrymen's chief concern was not the enemy or even that General Lee was exposed, but that they needed water. During the following morning the scene would be repeated more dangerously.

When it grew dark the fighting stopped and Stuart and his staff spent the night of May 5–6, 1864 near Parker's Store. To the extent that Confederate cavalry had been engaged in the previous day's battle, they had fought on foot. On the Federal side, other than the attack by Wilson along the Caparthin Road, Meade had not put his cavalry to use. Early on the morning of the 6th, Jeb seemed determined to handle things differently. It was Friday, six days before the day he would die.

He was up before dawn, and off to where Rosser's brigade was camped. That brigade had originally been commanded by Turner Ashby, then Grumble Jones, and now by one of Jeb's favorites. It had fought hard on the 5th, and it was that day that it was christened "the Laurel Brigade" by General Rosser. The practice of wearing an embroidered five-leaf laurel, often within a heart-shaped cloth badge sewn to a uniform jacket or hat, preceded the naming of the brigade, but its historian recorded that its members traced the origin of the name to May 5, 1864.[2]

Stuart described the brigade as "very much reduced by hard fighting" in a message to General Lee later in the day.[3] In reply, Lee sent a message that "it is very important to save your Cavalry and not wear it out," but also that "you must use your good judgment and make any attack which may offer advantages."[4]

Very much reduced or not, Jeb sent Rosser forward, across the Po River and past the Chancellor House. Major E.V.B. White and his "Comanches" were in the lead, and Rosser directed him to "run over everything you come to" and "push them as far as you can."[5] That White did, driving in the enemy's pickets and accelerating to a gallop, the rest of the brigade following. They were not in the Wilderness, but in a pine forest, the trees of which were far enough apart to allow horsemen to ride full tilt, but still dense enough that they could not see long distances ahead. The Comanches had their blood up, and the ardor of the thundering charge carried them further and faster than caution should have allowed. They ran headlong into Federal infantry and dismounted cavalry, which delivered a punishing volley, emptying saddles and dropping horses.

The Federals started to counterattack but Rosser sent in the 11th Virginia, commanded by Major E.H. McDonald, and drove them back, only to find entrenched Federal infantry that delivered another stunning blow to the charging Rebels. The 11th fell back and Rosser sent forward the 12th Virginia, under Colonel Thomas E. Massie, followed by the 7th Virginia, under Colonel Richard H. Dulaney. It was another wave crashing against another seawall, and both regiments rolled back across a field strewn with Laurel Brigade casualties.

A battery of Horse Artillery under Captain James W. Thomson was on its way, but only one gun arrived. It was commanded by Lt. John W. "Tuck" Carter, who ordered the gunners to pull down a rail fence atop a low hill so that the gun would have an unobstructed field of fire through the pines at the enemy. The cannon roared, lobbing shells over the heads of Confederates still on the field, many of whom—those able to ride or walk—fell back to rally and re-group behind the low hill occupied by the single piece of artillery.

The enemy did not attempt to follow up on its repulse of the three charges, and for a few moments the field was quiet, the Rebels waiting for the next stage of the contest. It came in the form of Federal artillery—five or six guns—positioned on a small rise opposite Carter's lone cannon. Their fire was sudden and tremendous. Confederate soldiers and horses were swept from the hill in dazed and bloody confusion.

In the woods behind Carter's gun the Confederates tried to rally and reorganize. Rosser sent in 150 dismounted men under Major McDonald to meet the anticipated Federal attack. What came were more waves of canister and case shot, punctuated by volleys of rifle fire, much of it focused on Carter and his gunners. Wounded horses kicked and plunged. Men hugged the ground, returned fire, or searched for comrades. The soldiers got behind the crest of the hill, but many of the enemy's artillery shells, aimed at Carter's lone gun, passed over and exploded among them.

The Laurel Brigade had lost its cohesiveness. Major White commanded about thirty men behind and to the right of Carter's gun. Further to the right were about a dozen soldiers of the 11th Virginia, commanded by Lt. Isaac Parsons. Stuart was on the scene, riding back and forth, calling on officers and men to be steady. Rosser remained mounted and beside Carter's gun, and Carter's cannoneers continued to return fire as rapidly as they could. The men behind the crest of the little hill expected to see Federal horsemen come swarming over the top of it and into their decimated ranks at any moment.

None came. Rosser had been severely punished, but so had the Federals. Carter's shells and canister and the sustained, repeated attacks convinced the Federals to stay where they were. The firing gradually died away. The historian of the Laurel Brigade wrote that it was the unit's bloodiest day of the war.[6]

Meanwhile, back at the main battle a great drama had unfolded. On the first day of wholesale fighting, May 5, both Ewell's Corps and A.P. Hill's, though outnumbered two to one, had held their own against Grant's Federal onslaught. Come nightfall Ewell's men had built rude breastworks for themselves, and had further gathered up abandoned weapons so that many of the men had two or three rifles at hand for the renewal of the contest.

In Hill's sector the men, expecting to be relieved by Longstreet, had simply been told to rest, and had neither built works nor truly sorted themselves out. Thus it came as a shock at 4:30 a.m. on the 6th when Hancock's reinforced corps once again crashed in. This time Hill's men could not long resist the murderous tidal wave and began streaming out of the woods, the bluecoats on their heels. For a few minutes only General Lee and his staff stood in their way and it looked as if the entire Confederacy had gone up. But then the head of Longstreet's corps was seen double-quicking up the

Orange Plank Road, two brigades abreast. They cut through the withdrawing Third Corps men and peeled off—Charles Fields' Brigade to the right,
Evander Law's to the left—to present a new brick wall for the Unionists to
surmount. First Corps artillery chief Porter Alexander described the close
call thus: "It was but a little after six o'clock when the terrific craches of
musketry, which bgan to burst out afresh in our front over the general roar
of the morning, told Hancock & Meade & Grant that Longstreet had
arrived."

Hancock's men, disordered by their advance through the woods, now
faced a counterattack by the Rebels' fresh First Corps. An immensely
relieved General Lee himself sought to lead the counteratttack, but some
Texas troops took hold of his horse Traveller's bridle and would not allow
it. Colonel Venable finally went to Longstreet to try to reason with his chief,
and according to Old Pete he replied, "I asked that he would say, with my
compliments, that his line would be recovered in an hour if he would permit
me to handle the troops, but if my services were not needed, I would like
to ride to sompe place of saftey, as it was not quite comfortable where we
were."

Lee promptly resumed his role as overall commander and allowed
Longstreet to control the tactical situation. Longstreet did more than that.
He not only stopped Hancock in front but launched a surprise flank attack
that began to roll up the Union left "like a scroll." From the edge of the
abyss the Confederates were now looking at an even greater victory than
Chancellorsville, with every prospect of seeing the Yankee army fleeing
once again back above the river. Over at Ewell's Corps on the left, John B.
Gordon had been anxious to launch a flank attack all day, and once finally
given permission near dusk he caved it in, capturing two Federal brigadier
generals and nearly 1,000 prisoners.

Porter Alexander could find no spots to place his artillery during the
battle so was asked to visit Jeb Stuart over on the right in case the cavalryman
had espied any openings. The two old friends toured the flank but in the
dense, flat woodgrowth could find none; Alexander wrote later:

> One incident I recall was our skirting an open field, with a pine
> thicket on the far side, say 200 yards off. Gen. Stuart thought that
> federal pickets held the pines, & turning to a courier with him, said,

"Ride out there & see if you can draw any fire." The courier had scarcely shown himself when there were several shots, & he came back with a bullet through his horse's nose. And it seemed as if the horse resented it, for he kept up a constant snorting & blowing blood on Stuart & myself as long as we were together.

Jeb returned to Parker's Store that evening and sent a telegram to Flora. "I am safe and well."

Someone else, even more important than Jeb Stuart, was not well at that moment. History had repeated itself in nearly the same way at nearly the same place on nearly the same day of the year. Lt. Gen. James "Pete" Longstreet had been accidentally shot by his own men one year and four days after the wounding of Stonewall Jackson, approximately four miles from where Jackson had likewise been shot.

Longstreet and his staff were trotting east on the Plank Road shortly before noon on May 6. His First Corps of Lee's army had thrown back Hancock's Union Second Corps and had thence hit it with a four-brigade flank attack that had every indication of success. Brig. Gen. Micah Jenkins, who commanded a brigade in the Corps, was riding beside Longstreet and remarked, "I am happy. I have felt despair of the cause for some months, but am relieved and feel assured that we will put the enemy back across the Rapidan before night." Suddenly a volley rang out from nearby. Longstreet wrote later that he remembered feeling "a severe shock from the Minie ball passing through my throat and right shoulder . . . and my right arm dropped to my side." Jenkins was hit in the brain.

With a bloody froth bubbling from his mouth and throat, Longstreet whispered to Maj. Gen. Charles Field to "assume command and press the enemy." He would survive the wound but be out of action until October, and then would be unable to ride a horse or use his right arm. Jenkins died a few hours after being wounded. The Confederate assault, however, stalled out. E.P. Alexander wrote after the war, of that particular point in the battle, saying, "I have always believed that, but for Longstreet's fall, the panic which was fairly underway in Hancock's Corps would have been extended & have resulted in Grant's being forced to retreat back across the Rapidan."[7]

Although the unit responsible for the mistake has never been positively identified, the prime suspect is the 12th Virginia Infantry of Mahone's

Brigade. As with the North Carolinians who mortally wounded Jackson, they were thought to have mistaken the body of horsemen for the enemy.

One way in which history did not repeat itself with regard to Longstreet's wounding was that Stuart was not selected to command the fallen general's corps. Command evolved instead onto Maj. Gen. Richard Anderson. It did, however, provide Jeb with an opportunity to command infantry in battle one last time and to prove that he was absolutely qualified to do so.

Stuart was up early again on May 7, before dawn and, accompanied by Garnett, a few couriers, and Col. Walter H. Stevens, the army's Chief Engineer, he rode out to scout the enemy's position. After an hour of observation, but without spotting any movements, the party returned to Parker's Store. For all practical purposes, Fitz Lee was in command of the Cavalry Corps that day, and he arrived at Stuart's bivouac in the afternoon to report having engaged the enemy's cavalry near Todd's Tavern and repulsing several attacks.

In the evening, Gordon's Brigade of North Carolina cavalry arrived and was directed to take position on the Catharpin Road, which had been barricaded during the day by a small brigade of Federal cavalry. Gen. Gordon sent out a skirmish line and, accompanied by Lt. Garnett, rode out to determine the enemy's strength.

The skirmishers moved slowly across an open area. Men were seen riding ahead. Shots rang out and were returned before it was determined that they were coming from a returning Confederate scouting party. No one was injured.

Soon the barricade extending on both sides of the road came into view and Garnett, accompanied by Private Charles D. Lownes, courier from the 4th Virginia, rode forward. Two Yankee horsemen rode away from the other side and retreated slowly down the road. Garnett and Lownes rode up to the barricade of rails and limbs and earth and peeked through. Just then, preceding the sound of the guns that fired them, two shells from enemy cannon came hurtling over, only a few feet above the barricade and the heads of a regiment of North Carolinians coming up the road behind Garnett and Lownes.

The regiment dismounted and moved away from the road. Garnett rode back to Stuart to describe what he'd seen, and about sunset Jeb, with a portion of Rosser's brigade, took position on Gordon's left and advanced far enough to find the enemy. Fighting broke out, Rosser's men pressed the Federals with Rebel Yells and the enemy fell back, but it was becoming too dark to continue, and after driving the Federals for nearly a mile contact was broken off.

The two sides remained in close proximity for a while longer, but after delivering an order from Stuart to General Gordon, Garnett was directed to ride among the North Carolinians, and, speaking in a low voice to the officers, tell them to direct their men to fall back quietly, as any conversation in a normal tone was clearly audible to the enemy.

Despite that warning, or more likely because of it, one "old Tar-heel" climbed up on a stump, tucked his thumbs under his arms in an imitation of a chicken, and emitted a loud clear rooster's crow that could be heard for hundreds of yards. Immediately a shot was fired from the direction of the Federals that passed in front of Garnett's horse and struck the stump where Chicken Man was performing. He rolled off and onto the ground amid the cheers and laughter of his comrades.

Their cover, such as it was, blown, the Rebels shouted and cheered at the Federals as they withdrew, and the Yankees responded in kind, alternating between groans, name-calling, and an exchange of epithets that "were neither euphonious nor endearing."[8]

On Sunday, May 8, after spending the night near Shady Grove Church, Stuart and his staff were once again up and mounted before dawn. Evidence had appeared that Grant's army was moving toward Spotsylvania Courthouse, and in response to Stuart's report, Lee had dispatched Longstreet's Corps, now commanded by Richard Anderson, in that direction at 10 p.m. on the night of the 7th. Jeb and his mounted military family jangled past the veterans of the First Corps who were marching steadily toward the sound of guns in the distance.

The noise ahead was coming from Fitz Lee, who was already engaged with the Federal van. Meade had directed Sheridan on the 7th to clear the Brock Road for the infantry to use, but Hampton and Rooney Lee kept them from doing so. When Meade arrived at midnight and found Sheridan's men asleep, he ordered them up and back to clearing the road so that Warren's infantry corps would be able to pass. However, during the night Fitz's men had cut trees and barricaded the road, and when Federal horsemen under Wesley Merritt began trying to force their way through, at 6:10 a.m. on the

8th, they found stubborn, dismounted cavalrymen supported by a battery of Horse Artillery who stopped their advance for five hours. Finally, shortly before Jeb and the lead infantry division arrived, Fitz fell back to a low ridge called Laurel Hill. By coincidence, the place of Jeb Stuart's birth was a farm near Ararat, Virginia named Laurel Hill.

Jeb could not be delayed, and decided that in order to get to the front of the infantry column, which was led by two brigades under the command of Brig. Gen. Joseph B. Kershaw, it would be necessary to take a short cut. With his staff and couriers he struck out cross-country with no roads or paths to follow and only the sound of the fighting to guide them.

Galloping, they entered an open field and found themselves on the right flank of a skirmish line of infantry. Believing them to be friendlies, Stuart and his entourage kept on, but when they came within 300 yards the infantry opened fire, and Stuart veered off to the right into a patch of woods. Nobody was shot, but once inside the woods, Garnett's horse plunged both front feet into a stump hole that was filled with dead leaves. They fell, but Stuart and the rest continued on at a lope. Garnett's left leg was caught beneath the horse and was severely bruised. The animal had trouble getting up and Garnett lay beneath him until he finally struggled out of the hole and the lieutenant was able to remount and hurry after the rest of the staff.

Stuart arrived at the head of Kershaw's infantry and, being the ranking officer on the field, assumed command. As Rebel foot soldiers came swinging up the reverse slope of Laurel Hill he directed them into position, singing *Lorena* as he did so.

He was mounted on General, and a South Carolinian wrote of him later, "He was a fine-looking officer and rode a fine, dark dapple-gray horse. He, the general, wore a black plume in his hat."[9] This soldier's observations, seemingly benign, are significant in determining who killed Jeb Stuart.

Stuart and the infantry arrived almost simultaneously with Warren's Federal Fifth Corps, only about 100 yards north of Laurel Hill. Believing that only cavalry blocked the way, Warren ordered an immediate attack, which dashed against the newly formed wall of Confederate infantry and was thrown back. The Confederates had won the race to Spotsylvania just in time. More assaults followed with the same result, and about noon the Union troops began building earthworks on the northern end of the clearing in front of the Confederate barricades.

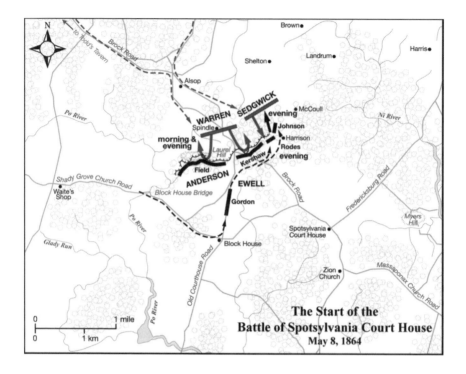

The Start of the
Battle of Spotsylvania Court House
May 8, 1864

In the afternoon, Sedgwick's Sixth Corps arrived at Laurel Hill and extended Warren's line to the east. At approximately 7 p.m., both Federal corps launched a simultaneous attack, but once again they were repulsed. After regrouping, they attempted to move around the Confederate right flank, only to find that Ewell's Second Corps was now arriving, just in time to repulse them again.

Meade had not done much to impress his new commanding general, Grant, that day, and in the finest military tradition he blamed his subordinates—Sedgwick for being too slow, Warren for having lost his nerve, and the cavalry for not accomplishing any of the road clearing they'd been ordered to achieve. While the fighting was getting started at Laurel Hill, Wilson's Union cavalry had reached and occupied the community at Spotsylvania Court House at 8 a.m., on the Brock Road a few miles in the rear of the Confederate position. One of Wilson's brigades under Col. John B. McIntosh rode up the Brock Road, intending to attack the Confederate position from the rear. Considering that Stuart had only a regiment of cavalry available, the threat might have been significant, but by then more of Anderson's infantry were approaching. When the blue horsemen ran into the gray foot soldiers, McIntosh, following orders from Sheridan, withdrew up the Fredericksburg Road.

Other than being the place at which Lee won the footrace against Grant to Spotsylvania, and other than providing Stuart with an opportunity to command infantry in battle, Laurel Hill had another significant effect on the war and particularly on Jeb Stuart.

Meade had not been impressed with Sheridan's handling of the cavalry or its performance, and after learning of Wilson's failure, Meade exploded and rained all over Sheridan, who, in finest short-man fashion, thundered and lightninged right back. Their loud exchange included various expletives that were not deleted, during which Sheridan told Meade that he could finally whip Stuart if given the chance. Meade bustled off and reported the entire encounter to Grant, repeating the coarse language and the latter part of the conversation about whipping Stuart. Grant, more amused than angered, replied, "Well, he generally knows what he is talking about. Let him start right out and do it." Meade, probably secretly hoping that Sheridan would get some serious comeuppance, complied and ordered Sheridan to proceed. On May 9, Sheridan and his entire command—at least 10,000 and possibly 12,000 horsemen—left the Federal army and departed on the ride that would lead to Yellow Tavern.

In the confusing fog that can be Civil War history, in which different generals and battles and military units parade by endlessly, and in which cavalry battles come in a variety of flavors, from Brandy Station to Buckland Mills to Trevilian Station, it is understandable that one might assume Yellow Tavern was just one more of many clashes of horsemen, brought on as part of some larger campaign or as the result of one side raiding the other. It might be thought of as significant only because Stuart was mortally wounded there; but Yellow Tavern was much more.

Yellow Tavern was, as Sheridan wanted it to be, his opportunity to demonstrate that he could whip Jeb Stuart. If a graph was prepared to show the effectiveness of Confederate cavalry in the eastern theatre versus the effectiveness of Federal cavalry in the same theatre, the point at which the lines intersected would not be Brandy Station but Yellow Tavern. The line might flatten out at a new elevation for the Federals at Brandy Station, just as there would be Confederate spikes at Buckland and other places, even after Yellow Tavern, but the Confederate horsemen were never the dominant mounted force in the East after May 11, 1864, as they had been before that date.

The reason was not simply the loss of Stuart. Wade Hampton, as well as Fitz Lee, would command superbly for the remainder of the war; but Confederate resources, particularly horses and men, were nearly exhausted by the winter of 1863–64, whereas Federal resources, including horses, had finally reached their maximum propensity to produce. And then there was the Spencer carbine, a repeating rifle that became standard issue to the Federal cavalry, far outclassing the Confederate muzzle-loaders.

There was also the issue of leadership. Grant and Sheridan were just what the doctor, and president, ordered, for the Army of the Potomac. Hot-tempered, banty-legged, Phil Sheridan, at 5' 5", did not inspire much in the way of romanticism or idolization, and critics have pointed out that anyone given command of 12,000 well-mounted troopers with repeating rifles had a pretty good chance of winning some victories against half-starved horses and scarecrows with single-shot carbines, but the fact is that Sheridan did what it took to win the war. Like Grant and Sherman, he was the kind of no-nonsense, no-bluff bulldog who would put the North's vast resources to work like no Pleasonton or Stoneman had been able to do.

The orders Meade delivered to Sheridan, however reluctantly, were to consolidate his command, take three days' rations and forage, and head for Haxall's Landing on the James River, which was a Federal supply depot about 50 miles southeast of Spotsylvania and some 15 miles southeast of Richmond, from which Maj. Gen. Ben Butler's Army of the James was supplied. Because Sheridan's route would take him directly toward Richmond, it was inevitable that the Confederates would interpret the move as a raid on their capital and that Jeb Stuart would seek to interpose between the city and Sheridan with a sizeable force of his own cavalry.

This, of course, was Sheridan's plan and purpose. He later wrote, "'I sent for Gregg, Merritt, and Wilson and communicated the order to them, saying at the same time, 'We are going out to fight Stuart's cavalry in consequence of a suggestion from me; we will give him a fair, square fight; we are strong, and I know we can beat him, and in view of my recent representations to General Meade I shall expect nothing but success.'"[10]

Sheridan made no attempt to be subtle or secretive. His column of horsemen, artillery, wagons, ambulances, and pack mules, which began at Todd's Tavern, stretched 12 miles east along the plank road toward Fredericksburg and then southwest on the Telegraph Road toward the North Anna River and then southeast toward Richmond.

A "fair, square fight". . . Sheridan versus Stuart for the title . . . winner take all . . . .

While Sheridan was arguing with Meade and then preparing for the title match, Stuart and his military family enjoyed their last evening together.

On Sunday, May 8, after a full day of battle, Jeb, Lt. Theodore Garnett, Major Andrew Venable, Major Henry McClellan, Major Norman Fitzhugh, and other members of the staff spent the evening and night at "the Old Block House," a feature near the Po River and Laurel Hill, for which streets in Spotsylvania are named today. It was not a lively affair, and would have been less so if those in attendance could have known what lay immediately ahead. As Lt. Garnett described, they drank their coffee, smoked their pipes, and turned in "without much of the light laughter & cheerful chit-chat which usually enlivened our campfires."[11]

As usual, Jeb and his crew were in the saddle before the sun was up on May 9. They rode from the Block House to Spotsylvania Court House, where Fitz Lee was supposed to report, unaware of Sheridan's movements or plans. Several dozen wounded cavalrymen were lying on the lawn of the courthouse, and Garnett walked among them looking for friends and finding at least two—Private A.J. Shepherd and Private Alexander Hunter, the latter being a member of the original "Black Horse Cavalry," Company H, 4th Virginia. Both would survive their wounds.

After a few moments of waiting, couriers from Fitz Lee arrived to report that a skirmish had begun in Lee's front and that it had the earmarks of getting larger. Stuart and his staff immediately headed to Lee's assistance, but before arriving they met his men falling back in a "slow & leisurely retreat." The enemy's force was too strong to resist, but mercifully it was not pressing hard. Even their artillery fire was unthreatening, with all of the shells flying overhead and many bursting as much as a mile in the rear.

Stuart sent Garnett to find the extreme right of the Confederate line of infantry, supposing it to be not very far from the site of Fitz Lee's ongoing skirmish. The young staff officer rode over a mile in a straight line and found no Confederate infantry, pickets or videttes who might tell him where to look. Finally, after half an hour he came to a "thin line of men, who were 'digging dirt' very leisurely," belonging to Brig. Gen. Harry Hays' Brigade of Louisianans of Early's Division of Ewell's Corps. They admitted to being the right wing. Garnett rode back to Stuart and reported what he'd seen, which caused Stuart to gallop off in haste to find General Lee in order to strengthen the line. This was done, after which Stuart's staff officers agreed that Grant may have just lost out on one of the best chances he ever had to shatter Lee's army. As it turned out, the line that was reinforced that morning would be the target of Grant's army and the focal point for much of the battle of Spotsylvania during the next week.

The rest of the day was passed watching and anticipating. Lee had successfully outmaneuvered Grant, which was impressive in the short run but just another development in the long run. Grant would continue pounding, and when not pounding, would eye Lee's army as a hammer eyes a nail, then move in a manner that would keep Lee busy and on the defensive. Spotsylvania was Chapter Two in a book that could be titled "Year of Near Endings."

The next morning, May 10, Stuart kept his staff officers busy reconnoitering the enemy's position, while he and General Lee spent a couple of hours at a church near Spotsylvania Court House. From the upper windows of the church it was possible to see snatches of enemy movement, particularly wagons and artillery, which tended to kick up dust.

Shortly after noon a courier came in with news—Confederate pickets on the Telegraph Road had been driven in by an extremely large force of the enemy's cavalry riding in the direction of Richmond. Everyone immediately assumed that Sheridan was raiding the capital. Stuart gave orders, but he did not have an abundance of men to whom to give them. Most of Hampton's division was west and north, along the Po River, too far away to arrive in time to help. In addition, General Lee wanted to have cavalry left behind to reconnoiter, screen movements, and watch the flanks of the army. That left Lunsford Lomax's and Williams Wickham's brigades of Fitz Lee's division, and James B. Gordon's brigade of North Carolinians, between 3,000 and 4,500 men, about a third the number of Sheridan's force. Stuart was not daunted. He had beaten longer odds on more than a few occasions.

Jeb directed the troopers to make ready, and told Major Fitzhugh to stay behind and take care of "the wants of our people." By 1 p.m. the brigades of Wickham and Lomax were in pursuit, and by 3 p.m. Stuart followed, although Gordon's brigade had still not arrived to join in the trek after Sheridan.

Those who saw Jeb before he left, most of whom would never see him again, recalled that he seemed just as upbeat as ever. E. Porter Alexander sat with him under an apple tree and had a "last interview" as Stuart was preparing to ride away, and recalled that he "was in his usual high spirits & cheerful mood." Alexander and Stuart had served together before the war, and prior to Jeb's marriage both had been "desperate admirers" of Mary Custis Lee, the oldest daughter of Robert E. Lee. A month or so earlier, Alexander had been waiting to have his picture taken at a Richmond photography gallery when Stuart walked in with a lady, wearing a veil, on his arm. Not having seen Jeb since Gettysburg, Porter jumped up and rushed to embrace him but Stuart drew back and ushered the lady forward a step, saying "An old friend of yours." She held out her hand and Alexander touched his hat, saying, "I beg pardon. I have not the pleasure." The he realized that it was Mary Custis Lee, whom Alexander had not seen since 1858. Stuart thought the incident was hilarious, and the old friends laughed about it one last time beneath the apple tree.[12]

Now mounting and beginning to ride, Stuart broke into *Miss Lucy Long*, the song for which the horse Jeb had given General Lee was named.

And now that we are married,
I expect to have some fun,
And if Lucy doesn't mind me,
This fellow will cut and run.

Oh, take your time Miss Lucy.
Take your time Miss Lucy Long.
Take your time, Missy Lucy,
and pour your coffee out.

The songs did not stop there. Garnett recalled that during the first three or four miles of their ride that "the cheerful smile, the hearty laugh, the merry hum of his voice as he ran over and over some favorite song" continued. One that he sang was *Her Bright Smile Haunts Me Still:*

It's been a year since last we met
We may never meet again
I have struggled to forget
But the struggle was in vain.
For her voice lives on the breeze
Her spirit comes at will,
In the midnight on the seas
Her bright smile haunts me still.
In the midnight on the seas
Her bright smile haunts me still.

And another was *Ever of Thee I'm Fondly Dreaming:*

Ever of thee I'm fondly dreaming,
Thy gentle voice my spirit can cheer;
Thou wert the star that, mildly beaming,
Shone o'er my path when all was dark and drear.
Still in my heart thy form I cherish,
Every kind thought like a bird flies to thee.
Ah! never, till life or memory perish,
Can I forget how dear thou art to me;
Morn, noon and night, where'er I may be.
Fondly I'm dreaming ever of thee.

If the melancholy nature of such songs belied feelings of foreboding it did not show at first. If he was, as he'd sometimes hinted earlier, having a presentiment of his own demise, he masked it well at the beginning of the ride to intercept Sheridan. When asked, however, he hinted that he might be harboring grave thoughts. His bugler, Private George W. Freed of the 1st Virginia, was riding directly behind him, and called out "General, I believe you are happy in a fight." A laughing agreement would have been a normal response, but Jeb turned rather suddenly and remarked, "You're mistaken, Freed. I don't love bullets any better than you do. It is my duty to go where they are sometimes, but I don't expect to survive this war."[13]

It was not the first time he'd said such a thing, nor would it be the last.

After the first four miles they stopped at a country store and Stuart talked to the owner and three ladies who were on the porch. Then they continued for another 16 miles. He seemed to have gotten contemplative. Garnett was riding "boot to boot with him all the way" and Stuart did not utter a word. At the end of the ride was Mitchell's Store, near the community of Chilesburg, and here they caught up with the rear of Fitz Lee's column.

It was dusk, and several squads of dismounted horsemen were walking back to collect their horses as Stuart and his staff rode up. One man stepped in front of Stuart's horse and was nearly run over, but he jumped out of the way and in doing so looked up and recognized the rider. "Hurrah boys," he shouted, "here's old Jeb!" Immediately a loud, shrill Rebel Yell was taken up, but Stuart patted the air with his gauntleted hand and said, "Don't holler, boys, until you get out of the woods."[14]

Further on, Jeb found Fitz Lee near his skirmish line, leaning on the gate of an empty farm house. Fitz's men, particularly Wickham's brigade, had caught up with and had been skirmishing with Sheridan's rear guard. They had had the shortest distance to travel to catch up with the Federals, and they had done their best to harass and slow them down, although it was growing too dark to continue doing so.

Fitz and Stuart conferred and Jeb called Lt. Garnett over and told him to ride back along the Telegraph Road until he found Gordon's brigade, which was the last in line, and tell Gordon to come on to Mitchell's Store.

Gordon's men had ridden further than anyone that day, more than 40 miles, having been at Locust Grove on the westernmost edge of the Wilderness when summoned to join in the chase after Sheridan, and they had not reached Spotsylvania by the time Stuart rode out at 3 p.m. Garnett rode nearly six miles before he found them, near a place called Mud Tavern, and by then they were going into camp. Forage and corn were being supplied to the horses by the quartermaster, who had found a farmer in the region able to supply it. Garnett knew the orders he brought would not be welcome.

Garnett dismounted and walked to a house where he could see an officer on the porch. He called out, asking the whereabouts of General Gordon, and Gordon proved to be the man he was calling to. Garnett walked to him and delivered the orders.

"By God, my men shall not move one foot till they feed up," Gordon exclaimed, and then gave Garnett an account of the day's long ride, during which he had not allowed even one stop for food or water. Garnett was not feeling particularly frisky either, so when General Gordon softened his tone and invited the young staff officer to come rest on the porch for a few moments, he accepted readily. In moments they were both asleep, and by the time Gordon shook Garnett awake, the brigade was mounted and ready to move.

On the way back to Mitchell's Store, Garnett rode ahead to alert the picket at the edge of Fitz Lee's camp that Gordon's brigade was coming in. As he was talking to the soldier in the road, a shot was fired at them, then another and another, a total of five or six. Garnett and the picket called out that they were friends and to stop shooting, but more bullets came their way. General Gordon rode up just then, having seen what was happening and being extremely angry about it. He sent men to the camp of a company of the 4th Virginia, which was on picket duty and was the assumed source of the shots. In the camp, however, almost all the men were still asleep and nobody was missing. The shooting stopped, but Garnett and the rest never figured out who had fired at them.

At Mitchell's Store while Gordon was approaching, Generals Fitz Lee, Lomax, and Wickham reported to Stuart and the four officers discussed options. By then the size of Sheridan's force was well-known, and either Lee or Wickham opined that Stuart didn't have enough men available to stop the Yankees. Jeb's response was immediate and almost angry. "No sir! I'd rather die than let him go on."[15]

At the end of the conference, Stuart directed Lee to have his weary men remount soon and expect to ride all night.

Sheridan had, earlier that day, traveled 22 miles from Todd's Tavern and reached Jerrell's Mill on the Ta River. It was there that Wickham's brigade came within pistol range of Sheridan's rear guard, which was the brigade under Brig. Gen. Henry E. Davies of Gregg's division. Wickham attacked, and Davies' men were able to repulse them, but not easily, not without some brushes with chaos, and not permanently.

The Federals destroyed Jerrell's Mill, including grain and flour stored there, then moved on. Wickham's men continued to hit and run, picking off as many Federals as they could, then falling back. Five miles past Jerrell's

Mill, as Davies neared Mitchell's Store, the Federal brigadier decided to set a trap. He directed the rear guard, upon approaching a bend in the tree-lined lane, to pretend to retreat in panic. Around the bend, the 1st New Jersey and 1st Pennsylvania regiments dismounted and hid behind brush and trees on both sides of the road.

It worked like the proverbial charm. Wickham's men saw what they thought was the beginning of a rout, gave s Rebel Yell and flew after their enemy. Rounding the bend a sheet of flame and lead mowed down dozens. After the survivors pulled back, Wickham continued to dog the enemy but he kept his distance and waited for the rest of Stuart's men to catch up.

Sheridan went into bivouac for the night on the north side of the North Anna River, whereas Stuart reached about five miles north of there at nightfall. The all-night ride Stuart had alerted Fitz Lee to expect would not be needed just to catch up with Sheridan. Stuart anticipated that Sheridan was headed for Beaver Dam Station, which was south of the North Anna, on the Virginia Central Railroad and not far from Richmond, and from there he expected the Federals would move east to threaten the Fredericks-burg and Potomac Railroad. Accordingly, he decided to send Fitz, with Lomax's and Wickham's brigades, to continue on Sheridan's trail while he and Gordon's brigade rode to Beaver Dam Station by a roundabout route.

He had another reason for wanting to put plenty of Confederate horse between that place and Sheridan. Flora and their two children were staying at the Fontaine home, just a mile from Beaver Dam Station.

But whereas most of Sheridan's long column was going into camp, Wesley Merritt decided to take no chances and dispatched George Custer and his brigade to go ahead to Beaver Dam Station. The Federals knew there would be supplies and railroad rolling stock there, and Custer's orders were to put everything to the torch and tear up the tracks.

Custer accomplished this with ease. The station and its sheds full of supplies were lightly guarded by Rebels who were driven off easily. The Federals took everything they could use, then set fire to everything else. Blue-coated raiders were finally getting to enjoy the sort of fiesta that gray-backs had reveled in at Manassas Junction, Tunstall Station, and Burke's Station during the preceding year.

About one million rations of bacon, half a million of bread, plus flour, sugar, molasses, liquor, medical supplies, tents, and small arms went up in flame. Two locomotives and three long trains of cars were destroyed, and Custer's men ripped up rails of the Virginia Central for five miles on each side of the Station. In one of the trains, Custer's men discovered nearly 400 Federal prisoners, including two colonels, a major and various other officers, enroute to Confederate prisons, and released them with great satisfaction.

Flora and the Fontaines watched the fire from the Fontaine Home in Beaver Dam, for which the station was named, only a mile away, and wondered how much time remained before mounted, blue-coated soldiers would arrive.

It did not happen. Stuart and Fitz Lee left Mitchell's Store about 1 a.m. on the 10th, and Jeb led Gordon's sleep-deprived, saddle-sore brigade to Davenport's Bridge. There he spotted Merritt's cavalry, particularly the 5th Michigan, crossing the North Anna. The Confederates were more familiar with the country than their opponents, and Jeb sent most of his command to cross the river at what Merritt described in his official report, as "blind fords," which were concealed only to those who didn't know where to look. As a result the Michiganders were surprised when they found themselves confronted by a superior force of Rebels in their front as they hastened to catch up with the rest of Merritt's men. They charged and managed to break through, but not without the loss of several men and officers, most of whom were forced to surrender.

In the meantime, Fitz Lee came within sight of Sheridan's main column just as the troopers were breaking camp. Lee placed his available guns, a battery and a section, and began shelling the enemy's rear, which was now a part of Wilson's division.

Word of the approach of Sheridan's huge column was the big news in Richmond, and people were scurrying to make ready. Word went out that all soldiers in the City not attached to a specific unit stationed in the capital, whether on furlough or there for other reasons, were to report to Capitol Square and there to be formed into companies to man the city's breastworks. One such soldier was Lt. Frank Robertson, assistant engineer on Stuart's staff. He had suffered from a heart condition since before the war, and the Gettysburg campaign brought it back. He had not been able to report back to Stuart since leaving the Bower in mid-July 1863. Still, Stuart had recently given him some work to do, on April 19, being the copying and preparation of a map of the Chancellorsville battlefield, and Robertson was working on that project when the call to arms went out. He reported and was assigned to a company that manned stationary artillery defending south Richmond, in case Ben Butler decided to take a run at the city also.

The fight at the North Anna River did not last long. Sheridan had not found the ground where he wanted to stage his title match, and knew there would be plenty more to choose from in the 27 miles that lay between there and Richmond. Stuart, of course, had still not managed to get ahead of Sheridan so that he could force him to fight a major battle.

Fitz Lee's two brigades crossed the river and went to Beaver Dam Station, where Stuart caught up with him. They gazed at the smoldering destruction, and smoldered themselves.

From Beaver Dam, Jeb directed Fitz to head toward Hanover Junction, which was a Confederate supply depot on the Fredericksburg and Potomac Railroad, while Gordon was to continue following Sheridan. He also sent the 2nd Virginia to Ashland, an important Confederate center on the Fredericksburg and Potomac Railroad, about 15 miles north of Richmond. The detour to Hanover Station, southeast and near the North Anna, with the bulk of the Confederate cavalry accomplished two purposes. If that was Sheridan's next target, then Fitz might beat him to it or at least catch him there. If it was not, and Sheridan stayed on the Telegraph Road, Fitz had a chance, with some hard riding, to get ahead of him and between the Yankees and Richmond.

In the meanwhile, Jeb had personal business to tend to. With Major A.R. Venable, he rode to the Fontaine home to make sure Flora and the family were okay.

Flora came out to meet them in front of the house. Jeb did not even dismount and stayed for mere moments, but he took both children up on the saddle for a hug and a kiss, exchanged a few words with his wife, and then bent low from the saddle and kissed her, bidding her an affectionate farewell. Flora would have that kiss to remember, their last and the final romantic kiss of her life, for the next 59 years.

Riding away, Jeb and Venable said nothing for several minutes, then Stuart spoke: "You know Reid, I don't expect to survive this war." He paused. "And if we are to be conquered, I don't want to live to see it."

Sheridan's column moved parallel to the Fredericksburg and Potomac

Railroad, toward Ashland, then took the Mountain Road, which went south from Beaver Dam Station toward Richmond and then intersected and joined the Telegraph Road to become the Brook Turnpike about six miles north of the city. At that road juncture was an abandoned inn, once painted the color of egg yolk and sunshine, called Yellow Tavern. Stuart rode with Fitz Lee's column paralleling the North Anna River to Hanover Station. He sent messages to General Bragg in Richmond, and did not paint a particularly pretty picture:

> Should he [Sheridan] attack Richmond I will certainly move in his rear and do what I can; at the same time I hope to be able to strike him if he endeavors to escape. His force is large, and if attack is made on Richmond it will be principally as dismounted infantry, which fight better than the enemy's infantry.[16]

The rest of May 10 was a day of riding rather than fighting. When Stuart and Fitz Lee reached Fork Church, they halted for a few moments' rest. There was a field of clover and Jeb's purpose in stopping was more for the benefit of the horses than the men. Stuart and his staff lay down in the clover, Garnett next to the general. The sun was going down but they still had miles to go to Hanover Station, and Jeb had let everyone know that he planned to keep going to Taylorsville, beyond the station, before halting.

Jeb had his hat over his face shading his eyes, but he removed it and turned to Garnett and said "I know where you want to be."

The statement did not sound as odd to Garnett as it might to anyone else. His family lived just seven miles away.

"Yes," Garnett replied, "I expect you do."

"Well go on," Jeb said, "and join me in the morning wherever you can find me."

Garnett did not argue, but mounted his exhausted horse for another ride to his mother and father's house, a stable and feed for the horse, an honest-to-God bed for himself.

Stuart and Fitz Lee did not reach Hanover Station until after dark. The Confederate soldiers were worn out, and even though he did not want to do so, Stuart allowed them to go into camp, but only until 1 a.m. Sheridan made it to the South Anna River, only twenty miles north of Richmond. Jeb sent another ominous wire to Bragg at 9 p.m.:

> There is none of our cavalry from this direction between the enemy and Richmond. Has the enemy made any demonstration upon Richmond? Please answer tonight if practicable as I am very anxious to give my command a night's rest if compatible with duty.[17]

Stuart insisted on taking his staff on to Taylorsville, which he'd planned to reach all day, but before leaving he summoned Major McClellan and told him to watch Fitz Lee and his troopers, and not to close his eyes until he saw them ready to move out an hour after midnight. McClellan was no more rested than anyone else, but he did as he was told, and then rode to Taylorsville to report to Jeb. He found him flat on his back under a blanket next to Reid Venable, his head on a saddle, snoring. Despite his seemingly inexhaustible supply of energy, Stuart was just as worn out as everyone, and McClellan had trouble waking him, having to pull him over on his side before he opened his eyes. He told Stuart that Lee's men were mounted and on the way. The rest of the staff were roused and, drained, McClellan threw himself on the ground, thinking he might get just a few moments of sleep while everyone else pulled themselves together. Within seconds he was nearly unconscious, and when the other staff officers and couriers were preparing to ride away he vaguely heard someone say, "General, here's McClellan, fast asleep, shall I wake him?"

"No," Stuart answered, "he has been watching while we were asleep. Leave a courier with him and tell him to come on when his nap is out." McClellan, like Garnett before him, did not argue.

Richmond was in a panic. Church bells and alarm whistles blew most of the night. Butler's Army of the James had made a demonstration at Drewry's Bluff and the news of the loss of Beaver Dam Station convinced the citizens that the long-expected, concentrated Federal attack on the capital had come at last. Many ladies sat up all night wearing their best clothes and jewelry, determined to present the best appearance possible for whatever untoward events would unfold. The home guard was in the trenches, and in addition to every available soldier, government clerks were given rifles and a story to tell their grandchildren. Colonel Josiah Gorgas, the Confederate chief of ordnance, wrote in his diary that a "brigade" of old men, in uniform, had turned out and were sent to the north side earthworks. At 5 a.m. on the 11th he went to the office of Secretary Seddon and found him preparing to destroy records, convinced that Richmond would soon be evacuated.

Stuart headed toward Ashland, and it was there that Garnett and McClellan caught up with him shortly before 6:30 a.m. Sheridan had dispatched a raiding party to burn the depot and railroad stock there and they were just beginning that task when the Rebels arrived and captured a good many of them. Some flat cars and a cord of wood beside the tracks were blazing merrily, and when Garnett rode close he heard a Confederate soldier telling the prisoners, with mock gravity, that he had been ordered to throw each of them into the fire as well. The Yankees were not amused.

Lomax, by 8 that morning, had reached Yellow Tavern at the intersection of the Telegraph Road, down which the Confederates were approaching, and the Mountain Road, down which the Federals were approaching. Stuart had finally accomplished his goal of getting in front of Sheridan, between the enemy and the capital city, and he had beaten him with almost three hours to spare. However, even though Stuart believed Sheridan was heading for the intersection, he couldn't be certain.

Stuart rode toward the tavern. McClellan was beside him and while they discussed "many matters of personal interest," the major thought the general seemed more quiet, "softer," than usual, even though he was communicative.[18]

When Stuart summoned Garnett, the lieutenant didn't notice any particular softness. Instead he thought that the cavalry chief seemed impatient. Not only was he uncertain of Sheridan's exact whereabouts, his command was also scattered, with Gordon's brigade behind and following the enemy, Lomax's brigade ahead waiting for an enemy that might not arrive, and Wickham with him on the Telegraph Road, still more than an hour from Yellow Tavern.

He handed his own fieldglasses to Garnett, the pair now on display in the Museum of the Confederacy, and told him to head out in the direction of the Mountain Road, cross-country, and to not return until he could tell him *exactly* where the enemy was. Stuart then left Wickham's brigade behind and galloped closer to Yellow Tavern with staff and couriers, while Garnett left the Telegraph Road and trotted away west.

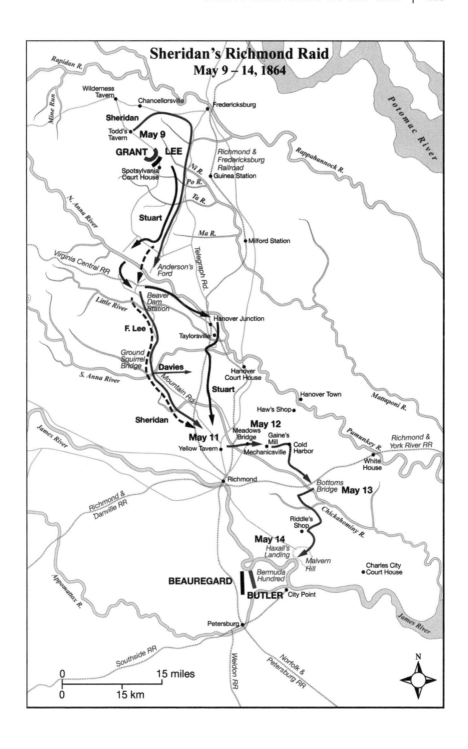

Sheridan's Richmond Raid
May 9 – 14, 1864

After riding a couple of miles Garnett saw a dust cloud ahead, moving away from him. He stopped at a cabin and learned from its occupants that the dust was kicked up by a Federal raiding party that had been sent out to burn Dilly's Mill. Garnett continued, but before getting much further, he heard the sound of guns in the direction of Yellow Tavern, and suspected that the exact location of Sheridan's column had become known. He turned around, spurred his horse into a gallop, reached the Telegraph Road again and turned south, passing Wickham's troopers, but pausing a moment to talk to Lt. Col. Robert Randolph of the 4th Virginia, who was normally "so bright and cheerful" but that morning seemed unusually dispirited. Randolph would be mortally wounded the next day at the Battle of Meadow Bridge.

Garnett galloped across the bridge spanning the Chickahominy River and on to the tavern, where he found Stuart riding along the front line, directing skirmishers who were doing battle with a heavy line of dismounted Federals.

Despite Lomax's arrival at 8, Stuart's arrival at 10, and Sheridan's not arriving until 11 a.m., Jeb did not interpose the men at his disposal between Sheridan and Richmond. He did not know how soon Wickham would arrive and certainly not Gordon, and in his current position he was on Sheridan's left flank, whereas, if he tried to block the Federals from riding south on the Brook Turnpike, they might simply ride over him and then have an open path to Richmond, at least until they reached the northern earthworks. He had already sent Major McClellan to find General Bragg and ascertain the number of troops manning those defenses, which was information that would help him decide the best course of action. If there were enough men in line in the trenches, he might be able to use them as an anvil and deliver a significant hammer blow to Sheridan.

Accordingly, when the enemy outflanked the left of Lomax's line and took possession of the tavern, so that their backs were to the Brook Turnpike and the fabled road to Richmond, Stuart did not regard it as a significant inconvenience. The longer he could hold Sheridan in place, the more time he would have for Wickham and Gordon to arrive so that he might have enough of a force to do some serious damage to Little Phil.

About a half mile north of the tavern there was a depression in the road that would serve as a good defensive position, and Stuart directed Lomax's men to make a stand there. Colonel Henry Clay Pate of the 5th Virginia was on hand, assembling and positioning his dismounted men on the left end of the Rebel line.

Pate and Stuart had had a rough relationship. Their history stretched back to Kansas, when each was dealing with John Brown, during which time Jeb once commented that Pate "could not be a corporal in the Missouri army." Later, when Pate became a Lt. Colonel in the Army of Northern Virginia, he feuded with Tom Rosser, Jeb's friend and commander of the 5th Virginia. The fuss spiraled down, past dispute and acrimony, into a full-blown, drawn-out court martial in which Jeb was a witness for Rosser. The men were usually openly contemptuous of each other.

Now, on the day when both were destined to receive their death wounds, the 5th Virginia was under Pate's command and was in an exposed place on the battlefield. Jeb had directed a battery of Horse Artillery to be placed nearby in a patch of woods on the west side of the Telegraph Road, and its guns were banging away at the Federals, who were obviously gathering on the Mountain Road for an assault. Having the guns close at hand was helpful, but the 5th was still in an open field with only a slightly sunken road for protection. The enemy would probably be able to flank them from the south, and there were more than enough Federals available to engulf the lone regiment.

Nevertheless, Stuart sent Garnett to tell Pate to "hold that position at all hazards." Pate was on foot, his saber in his hand, directing his men to the best positions available when Garnett delivered the order. Pate stared at him, unblinking and unsmiling. Thinking perhaps he'd not heard, Garnett leaned closer from his horse and repeated the order, "Colonel, General Stuart says to hold this position at all hazards," but Pate still did not reply and did not give Garnett any sort of message to take back to Stuart. Garnett, surmising that Pate must think that Stuart had placed him there "as a veritable death sentence," rode back.[19]

Pate's position was so perilous that Garnett soon realized he might not be able to escape it. A wheat field on the east side of the road was the only way back to Stuart that was not completely under the command of the enemy's guns, but the field was wide open and not out of rifle or cannon range. Garnett dashed into the field at an all-out gallop, his horse seeming to understand their peril as much as the lieutenant. Then the animal suddenly snorted and took a hard left turn, just in time to avoid tumbling into a deep ditch. Garnett rode along its edge for about a hundred yards but could not find a place to cross, and he was riding in the direction of the Federals. Finally, as a last resort, he wheeled the horse around, took a running start and leaped the ditch. By the time Garnett rejoined Stuart, the 5th Virginia had managed to repulse one attack, but had then been overwhelmed and Pate was killed instantly by a bullet that hit him in the forehead.

The more popular, oft-repeated version is that Stuart delivered the order in person, and that the two men looked each other in the eye, Pate said, "I shall do it," extended his hand, and the two shook, all their past differences put aside.

Another, more detailed version had Jeb riding up to Pate and holding out his hand, which Pate took, smiling. "Colonel," Stuart said, "you have done all any man could do. How long can you hold?"

"Until I die," Pate replied.

"You're a brave man," Stuart said and again they shook hands.

It could have happened. Jeb might have done that before the 5th took position, when Garnett wasn't present, then sent Garnett to reinforce the importance of the issue. Pate may have stared contemptuously because he was insulted that a young staff officer would come along and tell him to do something he'd already assured the commanding general he would do, spoiling the great romance of their reconciliation. The last day of a man's life might be an ideal time to conduct oneself completely out of character with all obvious attitudes held during the previous half decade. Perhaps the best evidence of that possibility is the fact that Jeb would speak highly of Pate's gallantry the next day, as he, Stuart, lay dying. Yet Garnett, who was there and who later heard the popular story, wrote of it, "of this, I can recall nothing."[20]

As soon as Garnett returned to Stuart, the general sent him off again, this time to General Wickham with orders to come on as quick as he could and, upon arriving on the Confederate right, to attack vigorously whatever he found in his front. Garnett galloped off again, but he was unable to locate Wickham. Hearing firing on the Confederate right, he found the 4th Virginia, which was a part of Wickham's brigade, sullenly retiring. He reined in beside Captain Aleck Payne of that regiment and stopped to ask him where Wickham might be and to tell him the orders he was carrying. Payne replied that it would be impossible for the brigade to advance further, that the enemy was dismounted and in heavy lines in the timber and that his regiment had just attempted to attack but had been driven back. Nevertheless, it appeared that their assault on the Federal left had served Jeb's purpose, as the Federals were falling back from the Telegraph Road, thereby relieving the pressure on the Confederate left.

As Garnett was talking to Payne a messenger from Gordon arrived on a horse so exhausted that the messenger begged Garnett to take the dispatch the rest of the way to Stuart. Garnett agreed and returned to Stuart with the message, which was that Gordon had skirmished with the enemy's rear guard at Ground Squirrel Bridge, some 12 miles up the Mountain Road the previous evening. Stuart slapped his thigh and said "Bully for Gordon," but then in almost a whisper said, "I wish he was here!"

In the southern defenses of Richmond, Frank Robertson was becoming bored. He and his companions could hear the firing in the direction of Yellow Tavern, but nothing was happening along the southern front. A friend named Willie Worthington sent a young house servant on a horse with a basket of food, and Robertson asked the commander in the area if it would be okay if he and a companion went into a clump of bushes for lunch. Given permission, they ate the food, then mounted double on the horse, left the servant boy to return with the basket, rode back into town and reported to the arsenal on 7th Street, where they were issued rifles and cartridge boxes. They then walked to the earthworks on the north side of the City, picking up another fellow "pretty much similarly situated" on the way. They didn't stop at the breastworks but continued on, planning to find the northernmost skirmish line, most likely to see action. Before they arrived, however, a shot fired from the direction they were headed slapped into a gatepost where they had paused to rest. This modified their plans, and after conferring further, they turned about and "bravely marched back to town."[21]

In another part of Richmond, Heros Von Borcke decided that his services were needed on the battlefield. As he described the situation in his exaggerated manner, "The sound of our light guns, which I recognised so well, did not fail to rouse me into a state of excitement; and as an old warhorse prances and curvets at the shrill ringing of the trumpet, I felt the blood pour like electric fire through my veins, and rushed about in feverish uneasiness. I fancied I heard my sword rattling in its scabbard to summon me to the scene of conflict by my General's side. . . ."

Having no horse of his own and unable to find one to borrow, he finally "impressed by force" a "miserable little pony" from a government wagon and headed toward the sounds of the guns north of the city. He passed the defensive earthworks and the last of the infantry pickets on the Brock Turnpike and ventured into territory that, for all he knew, might be in the hands of the enemy.

It was. After crossing a bridge some Federal cavalry came out of the woods on either side of the rode and came at him, shouting and firing their revolvers. Von turned his pony around and spurred it into its fastest gear, which was just enough to get him back to friendly pickets in a chase he described as covering several miles, meaning it was probably half a mile.

He claimed that he then went to Braxton Bragg, who he said was commanding the Confederate infantry, apparently along the city's defenses, to urge him to send troops to support Stuart, but his appeals were denied and he trudged back to Richmond. Just before reaching a friend's house, blood began to flow from his mouth. His exertions had re-opened his wound, and he nearly fainted before being found by his friends, was carried to the house and put to bed.

Major McClellan made the trip on the Brock Turnpike from Yellow Tavern to Bragg's headquarters without running into either the Yankees who chased Von Borcke or Von Borcke himself. He delivered his message from Stuart to General Bragg and, in response to Jeb's inquiry about the number of men available to occupy the earthworks, was told that some 4,000 were in position and that Bragg was confident they could not only hold the line, but that three more brigades were on the way from Petersburg.

Returning, McClellan found Sheridan's force between where he was on the Brock Turnpike and where Stuart was on the Telegraph Road, so he made a wide detour and rejoined his commander at about 2 p.m. Jeb was pleased with the information McClellan brought him, and he sat down with the major, near a battery of Horse Artillery on the right of the Confederate line just north of "Half-Sink," a point where a bridge crossed the Chickahominy bottomland, to discuss what had happened in his absence and what Jeb was hoping would occur soon.

Wickham held the Confederate right and Lomax the left, with a battery of artillery anchoring the left end and Lomax's line extending along the Telegraph Road, then crossing it to a hill where another piece of artillery was positioned. Two more guns were in the road. Everyone was dismounted except part of the 1st Virginia, which was acting as a mounted reserve.

Stuart and McClellan talked for nearly an hour, waiting for Gordon's arrival and/or the enemy's attack. Jeb was hoping that once the three brigades from Petersburg arrived that they would advance up the Brock Turnpike, at which point they would have Sheridan trapped between two jaws of a vice.

Near the end of their conversation, Stuart wrote or dictated the last military dispatch of his life, dated May 11, 1864 at 3 p.m. from "Headquarters near Half Sink Bridge." After a wartime career in close association with the greatest leaders of the Army of Northern Virginia—Lee, Jackson, Longstreet, Hill, and others—it is rather ironic that his last message went to Braxton Bragg, one of the least admired generals in the Confederacy. The dispatch informed Bragg of the position of the enemy and that Gordon was on his way to join Stuart. The key part of the message was "Now General, if we can make a combined attack on them with Hunton's brigade [Eppa Hunton, then commanding troops in the Richmond defenses] I cannot see how they can escape." Bragg characteristically ignored the advice of a general more capable than he, kept all of his infantry where it was, and effectively sealed Jeb's fate.

A little before 4 p.m. the lull in the battle ended. Sheridan launched a mounted attack on the Confederate left and Jeb climbed aboard General and, as always, hastened to the point of greatest danger. McClellan tried to follow but his horse was so exhausted that he was left behind.

The enemy's attack hit the 1st Virginia, captured two guns of the Confederate battery there, and forced the Rebels back. Stuart rode into the middle of the action. Several troopers saw Stuart approaching and one, a private in Company G, heard him say, "Boys, don't stop to count fours. Shoot them, shoot them!"

That is what the Virginians did, and they were able to bring down so many horses and riders that the road became blocked and the enemy's assault was stalled. Jeb saw this and rode over to where about 80 men, primarily belonging to Company K of the 1st Virginia, most of them Marylanders under Captain Gustavus "Gus" W. Dorsey, were located along a fence. He rode slowly, alone, and was whistling. He took position between two dismounted troopers, fourth Corporal James. R. Oliver and Private Frederick L. Pitts, with General's head extending beyond the fence and Stuart's right boot brushing against Oliver's left elbow.[22]

Bullets were still flying and a portion of the mounted 1st Virginia reserve made a charge up the road, but were driven back and the Federals—Custer's men—followed up, coming at the Confederate line again.

Jeb drew his revolver—not the heavy, unwieldy LeMat, with its nine shot cylinder and extra 10-guage shotgun barrel that he is often portrayed as favoring—but his exquisite, smooth-actioned .36 caliber Whitney.

"Bully for old K! Give it to 'em boys!" he shouted, and began shooting at the Federals, who were now falling back again, some of whom were within only 15 or 20 feet of Stuart.

All six shots fired, Jeb commanded, "Steady men, steady."

Suddenly he jerked so violently that his hat fell off. He pressed a hand to his side and dropped his head.

Troopers stared in disbelief. A crimson stain was visible. Captain Dorsey was close enough to reach up, steady him in the saddle and ask Stuart about his condition.

Stuart replied calmly, "I'm afraid they've killed me, Dorsey."

NOTES

1 William M. McDonald, late captain, C.S.A., *A History of the Laurel Brigade: The Ashby Cavalry of the Army of Northern Virginia and Chew's Battery,* p. 225 (Baltimore: Mrs. Kate N. McDonald, 1907)

2 *Ibid.* at 229-230.

3 ORs. Vol. LI, part 2, p. 893.

4 Wert at 342.

5 McDonald, supra, at 234.

6 *Ibid* at 233-34.

7 E. P. Alexander, *Fighting for the Confederacy: The Personal Recollections of General Edward Porter Alexander,* p. 360 (Chapel Hill: University of North Carolina 1989).

8 *In the Saddle with Stuart* at 57.

9 Wert at 344.

10 Phillip Sheridan, *Personal Memoirs of Phillip Sheridan,* Vol. 1, p. 370 (London: Chatto

& Windus, Picaddilly, 1888).

11 *In the Saddle with Stuart* at 58.

12 Edward Porter Alexander, Gary W. Gallagher, ed., *Fighting for the Confederacy: The Personal Recollections of General Edward Porter Alexander* 335, 374 (Chapel Hill: University of North Carolina Press, 1989).

13 *In the Saddle with Stuart* at 58.

14 *Ibid* at 62.

15 Wert at 348.

16 Burke Davis, *JEB Stuart: The Last Cavalier*, 391 (New York: Rhinehart & Co. 1957).

17 *Ibid.* at 391-92

18 *I Rode With Jeb Stuart* at 411.

19 In a later account, Garnett theorized that Pate's behavior and failure to speak was due to the fact that the Colonel was "quite deaf." Wert at 353, citing the Garnett Family papers at the University of Virginia.

20 *In the Saddle with Stuart* at 67.

21 *In the Saddle with Stuart* at 93.

22 "Stuart's Death; How it Occurred," in the "Confederate Column" of the *Richmond Times-Dispatch,* September 22, 1907.

CHAPTER 11

AND GOD'S WILL WAS DONE
May 11–13, 1864

While I draw this fleeting breath,
when mine eyes shall close in death,
when I soar to worlds unknown,
see thee on thy judgment throne,
Rock of Ages, cleft for me,
let me hide myself in thee.
        —*Rock of Ages,* Verse 4

It happened quickly during a raging battle. Men who saw parts of it filled in the rest of the story with what they surmised must have happened. Men who didn't see any of it but who were nearby, or who heard an account from someone claiming to be an eyewitness repeated what they heard and sometimes claimed the story as their own. Years went by and surmising, speculating, overhearing, and wishful thinking were repeated and refined until each teller became certain of the way it all happened. Hearsay became what a man witnessed. Guesses became memories. The memories became permanently imprinted on men's brains.

Children, neighbors, and friends asked to hear the story again and it improved with each telling. There were no books easily available, and certainly no Internet to consult. Listeners who heard the story "from the horse's mouth" passed it on. It grew, or became more detailed. Nobody intended to lie. They liked telling about what they saw, enjoyed the distinction, or were proud to have known someone who was actually there, who saw it, helped make it all happen, who knew the REAL story.

For stories about incidents that happened during a war, there is another factor to consider. Many veterans, then as now, did not enjoy talking about or reminiscing about what they saw during the war once it ended. This was particularly true for men who were defeated, and for men who were involved in particularly painful incidents. Often the returning soldiers declined to relive what they saw and did—put it out of their minds—for decades. Memories, though stark, did not always become imprinted on their brains, particularly if left to molder for years.

For the Civil War in particular, the passage of time changed everything. By the 1890s, participation in the war was not merely acceptable to remember and discuss, but was a source of great pride and social standing. Veteran organizations, the Grand Army of the Republic, the United Confederate Veterans, local camps of each, and groups from particular regiments held reunions, meetings, and annual sessions. The old memories were pulled out, dusted off, and shared. When there were gaps, when a man could recall being in a place but was not able to re-capture details, it was handy to have old friends who were able to be more specific, to supply one with one's own memories.

As with the death of many great men there are different versions of how Jeb Stuart was mortally wounded. Some are of the car wreck nature, with every witness giving a somewhat different account. Others are of different automobiles in other locations.

The most commonly accepted version, immediately after the wounding occurred and to this day—the version provided in all four of the major biographies of Stuart[1]—is based on the eyewitness testimony of Captain Agustuvas "Gus" Dorsey, commander of Company K, 1st Virginia Cavalry. That is the version that begins at the conclusion of Chapter Ten.

Yet there is another, different account of Stuart's wounding, and its credentials are just as impressive as Dorsey's.

It was supplied by Lt., later Major, John R. McNulty of the Baltimore Light Artillery, under Major James Breathed. He recalled after the war that he and Breathed were the last two men to fall back after the two guns of the Confederate battery were lost, and they met Stuart, holding a flag, on the back slope of a ridge behind the front lines, and that the general then led a charge against the enemy and was shot while doing so. He recalled seeing Stuart at the base of the hill, near a creek after he'd charged the enemy, surrounded by about 30 men. "These men were not Dorsey's men, but the general's staff, couriers, escort and such individuals as are always passing to and fro on a battlefield, and with these Stuart charged across the creek bottom."[2]

McNulty's version received some support from Jeb's brother-in-law, Dr. Brewer, which he provided to newspaper reporters shortly after Stuart's death and presumably originated from Stuart himself:

> He had formed a line of skirmishers near the Yellow Tavern when, seeing a brigade preparing to charge on his left, General Stuart with his staff and a few men dashed down the line to form troops to repel the charge. About this time the Yankees came thundering down on the general and his staff. Twelve shots were fired at the general and his small escort, at close range, the Yankees evidently recognizing his well know person. The general wheeled upon them with his natural bravery which had always characterized him, and discharged six shots from his revolver at his assailants. The last of the twelve shots fired at him struck the General in the left side of his stomach. The General did not fall, knowing he would be captured if he did, and nerving himself in his seat, wheeled his horse's head and rode for the protection of his lines. Before he reached them his wound overcame him and he fell or was helped from his saddle by one of his ever-faithful troopers, and from there was carried to a place of security.

McNulty's version was supported in much greater detail by Lt. Elijah Colner of the 1st Virginia, who wrote that after Breathed and McNulty met Stuart on the back side of the hill, that Breathed told Stuart it was possible to retake the battery just lost to the enemy, with two squadrons, and that Stuart ordered the 1st Virginia to charge in columns of fours in order to do so. However, when the column rode over the top of the ridge, Captain Hammond of the regiment, who was in the lead, was shot from his horse, causing Stuart to wave his saber in the air, shout "Forward men," and lead them on.

Colner said, "The command quickly drew back over the hill, and in a few minutes the General came back, supported on his horse by Private Bruce of Captain Dorsey's company."[3]

Another account that partially supports and partially conflicts with Colner's was contained in a letter to the editor of the *Richmond Times Dispatch* and printed in the issue of March 19, 1909. The author was an orderly sergeant in Company E of the 1st Virginia named B.J. Haden. The purpose of his letter was to take issue with an account published in the *New York Sun* which contained an interview with an artilleryman in Wickham's brigade, presumably of Breathed's battery. That artilleryman recounted seeing Stuart lead a small group of men in a charge and then watching a man on foot draw his pistol and shoot the General, who fell from his horse, after which the horse was shot. One of Haden's principal gripes about that account was that due to the density of the pine forest, "there is not a man living or one that ever lived, who could tell you who shot General Stuart."

Instead he offered his account, which was that he saw Hammond's company ride toward the Tavern, not to meet an attack but to attempt to draw the enemy into a trap. He wrote that after they had passed that General Stuart rode up to within three feet of Haden, but that just then bullets began hitting nearby and he, Haden, returned to his command. Hammond's squadron came thundering back, the captain dead and Federals mixed in with the retreating Confederates, and shortly thereafter he heard that Stuart had been wounded right where Haden had left him, and had been helped from the field by Private Bruce of Dorsey's Company K.[4]

If these accounts, told by supposed eyewitnesses, seem surprising and inconsistent with the commonly accepted version, consider that Colner knew of Dorsey's description of Jeb's wounding and said of it:

> Captain Dorsey's narrative, as far as is known to me, is almost an entire misconception of the facts, for it conflicts essentially with Major McNulty's account and my own, substantiated as it is by eyewitnesses to the sad scene that terminated in the loss to Virginia of her greatest cavalry chieftain. Captain Dorsey is undoubtedly mistaken. The state of affairs was occasioned, I think, by a lack of personal knowledge of the operations of the forces on the north side of the hill, his [Dorsey's] command being engaged a little beyond the crest of the hill.

Consider further that one of the most respected historians of the Civil War, Robert E.L. Krick, has compiled twenty different versions of how Stuart was wounded, most of them from putative eyewitnesses.[5]

Still, the Dorsey account is regarded as the most reliable, and it is consistent with the other reports from veterans over the years as well as staff officers and others who were with Stuart prior to his death or who heard it from the stricken general's own telling.

Along with the difference in how and where Stuart was wounded is the question of who deserves the credit for pulling the trigger and loosing the fatal bullet.

The man most frequently identified as being Jeb Stuart's killer was old enough to be his father. John Huff was a 48-year-old member of the 5th Michigan Cavalry. A Canadian by birth, he was formerly a member of Berdan's Sharpshooters, and is therefore attributed with being a crack shot. On May 1864 he was not using a Sharps carbine, or any kind of carbine, but a .44 caliber revolver. Most sources say it was a Colt, but some say it was a Remington.

The traditional story is that Huff was on foot, retreating after being unhorsed in Custer's counterattack, and that he passed within about 30 feet of Stuart, saw the big Rebel officer, paused, fired one shot, and then continued on his way into Federal lines.

There is very little record of how or why Huff or others decided that he shot Stuart, and one or two accounts say that he never claimed to have done so. The most official of the records is the report filed by Colonel Russell A. Algers of the 5th Michigan, which said the following:

Reforming the line, the Sixth Michigan, Major Kidd, having joined me, I received an order from the general commanding the brigade to charge the enemy in my front and right, as he was going to charge a rebel battery stationed on the right of the road. This order executed, and arriving at a point commanding a hill in rear of the rebel battery, my attention was called by Captain Judson, of this regiment, to an officer, accompanied by a large staff and escort, carrying a battle flag, who was just coming on to the hill from the rear. This officer was shot from his horse by Private John A. Huff, Company E, formerly of Berdans Sharpshooters. He was immediately carried to the rear by his staff. About thirty minutes later the hill was carried, and a woman and negro informed me that General Stuart had been shot on the hill mentioned, and first brought to their house and afterward carried away in an ambulance. Rebel accounts agree with the statements made by this woman and negro; also what was seen by us.[6]

Who was carrying the flag? The escort or the officer? Surrounded by a large staff and escort? Not according to Dorsey. Shot from his horse? No. Immediately carried to the rear by his staff? Perhaps. Taken to a house? No, unless the woman and the negro meant only that he was taken to the vicinity of a house.

We don't know who told Algers that Huff deserved the credit. In all likelihood, once the word spread that Stuart had been mortally wounded, Huff or his companions put two and two together and came up with a conclusion that has survived for decades.

The Stuart family accepted Huff's claim, assuming he made one, even to the point of believing that Huff literally requested permission to kill Stuart. This came about because a few years after the war Colonel Algers called at the home of General Phillip St. George Cooke, the father of Flora Stuart, while Mrs. Stuart was visiting. Upon being introduced to the widow he said, "Mrs. Stuart, I am sure that you would rather not meet me, as I am responsible for all of your tragedy and sorrow. It was I who gave the order to the sharpshooter to shoot General Stuart." Flora turned away "in her fresh grief . . . unable to reply to his confession." Stuart's granddaughter, Marrow Stuart Smith, recorded that Huff asked Alger, "I can shoot General Stuart, shall I?" to which Alger assented.[7] The likelihood of that having happened is too remote for serious consideration.

Custer chimed in about the matter to say in his report on the battle that:

> His defeat was complete. He fled, leaving a large number of dead and wounded in our hands. Among the dead was found the body of the notorious Col. Henry Clay Pate.
>
> From facts obtained on the battle-field and from information derived since, I have every reason to believe that the rebel General J. E. B. Stuart received his death wound from the hands of Private John A. Huff, Company E, Fifth Michigan Cavalry, who has since died from a wound received at Haws Shop.[8]

More than one historian has suggested that Custer promoted the Huff story in order that one of the regiments in his brigade would receive the credit for killing Stuart, as though George Custer was the sort of man who would embellish the facts merely for the sake of personal aggrandizement.

Private Jim Oliver, on foot next to Stuart, said that the killing shot was fired by one of several mounted Federals who was almost immediately shot himself. "[A] body of Federal cavalry, charging in columns of fours . . . got to our line of battle . . . [and] . . . filed to their left and in front of our command, passing within ten or fifteen feet of our line and General Stuart. Under our fire they broke into twos, threes and fours, firing at us as they passed on at a trot. But one of them checked his horse directly in front of General Stuart and turning toward him, fired at the general and as quickly rode on, but immediately he fell, dead or wounded. This I saw very distinctly. . . ."[9]

Huff, who was not wounded that day, left no personal account of the incident, and died before he had much opportunity to do so. He was shot in the head 17 days later, on May 28, 1864, at Haws Shop in Hanover County, Virginia, seven miles east of Yellow Tavern. He was not killed immediately and spent two or three weeks in a military hospital before being sent home, to Armada, Michigan, where he died on June 23, 1864, survived by a wife and two daughters. He is buried in Willow Grove Cemetery in Armada.

Dr. Brewer said that twelve shots were fired at Stuart, which, if accurate, could only have been something Jeb told his brother-in-law. Unless simply added for dramatic effect by either Brewer or the reporter, this statement indicated that shots came close enough and far enough apart for Jeb to take note of them and understand they were meant for him. The one that hit him could have come from any number of would-be assassins, although that doesn't mean that Huff could not have been the shooter.

Chief among the other shooter candidates is Shedrick L. Pealer, of the 1st New York Dragoons, aka the 19th New York Cavalry. Pealer's company commander, Captain Andrew J. Leach, was an eyewitness to the basis for Pealer's claim and he provided it for the regimental history of the 1st Dragoons, published in 1900. He recalled that the dragoons were deployed on a road with artillery on their right, and, 80 to 100 rods in their front, on an elevation, was a farmhouse "with the usual outhouses and negro quarters" and a rail fence. General Sheridan himself came along and told Leach to occupy the buildings, find out what the Confederates were doing, if that wasn't obvious, and to report back to him, so Leach took 20 men and got to the buildings, at which point:

> [M]y men called my attention to a rider upon a white horse, evidently an officer of rank, who was riding along their lines, seemingly superintending their formation. One of my men, Shedrick L. Pealer, called my attention to him particularly, and said, "I will try him a shot;" and resting his carbine across the corner of one of the huts, elevated the sights, and fired. The officer fell, and created general confusion, which could be plainly seen from our position; and that part of their line moved back into the woods and out of sight.
>
> I reported what I had seen to General Sheridan in person, the men were soon recalled, and the fight ceased. I afterward learned that Gen. J. E. B. Stuart rode such a white horse, and was killed that day, and it was reported through Confederate sources that Stuart was struck by a "chance shot;"' but I have always believed that it was the shot of Pealer that killed him. As further confirmation, it is well known that he was killed in front of our line, and killed by our regiment. Other members of my squad fired at this same officer, but none seemed so deliberate as this; and the fall was noticed immediately after the shot. I was certain at the time that that shot killed the officer, but I did not realize or even know then that it was Stuart, the famous cavalry leader, as I had not learned that he rode a white horse. It is certain that thereafter we saw no more of a conspicuous officer on a white horse.
>
> Shedrick L. Pealer was killed at Cold Harbor, May 31, 1864, and we lost one of the bravest and best of soldiers.[10]

The most discrediting aspect of Leach's and therefore Pealer's claim may be the same fact that most convinced Leach—that Stuart rode a white horse at Yellow Tavern. Stuart's horse that day, General, was a gray, and while it is absolutely correct that grey horses turn whiter and whiter as they age, so much so that genuinely white horses are sometimes referred to as "grays" (so much so that the Indians at the Little Big Horn who saw the men of E Company mounted on grays called them white horses), but General was probably not such a horse. He was a dapple gray and, as recalled by the South Carolinian who took note of Stuart and his mount at Laurel Hill, was a "dark dapple gray." Jeb did not own any other gray or white horse at that time of this life. He only had General and "the Pony," a bay, after losing three of his best horses to glanders during the winter.

Additionally, Leach wrote that "the officer fell" and "the fall was noticed immediately after the shot," whereas according to the Dorsey account Stuart remained mounted, was led away and was helped to dismount only after General became unmanageable.

The house that Leach wrote about might have been the Crenshaw House, which was on the battlefield near the front line, or another farmhouse where Colonel Pate's body was placed after his death, but both were located behind the Confederates' position instead of 80 to 100 yards in their front.

It is possible that the officer Pealer picked off was Colonel Henry Clay Pate, but the nature of the fighting makes that unlikely. Pate was almost certainly on foot when he was killed and if he was riding a white horse no record of that fact has been located. Captain James Breathed, commanding the Horse Artillery, was wounded at Yellow Tavern, but it occurred in hand-to-hand combat with a Federal officer who Breathed killed. Captain Hammond of the 1st Virginia was shot from his horse near where Stuart was shot, but it was apparently during a charge and the color of his horse isn't known. It has also been suggested that Pealer wasn't even at Yellow Tavern, but at Meadow Bridge the next day, and that the officer he shot was Brig. Gen. James B. Gordon, who was hit by a shot from approximately 400 yards away, although it hit Gordon in the arm and did not unhorse him.

In any event, the man Pealer shot could have been any Rebel who happened to be riding a white horse at the battle and who was killed or wounded . . . or it might have been Jeb Stuart.

One reason Pealer's claim is given credit is because at least one account stated that Huff fired the fatal shot from 400 yards away, which is an absurd distance for a pistol shot to be accurate. An intrepid supporter of Pealer's claim even conducted a test, firing both a .44 revolver and a Spencer carbine at a four-foot target after "marking off the distance," presumably 400 yards. He hit the target three out of five times with the carbine and zero out of five with the revolver.[11] The caliber of the bullet that hit Jeb is unknown because it was either not removed from his body or because, as is stated in more than one account, it passed completely through him and exited near the spine.

That bullet, whether a .44 caliber pistol ball, a .50 caliber Spencer bullet, or something else, hit Stuart less than five minutes after 4 p.m. on May 11. Assuming the Dorsey/Oliver/Pitts version account is diagnostically correct, what followed after the wounding described at the conclusion of the previous chapter now continues, as it was supplied by men of Co. K, particularly Captain Gus Dorsey, Corporal Jim Oliver and Private Fred Pitts.

"General, are you hit?" Oliver asked.

"Yes."

One of Jeb's couriers, probably Private A.H. Carpenter of the 4th Virginia, was behind him and Jeb turned enough to tell him, "Go ask General Lee and Doctor Fontaine to come here."

Just then the normally calm, reliable horse, General, decided to get spooky. He began prancing, wheeling, and tossing his head. Stuart was slumped in the saddle and tried only minimally to control him. Dorsey helped Stuart to dismount and directed Pitts to bring his horse over so they could transfer Stuart to it, but Jeb, lying on the ground, protested, "Leave me Dorsey, get back to your men and drive the enemy. I'm afraid they've killed me and I'll be no more use. Go back."

Dorsey refused, saying that was an order he could not obey. "I would rather they get me too then leave you here. We'll have you out in a shake."

Pitts arrived with his horse, dismounted and took the reins of General, who was still restive. Dorsey, Oliver, and a Private Holland helped Jeb mount Pitts' horse and Pitts mounted General. Dorsey told his men to get Stuart back from the line of battle. Another Marylander in the company, Tom Waters, took the horse's bridle and turned him, and either Waters or Pitts led Stuart, on Pitts' horse, back from the line about a hundred yards. Oliver was on one side, steadying him and Private Robert Bruce was probably on the other. Stuart protested, but Dorsey said, "We're taking you back a little, General, so as not to leave you to the enemy." He directed Private Charles Wheatley to find an ambulance.

"Take the papers from my inside pocket and keep them from the Yankees," Stuart said.

Dorsey reached up and fished for the papers in the inside breast pocket of Stuart's battle jacket, found a small packet and pulled them out. A couple appeared to have been torn by the bullet but they were not blood-stained.

Other members of Company K had gathered around the little group but Dorsey directed them back onto the line. Pitts and Oliver returned as well, Pitts still on General, which he rode in a charge against the enemy a few moments later. Another of the company who had been close, Private Burgess, recalled later that the men knew the gunshot had done significant damage. "He was wounded mortally, as we knew when we saw where the bullet had entered his side and torn his gray jacket." Before he left, Pitts noticed that "his whole side was soaked with blood," and he surmised that Stuart was "seriously hurt."[12]

Dorsey, Waters, and Bruce helped him dismount again, and they set him down gently with his back against a tree to wait for the ambulance. Stuart neither spoke nor groaned, and he may have been going into shock.

Fitz Lee arrived, and was stricken at what he saw. Stuart turned over command to him. "Go ahead Fitz, old fellow. I know you'll do what's right." Eleven years later, when giving a speech at the Army of Northern Virginia Banquet, Fitz described those words as "my most precious legacy."[13]

Dr. Fontaine and Reid Venable arrived, as did Wheatley and the ambulance. Stuart was lifted up and placed in it, lying flat on his back.

Things were not going well at the scene of Stuart's wounding. The Federals were pressing vigorously, and several of the dismounted Confederates began falling back, others began running. Stuart saw this and didn't like it. He raised himself up and shouted from the ambulance, sounding very much like the commanding general he still was, "Go back! Go back! Do your duty as I've done mine. I would rather die than be whipped!"

As it turned out, Stuart's comment was more prophetic than anyone knew. Not only was he being whipped and not only was he going to die, but most of the men who stayed on the firing line were either killed or captured.

Lt. Garnett had been told by Stuart before the wounding that he needed to take 20 men to Richmond to bring back ammunition, but that he should first go the Crenshaw house, which was on an elevation on the other side of a deep ravine in the Confederate rear. There he was to obtain as much information as he could, either by observation or interviewing its inhabitants, about "by-paths" through farms between Yellow Tavern and Richmond, after which he was to return to Stuart to collect the 20 men and written orders for the ammunition.

When Garnett got to the house he found it had been turned into a hospital. Surgeons were tending wounded, but Mr. Crenshaw was present and gave Garnett detailed information to write down in his order book about paths that would get him to Brook Hill, on the outskirts of the capital city. Returning, he ran into Brig. Gen. Lomax and a cousin of Garnett, Lt. James Hunter, Jr., who was on Lomax's staff, at another farmhouse, and was told that the body of Colonel Pate was inside. Lomax, Pate's commander, was grieving, and Garnett felt obliged to go inside and pay his respects. He spent five minutes there, taking note of the bullet hole in Pate's forehead, and then remounted and rode with Lomax and Hunter toward the place where Garnett had separated from Stuart.

Just as Garnett separated from Lomax and Hunter so that they could each return to their commands, a squadron of Federal cavalry attacked a battery of the Horse Artillery. Garnett shouted a warning to Lomax, who galloped away and returned with a squadron of the 6th Virginia. Garnett joined them and Lomax, Hunter, and he led the attack, only to have it smashed to pieces, not by the enemy but by one of the Horse Artillery's limbered guns endeavoring to escape. It came barreling down on Lomax's men, its horses in a panic and its driver applying the whip. The cavalrymen had to swerve out of its way and the well-ordered attack that was intended stalled out. Dismounted troopers were falling back, some calling for ammunition, and the rest of the battery was captured. Garnett thought he would see Stuart arrive at any moment, as he always did where the fighting became hottest, but the general did not appear.

Garnett stayed a few more seconds, until bullets began kicking up dirt around and beneath his horse, then turned away. Another gun of the Horse Artillery, under Lt. William Hoxton arrived, ready to go into action, but Garnett convinced Hoxton that doing so would mean being overrun and losing the piece, so Garnett and the limbered gun rode to the bridge on the Telegraph Road where it crossed the Chickahominy. There he met Major McClellan and learned that Stuart was wounded.

McClellan had been left in the dust back at Half-Sink when Stuart rode to the sound of the guns. His horse was exhausted from the trip to Richmond, and McClellan traded it for another that he described as "a captured nag, a sorry animal,"[14] and by the time he arrived near where the General had been wounded, the ambulance had already departed. Now he and Garnett went in search of it.

A former staff officer had arrived at the ambulance before it left. This was Lt. Walter Q. "Honeybun" Hullihen, who had been an aide-de-camp for Stuart from April 29, 1862 to November 19, 1863. Since then he had served as an assistant adjutant general on Lomax's staff, but when he heard of Stuart's wounding he rushed to the scene in time to climb into the ambulance with the general and Dr. Fontaine.

In addition to Hullihen and Reid Venable there were at least three couriers, Private A.H. Carpenter of the 4th Virginia, and Privates Augustine Henry Ellis and William T. Thompson, both of the 13th Virginia. It is also possible that Private Charles D. Lownes of the 4th Virginia was there or nearby. They headed toward Atlee's Station. An 18-year-old private of K Company named McCormick also accompanied them a little of the way, the nose of his horse inside the rear of the ambulance. Carpenter noticed that after Stuart called to the retreating men to go back and do their duty, that although Stuart was quiet, he shook his head back and forth "with an expression of deepest disappointment."[15] McCormick saw the same thing, saying that Stuart had his arms folded and that he shook his head from side to side wearing a look of resignation

The ambulance did not drive away slowly or calmly. It was pulled by two mules that were not accustomed to the battle that was still raging nearby. As soon as they saw they were being allowed to depart they broke into a run and dashed down a steep bank so rapidly that the right rear wheel of the vehicle left the ground and flew into the air. Private McCormick was afraid it was going to overturn and drag everyone inside to death.

It did not, but continued at full speed until it reached the bridge at the Chickahominy. There Major Venable ordered a halt so that Dr. Fontaine could examine the wound.

They unwound Stuart's stained yellow sash, unbuttoned his vest and shirt, and then turned him on his side, presumably to look for an exit wound. To Hullihen Jeb asked, "How do I look in the face, Honeybun?"

"You are looking all right," Hullihen replied. "You will be all right." Dr. Fontaine was not so optimistic. He thought the bullet may have hit Stuart's liver, and that he might die at any moment.

Stuart recognized Hullihen's assurance for what it was. "Well," he said. "I don't know how this will turn out, but if it is God's will that I shall die I am ready."

By then some soldiers had gathered around the ambulance, and Jeb shooed them away, telling them, "Go back to the front. I will be taken care of. I want you to do your duty to your country."

Garnet and McClellan caught up. McClellan saw that the horrible rumor was true, and remembered that Stuart had told him on more than one occasion that in the event of his wounding, McClellan should not leave the field but should report to the officer next in rank. Conscious of that duty and knowing the general was in good hands, he left to find Fitz Lee.

Garnett stayed with the ambulance as it started up again. They moved rapidly, not only to get the general to safety and medical treatment, but because a storm was blowing in. Rain began falling in torrents. When they arrived at Atlee's Station they parked beneath a large oak tree to ward off some of the wet. Fontaine prescribed a shot of whiskey as a stimulant. Predictably, Stuart declined, saying, "No, I've never tasted it in my life. I promised my mother that when I was a baby."

Venable joined in, telling Stuart that the circumstances were different and that he should do as the doctor ordered. Wavering, Jeb held out his hands to Venable. "Lift me," he directed, and Venable helped him into a sitting position. "Old fellow," Jeb continued, "I know you will tell me the truth. Is the death pallor on my face?"

Venable looked and shook his head. "I hope not, there is some flush on your forehead." This seemed to reassure Stuart, and he assented to take a take the drink, his first and only. One wonders what he thought of it.[16]

The rain subsided and they continued, now at a walk. At Mechanicville they overtook a doctor who, upon learning that General Stuart was in the ambulance rode ahead and had hot coffee and biscuits waiting at his gate when they arrived. Jeb tasted the coffee but put it aside, "unable to take what had always been to him the greatest comfort."[17]

Garnett rode ahead from there to report the news to General Bragg in Richmond and to make certain a bed was prepared and waiting for Stuart when he arrived. Garnett entered the city about 10 p.m. and went to the home of Dr. Charles Brewer and his wife, Maria, Stuart's brother-in-law and sister-in-law.

At Bragg's office he made a brief, to-the-point report that was met, Garnett, recalled, "with supreme indifference." Bragg, whom he called "his cold-blooded highness," expressed no sympathy by word or manner, indicated no interest in Garnett or his message, and sent no message back with him.

Garnett and his horse were utterly exhausted, having been in and under the saddle for a full week with little food or rest, punctuated by near-death battle experiences and now the critical wounding of the man Garnett most admired in life. He wrote later that he could not remember where he spent the night, although he believed it was at the home of Reverend Joshua Peterkin, who would have his own duty to perform regarding General Stuart two days from then.

The ambulance arrived at Dr. Brewer's home at 210 Grace Street, between Madison and Jefferson, at about 11 p.m., and Jeb was carried into the house and upstairs to a small bedroom. The house had a low wall around it on which yellow roses were blooming. His blood-stained uniform was removed and he was probably provided with one of Dr. Brewer's sleeping gowns. Dr. Fontaine tended and bandaged the wound. Now that his long trip, which had included long detours and side roads to make certain of avoiding the enemy, was over, Stuart seemed to be in less pain, and he drifted off to sleep for the night.

Stuart awoke before dawn, as was his custom, and asked Dr. Brewer to summon Heros von Borcke. The General seemed rested and strong, and the members of the household felt optimistic about his chances for recovery.

Brewer found Von Borcke and roused him at daybreak. The huge Prussian dressed as quickly as he could and hastened to Stuart's side, where Jeb greeted him with a smile and every appearance of having shaken any expectations of his demise.

"I'm glad you've come, my dear Von," he said. "You see they've got me at last, but don't feel uneasy. I don't think I'm so badly wounded as you were, and I hope I shall get over it as you did."

He told Von and others who were present about how he'd been wounded, saying that his hope and expectation would be that Bragg would attack from Richmond, which might have meant the annihilation of Sheridan's entire force, but that the odds, which Jeb thought were about 8,000 to 1,100, were too great for the cavalry to defeat Sheridan without Bragg's assistance. Von Borcke's summary of what Stuart said was as follows:

> At about four o'clock, the Federals succeeded by a general charge in breaking and driving back one of our regiments which General Stuart was rallying in an open field. When continuing their advance the enemy were met by the 1st Virginia and driven back again in confusion. Seeing near him some of the dismounted Federal cavalry, who were running off on the opposite side of a high fence, Stuart rode up to them calling on them to surrender, and firing at them as they continued their flight. He had just discharged the last barrel of his revolver when the hindmost of the fugitives, coming close up to the fence, fired his revolver at him, the ball taking effect in the lower part of the stomach and traversing the whole body. Stuart, finding himself severely wounded, and the enemy at the same time renewing their attack, turned his charger quickly round and galloped half a mile further to the rear, where he was taken from his horse nearly insensible from loss of blood, and sent in an ambulance to Richmond.[18]

His account sounds like a combination of Dorsey's and McNulty's versions, with the part about galloping half a mile to rear sounding like a combination of McNulty's and Von Borcke's well-established penchant for exaggeration.

Fontaine and Brewer both expressed hope that the wound was not fatal, and when McClellan arrived at about 11 a.m., he thought the general seemed calm, composed and in full possession of his mind. Quickly thereafter, Stuart began going downhill. Paroxysms of pain interrupted his attempts to speak, and Dr. Fontaine became more pessimistic.

Stuart began talking about the disposal of his papers and possessions. He directed McClellan to file or otherwise make proper arrangements for his official papers, and to make certain his personal effects were delivered to Flora. Then he said, "I wish you to take one of my horses and Venable [who was still present], the other. Which is the heavier rider?"

McClellan said he thought Venable was, and Stuart said, "Then let Venable have the gray horse and you take the bay."

Pausing a few seconds, he continued speaking to McClellan. "You will find in my hat a small Confederate flag which a lady of Columbia, South Carolina sent me with the request that I wear it upon my horse in a battle and return it to her. Send it to her."

McClellan knew nothing about such a flag, but he looked in Stuart's hat and found it inside the lining, stained with the general's sweat. Later he found the letter from the lady among Stuart's papers and fulfilled his request. One wonders what became of the artifact.

Continuing, he said, "My spurs which I have always worn in battle I promised to give to Miss Lilly Lee of Shepherdstown, Virginia. My sword I leave to my son."

The spurs he referred to were not the golden spurs that had been sent to him by a lady in Baltimore, and which served as the basis for his adopted acronym "K.G.S." for "Knight of the Golden Spurs," nor was their recipient the wife of Robert E. Lee, as was sometimes reported. They were a pair of silver spurs that Stuart had given to William F. Lee before the war, when they served together at Jefferson Barracks. When Lee, then a colonel, was killed early in the war, his wife, Lily Parin Lee, gave the spurs back to Stuart when he visited her in Shepherdstown on October 1, 1862. Now he wanted them returned to the widow of their rightful owner.

As he and McClellan were talking, the sound of guns came from the distance, outside the city, and Stuart quickened. "What is that, what does it mean?" he asked, and McClellan explained that troops were moving against Sheridan's rear on the Brook Turnpike, and that Fitz Lee intended to oppose them at Meadow Bridge. This was Stuart's plan from the day previous and he said with earnest, almost eager conviction, "God grant that they may be successful."

Then he sighed and turned his head aside. "But I must be prepared for another world."

The cannonading continued, and Stuart, ever thinking of one's duty, said "Major, Fitz Lee may need you." McClellan understood. He rose, shook the general's hand and bid him a final farewell. It was then about noon, and as McClellan started from the room, President Davis stepped in.

Davis took the hand just abandoned by McClellan and asked, "General, how do you feel?"

"Easy, but willing to die if God and my country think I have fulfilled my destiny and done my duty."

The president stayed only a few moments. Charles and Maria Brewer, Dr. Fontaine, Venable, Von Borcke, and others were there, and at about 12:30 Garnett arrived. Stuart was not as alert as he had been earlier, and Garnett took his hand and held it, sitting by the bed. As he said later, his grief was as great as if his own father was dying, and he was certain Stuart's loss would be a disaster to the Southern cause and an irreparable calamity to the army.

At 1 o'clock there were sudden shouts and noise from outside, and Stuart opened his eyes and showed some excitement. "What's that? Go and see!" he said to Garnett, so the lieutenant went outside and over to Broad Street. An ambulance was going by and he asked a bystander what was going on. "They have a Yankee general in that ambulance," he was told, "a prisoner captured out on the Brook Turnpike."

Garnett was skeptical, and for good reason. The occupant of the ambulance was actually one of Stuart's favorite brigade commanders, James B. Gordon of the North Carolina Brigade. He had been wounded in the arm at Meadow Bridge and was being taken to a hospital. Despite the seemingly minor nature of the wound, it proved fatal, and he died six days later. When Garnett returned to Stuart he was asleep.

Sleep, as well as comprehension, came and went. Garnett and Von Borcke took turns sitting beside his bed, feeding him ice, which Von said he ate in great abundance, and putting ice on his wound to try to relieve the pain. Dr. Fontaine tried to get him to take another drink of liquor, brandy this time, but Stuart refused. There was the matter of his promise to his mother and besides, the drink he'd had the day before was neither enjoyable nor helpful. At 3 p.m. Garnett left Stuart's bedside to eat with the Rutherford family, but he returned while Stuart was still alive.

The news of her husband's wounding reached Flora in the form of a telegram sent by Von Borcke the morning of the 12th. She was still staying at the Edmund Fontaine home near Beaver Dam Station, only about 30 miles from Richmond, but Sheridan had cut the telegraph lines, so the message had to be sent from Richmond to Lynchburg to Charlottesville and then to Beaver Dam Station so that it did not arrive until almost noon. One version of the story is that Major William W. Blackford was visiting, that he intercepted the telegram and arranged for a locomotive to take Ms. Stuart to Richmond before telling Flora of its contents, but that is not supported by Blackford's principal account, in which he mistakenly said he visited her on May 13, after which a train arrived with the news, and that by that time Stuart was already dead.

Another version is that she was upstairs bathing one of the children when the message arrived. The story handed down in the Stuart family is that Colonel Edward Fontaine, brother of Dr. John Fontaine, received the telegram in the morning and kept it from Flora until after she had had lunch, during which time he worked out transportation for her.[19] This version placed Flora at the Beaver Dam Station when the telegraph arrived, where she was helping to tend to wounded from the fight at that place from the day before. She returned to the Fontaine house for lunch and while Colonel Fontaine arranged for a train to carry her to Richmond, his wife broke the news to Flora.

She immediately took a carriage back to Beaver Dam Station where she boarded a train. With her were the two children, Jimmy and Virginia, a nurse named Tilda, two of the Fontaine daughters, and Dr. George Woodbridge, rector of the Monumental Church in Richmond, whose son was in Stuart's command and who was also visiting at the Fontaine home. The train was specially arranged for her by Colonel Fontaine and the only engineer available was an inexperienced volunteer. It only carried the party as far as Ashland, thirteen miles, after which Sheridan had torn up the tracks, but it took two hours to do so.

They had no further transportation available, but Dr. Woodridge asked around, explaining the parties' plight. Some wounded Confederate officers in an ambulance, upon hearing of the situation, gave up their mule-drawn ambulance and Mrs. Stuart and the party set out again on what must have been the most agonizing trip of her life.

The roads were poor, and soon after leaving Ashland a violent thunderstorm began with heavy rain and a lot of lightning and thunder. Occasionally they met soldiers going in the other direction and they invariably asked if they'd heard any news about General Stuart, to which they were almost always told, "No, but we heard the wound is not serious."[20]

About eight o'clock they reached the Chickahominy River, but the bridge had been destroyed by Confederate cavalry to stop or delay Sheridan. It was dark and still raining but they found a cavalry picket who directed them to a ford a mile or two downstream,. A Confederate officer had to guide them across, water came in over the floor of the ambulance, and it tilted forward and to one side.[21]

At another point a shot was fired over the vehicle, but the shooter turned out to be Confederate. The two children slept on the hard wooden side seat of the ambulance with a blanket, while Flora sat with her gold watch in her hand, watching the minutes and praying she would not be too late. She recalled that after it became dark—they would not arrive until after 11 p.m.—a vivid flash of lightning revealed the time and that it turned out to be the hour at which General Stuart died.[22]

At about 10 p.m., as they were approaching the outskirts of the city, Dr. Woodbridge, saw horses ahead in the dark and men lying along the roadside. Suddenly a horseman loomed directly in front of their mules' heads and Dr. Woodridge pulled them to a stop.

"Who's there? Stand!" came from the horseman in the road, who was a sentinel. Dr. Woodbridge explained who was in the ambulance and their purpose and the sentinel exclaimed: "Thank God! My cap snapped twice when you did not answer my repeated challenge," meaning he had attempted to shoot at them, and then added, "We are Lomax's men."[23]

At the Brewer home, Jeb had begun asking urgently when Flora would arrive. He drifted in and out of his senses, and also asked about Little Flora, gave orders to couriers, spoke of battles, and experienced jolts of sharp pain. One of his distinct commands, probably delivered dozens of time in the field, was "Make haste!" Around 5 p.m. his mind cleared, he asked again about Flora, and asked Dr. Brewer if he would live through the night. Charles was honest. He told him that death was "rapidly approaching." Stuart nodded and said, "I am resigned, if it be God's will, but I should like to see my wife . . . but God's will be done."

At about 7 p.m., those in attendance were Von Borcke, Garnett, Dr. Brewer, Dr. Fontaine, a Reverend Keppler, and Reverend Joshua Peterkin of St. James Episcopal Church. There may have been others; others so claimed, but it was a small bedroom.[24]

Keppler and Peterkin prayed aloud and Stuart asked that everyone sing *Rock of Ages*. He joined in the best he could.

At some point, if Von Borcke is to be believed, Stuart grasped his hand firmly, pulled him near, and said, "My dear Von, I am sinking fast now, but before I die I want you to know that I never loved a man as much as yourself.

I pray your life may be long and happy; look after my family after I'm gone, and be the same true friend to my wife and children that you have been to me." Von claimed those were Stuart's "last connected words," after which "the paroxysms of pain became more frequent and violent" until death relieved his suffering. Even if that is not exactly how it happened, there can be little doubt that Stuart's feelings for Von Borcke were as Von chose to remember them.

About 7:38 p.m., Jeb turned to Dr. Brewer and said, "I am going fast now. I am resigned. God's will be done." And so it was.

Flora arrived at about 11 p.m. She asked to see her husband and was told she could, no one having the heart to tell her he was dead. She was directed upstairs, she rushed to his side, and her life changed forever.

The next morning Garnett assumed the responsibility of contacting general officers whom he wanted to serve as pallbearers, but when he wrote of it later he could recall the name of only one, Brigadier General Joseph R. Anderson, a Virginian and former brigade commander during the Seven Days Battle who oversaw Tredegar Iron Works and the Confederate Ordnance effort. Other pallbearers identified in the newspapers were Brigadier General John H. Winder, Brigadier General George W. Randolph, Brigadier General Alexander R. Lawton, Brigadier General Samuel McGowan,[25] Brigadier General Robert Hall Chilton, plus Commodore French Forrest and Captain Sydney Smith Lee, of the C.S. Navy. Braxton Bragg was also listed in some papers as a pallbearer, and although he attended the funeral, the likelihood of Garnett inviting "his cold-blooded highness" to be a pallbearer is remote in the extreme.

No record has been found of how Stuart was dressed for burial, but it was probably the same uniform in which he was mortally wounded. Based only on wartime photos and uniforms in museums, he owned at least four different uniform coats during the war, probably more. One was a double-breasted general's frock with buff-colored cuffs and eight buttons on each side arranged in four sets of two; two were double-breasted battle jackets with buff-colored cuffs, one with six buttons on each side arranged in three sets of two and the other with nine buttons on each side arranged in three sets of three; plus one battle jacket with plain, or gray-colored cuffs and nine buttons on each side arranged in three sets of three. The frock and the battle jacket with plain cuffs survived and are in the Museum of the Confederacy and the Virginia Historical Society Museum respectively.[26] One battle jacket—that which Stuart wore on at least one, possibly both of his rides around McClellan—was given to John Esten Cooke, who displayed it on the wall of his study, along with a saber captured at Gettysburg and portraits of Lee, Jackson, and Stuart, for the rest of his life.[27]

That leaves at least one battle jacket with buff-colored sleeves unaccounted for. While this is only speculation, it seems likely that Flora and those close to Stuart would have wanted to dress him for burial in uniform, that no other general's uniform was readily available, and that the badly stained jacket in which he was wounded was not an artifact Flora was anxious to keep around the house. The condition of that jacket explains why his body was covered with a white sheet up to his chin when it was laid out on a billiard table at the Brewer home for viewing before his funeral.

The fact that his body was laid on a billiard table—probably selected for its size and location in the house—and that all but his face was covered with a sheet was a memory handed down through the family of General George S. Patton. The World War Two hero's paternal grandfather was Colonel George Smith Patton, who commanded the 22nd Virginia Infantry and who was killed in the Third Battle of Winchester the following October. He was in Richmond on May 13, 1864 and he put on his best uniform and took his eight-year-old son to what he recorded as being a private home, being that of the Brewers. There was a line of hushed citizens and soldiers filing by the billiard table where Stuart had been laid, his legs and torso covered with a sheet. The younger Patton, George William,[28] thought that the sheet was as smooth as marble and that it contrasted sharply with Stuart's red, wiry beard. The boy knew who Stuart was, and thought to himself that he couldn't really be dead because important people like that do not die. Leaving the house, the younger Patton caught the scent of the yellow roses on the front wall. For the rest of his life the smell of flowers brought back the memory of that day.[29]

The body was placed in a metal casket, which was then placed in a hearse drawn by four white horses, the forelock of each decorated with a black ostrich plume. There was no music, beating drums or military escort. Instead there was the sound of the most appropriate dirge available for Jeb Stuart—distant cannon fire. The enemy was shelling Drewry's Bluff and Confederate guns were responding.

The cortege reached Saint James' Episcopal Church at the corner of Marshall and Fifth streets at five o'clock. It was crowded with citizens and soldiers, including President Davis, General Bragg, General Ransom, and other civic and military officials of Richmond. The metallic casket was borne into the church and up the center aisle to the altar, with an organ pealing a solemn funeral dirge and an anthem sung by a choir. The casket was decorated with lilies arranged in the shape of a sword, plus a crown of bay leaves.[30] The service was read by Rev. Dr. Peterkin, assisted by other ministers, concluding with singing and a prayer. It was a simple service, "lacking for the honors that had graced the funerals of his peers,"[31] because Sheridan still threatened on the north and Butler on the south sides of the City.

The organ ground out slow, solemn music and the body was taken out again, back to the hearse with its black-plumed white horses, the congregation standing with heads uncovered as it was carried by. Carriages occupied by family, staff, friends, and admirers trailed after the hearse as it wound its way to Hollywood Cemetery, where Little Flora had been buried in November 1862, and where she was now to be joined by her daddy, as he had longed to do for so long. Rev. Dr. Minnigerode, of Saint Paul's Church, read scripture and led the mourners in prayer, "and all that was mortal of the dead hero was shut in from the gaze of men."[32]

Shortly after the funeral the Richmond City Council adopted a resolution honoring Stuart. It was not long and flowery, nor was it something the City Council did for every Confederate general who was killed. Stuart, however, had died defending the city, and the city fathers let it be known they considered him "not only . . . one of the first military characters of the age, but also a citizen whose eminent patriotism and pure life gave the best guarantee that his military capacity would never be otherwise employed than in the cause of freedom and for the welfare of his country." In concluding, after tendering its deepest condolences to the Stuart family, the Council resolved to someday "commemorate by a suitable monument their gratitude." In a separate resolution the Council appointed a three-person commission to report back at some future meeting with a design for that monument and its inscription.[33]

It was not unusual, in the weeks and months that followed, to see a large man, his horse tethered to a nearby tree, sitting beside the grave, sometimes for hours. It was Von Borcke, of course, "recalling his excellent qualities, and musing over the many glorious battles through which [they] had fought side by side."[34]

NOTES

1 *Jeb Stuart* by John Thomason; *Bold Dragoon* by Emory M. Thomas, *The Last Cavalier* by Burke Davis, and *Cavalryman of the Lost Cause* by Jeffrey Wert

2 A.K. Matthews, "Gen. Stuart's Death: How the Chieftain Received his Mortal Wound," *National Tribune*, Washington, D.C., June 23, 1887.

3 *Ibid.*

4 "Stuart's Last Battle," in "Our Confederate Column," p. 8 of Sec. B, *Richmond Times-Dispatch*, March 19, 1909; Haden provided another, slightly different version of what he witnessed in a story published in the *Confederate Veteran* magazine in August, 1914, at p. 352.

5 A.K. Matthews, supra.

6 ORs, Vol XXXVI, Part 1, page 828.

7 Marrow Stuart Smith, Sean M Heuvel, ed., *Life After J.E.B. Stuart: the Memoirs of his Granddaughter*, pp. 24-26 (Lanham, Md: Rowman & Littlefield Publishers, Inc., 2012).

8 ORs, Vol. XXXVI, Part 1, pp. 819-20.

9 "Stuart's Death; How it Occurred," in "Confederate Column" of the *Richmond Times-Dispatch,* September 22, 1907.

10 Rev. J.R. Bowen, *Regimental History of the First New York Dragoons* (Ann Arbor, Mich.: J.R. Brown, 1900).

11 http://civilwartalk.com/threads/jeb-stuart.48184/page-3

12 "Stuart's Death; How it Occurred," *supra.*

13 Speech of General Fitz. Lee, at A. N. V. Banquet, October 28th, 1875, *Southern Historical Society Papers.* Vol. 1, pp 99-103 (1876).

14 A.K. Matthews newspaper article, *supra.*

15 Burke Davis *JEB Stuart: The Last Cavalier,* 409 (New York: Rhinehart & Co. 1957).

16 Stonewall Jackson, like Stuart, did not drink alcohol but, also like Stuart, he agreed to do so after he was mortally wounded. In Jackson's case the cause of his abstinence was not a promise made to his mother, but first-hand experience from the Mexican War. He liked the taste too much.

17 *In the Saddle With Stuart* at 71.

18 Von Borcke at 443-44.

19 Marrow Stuart Smith, Sean M Heuvel, ed., *Life After J.E.B. Stuart: the Memoirs of his Granddaughter*, p. 25 (Lanham, Md: Rowman & Littlefield Publishers, Inc., 2012).

20 Editorial entitled "The Wounding and Death of General J.E.B. Stuart: Several Errors Corrected," *Southern Historical Society Papers,* Vol. VII, p. 141, January to December, 1879.

21 Marrow Stuart Smith, *supra*.

22 *Ibid*. According to Flora's granddaughter, the time revealed by the watch was 2 a.m., but Stuart died at 7:38 p.m. and Flora had reached his side before 2 a.m.

23 Editorial entitled "The Wounding and Death of General J.E.B. Stuart: Several Errors Corrected," *supra*.

24 The *Chicago Tribune* of May 25, 1864 contained a surprisingly detailed account of Stuart's last hours, including the names of several of those present at his death, listed as though everyone should know who they were, including "Dr.s (sic) Brewer, Garnett, Gibson, and Fontaine, as well as Reverends Peterkin and Keppler. It isn't known who was present named Gibson, although Stuart had a courier named Private Gilbert Gibson from the 6th Virginia.

25 One of the Richmond papers identified a pall bearer as General McCowan, which almost certainly should have been Brig. Gen. Samuel McGowan, a South Carolinian and brigade commander in the Army of Northern Virginia. Maj. Gen. John Porter McCown served in the western theatre. The same paper identified a pallbearer as General Lorton instead of General Lawton.

26 The battle jacket with plain cuffs has insect damage on the front that is sometimes mistaken for or incorrectly described as the bullet hole from Stuart's mortal wound. That jacket, as well as the accompanying gray trousers with double yellow stripes, Whitney revolver, and blood-stained yellow sash were given to the Virginia Historical Society by Stuart's granddaughter, Virginia Stuart Waller Davis, and whereas the revolver and sash were identified by the family as being from Yellow Tavern, the uniform was not. E-mail to the author dated April 28, 2014 from Heather Beattie, Museum Collections Manager, Virginia Historical Society Museum.

27 Cooke simply wrote of the jacket that it was the one Stuart rode on his "famous ride around McClellan in 1862," which was probably the first one but could have been either. The portrait of Stuart was the famous seated pose looking straight at the camera and wearing his frock coat, below which Cooke cut and placed a slip from one of Jeb's letters to Cooke that said "Yours to count on, J.E.B.Stuart " John Esten Cooke, Prologue to *Mohun, or the Last Days of Lee and His Paladins: Final Memoirs of a Staff Officer Serving in Virginia.*(New York: F.J. Huntington, 1869).

28 George William Patton, the father of Gen. George S. Patton, Jr., was born in 1856 and changed his name to George Smith Patton in 1868 in honor of his grandfather. He later became George S. Patton, Sr.

29 Robert F. Patton, *The Pattons: A Personal History of an American Family,* p. 56 (New York: Crown Publishers, 1994)

30 Alfred Hoyt Bill, *The Beleaguered City: Richmond 1861-1865*, pp. 216-271 (New York: Alfred A. Knopf, 1946).

31 *Ibid*.

32 "The Death of Major- General J. E. B. Stuart," *Southern Historical Society Papers*, Vol. VII, p. 109 (1879).

33 The complete resolution read as follows:

Whereas, the people of Richmond, in common with their fellow-citizens of the Confederate States, have to deplore in the death of Major General J.E.B. Stuart, not only the loss of one of the first military characters of the age, but also of a citizen whose eminent patriotism and pure life gave the best guarantee that his military capacity would never be otherwise employed than in the cause of freedom and for the welfare of his country; and

Whereas, they not only recognize their great misfortune , in common with the rest of their countryman, but bearing in mind that he yielded up his heroic spirit in the immediate defense of their city, and the successful effort to purchase their safety by the sacrifice of his own life, they are profoundly moved with sentiments of gratitude for his great services and of benevolent feeling for his glorious memory, and are desirous to express and to record their sense of peculiar obligation in a permanent and emphatic manner; therefore be it

Resolved, that the Council of the city of Richmond, in behalf of the citizens therefore, tender to the family of General Stuart the deepest and most heartfelt condolence, and earnestly request that remains of their great benefactor may be permitted to rest under the eye and guardianship of the people of Richmond, and they may be allowed to commemorate by a suitable monument their gratitude and his services.

34 Von Borcke at 445-46.

CHAPTER **12**

THE WORLD WITHOUT JEB STUART
After May 13, 1864

Let the curtain come down! Let the scene pass away.
here's an autumn when summer hath lavished its day;
We may sit by the fire, when we can't by the lamp,
and re-people the banquet—re-soldier the camp.
Oh! Nothing can rob us of memory's gold,
and tho' he quits the gorgeous, and we may grow old,
with our Shakespeare at heart, and bright forms in our brain
we can dream up our Siddons and Kembles again.
Well! Wealthy we have been, tho' fortune may frown
and they cannot but say we have had the crown.

> —Song by J. Hamilton Reynolds, sung by W. Balfe
> at a dinner given to Charles Kemble by the
> Garrick's Club, Jan. 10, 1837, copied by Stuart's
> Aide-de-Camp, Theodore Garnett into his
> *Continuation of War Sketches*, on Feb. 6, 1872
> (Stuart's birthday) suggesting that "Stuarts
> and Jackons" be substituted for "Siddons
> and Kembles."

THROUGHOUT THIS BOOK, beginning in the first chapter, there have been references to Stuart being "diminished" during the last months of his life, and yet, when one reads his letters and reports, as well as descriptions of how he acted, he sounds as full of life and joy as ever. What basis is there for saying he was diminished?

Compare the Jeb Stuart in his year of glory with the Jeb Stuart in his year of desperate struggle. The former Jeb loved three things and engaged in them as often as he could, viz, holding grand reviews of his cavalry, going to balls and parties, and, most of all, conducting raids on the enemy. However, in the ten months between the Gettysburg campaign and Yellow Tavern, he held only one review, apparently at the request of General Lee, he frequently declined invitations to balls and parties, and he conducted no raids on the enemy. That makes his last official raid the one he conducted from June 24 to July 1, 1863, a resounding failure. Might that failure have made him lose interest in conducting more?

Combine that behavior with his comments to comrades during the last year of his life, on at least four recorded occasions, that he did not expect to survive the war, and/or didn't want to survive if the South was going to be conquered. Consider the three principal career disappointments he experienced—being caught by surprise at Brandy Station and ridiculed publicly, failing General Lee during the Gettysburg campaign, and never being promoted to Lt. General. Consider the disappointments in his private life—inability to acquire and own a home; wife and children having to move from place to place as guests of friends and family; being dependent on his brother for financial support; a worrisome, pessimistic wife; fearing the government was going to seize the family salt works; worry about the health of his children; and long absences from his family. Pile on top of that the loss of so many people he loved—Little Flora, John Pelham, Stonewall Jackson, Von Borcke, Channing Price, Redmond Burke, William Farley, his sister, Vic.

Anyone who experienced what Stuart experienced during the last year of his life, in addition to the constant pressure of command, the stress of battle, the public scrutiny, and insufficient resources would, in today's world, be diagnosed with Post Traumatic Stress Disorder. Stuart, however, was merely diminished.

His death in May 1864 spared him from witnessing and participating in the agony that attended the Confederacy's last year and its death throes. Had he lived he would have done his duty but it is unlikely he could have significantly changed anything that happened. The South's defeat would not have destroyed him. He was too strong and too upbeat—to the point of effervescence—to be anything but the same buoyant Jeb Stuart. Yet, given the choice of dying as he did or surviving to experience the existences of Pete Longstreet, John Mosby, Wade Hampton, or Fitz Lee, as relatively benign and respectable as those lives became, Jeb would not have hesitated. He would have opted to be remembered as:

> Plume on a hat band, spurs made of gold,
> he who dies youthful never grows old.
> He who died youthful but lived every hour,
> God granted glory, the cavalier flower.[1]

Flora donned widow's black the day of Jeb's funeral, and continued wearing mourning clothes until she died in 1923.

Following the funeral she took her children and their meager possessions to the home of Alexander "Alick" Stuart, the brother who had always supported Jeb, in Saltville, Virginia. There she lived for the rest of the war, but not always peacefully. On October 1, 1864 a Federal cavalry force commanded by Brig. Gen. Stephen G. Burbridge attempted to capture the saltworks, which belonged to the Stuart family and which were of vital importance to Virginia's war effort. Confederates, many of them home guard, managed to beat back the offensive but the Federal force included a unit of black cavalryman, and a Rebel guerilla named Champ Ferguson commanded a group of irregulars who murdered several wounded Federal troops, black and white, for which he was tried and executed after the war.

Two months later the Federal cavalry came again, this time under Maj. Gen. George Stoneman, and they were successful. The saltworks were taken and on the morning of December 22, 1864, Flora awoke to find snow falling and the house surrounded by Federal troops demanding to be fed. The home in which she was taking refuge contained eight women, six children, and four slaves, and the latter spent the morning cooking for the Federal cavalrymen. Around noon the Federals began searching the house for valuables, and upon finding a locked room demanded the key. Inside the room were various trunks and items taken from the rest of the home to make more room in the areas with fireplaces, it being too cold to occupy the entire house. Included in the room was essentially everything Flora owned and she was certain she would lose it all.

Once the room was unlocked the Federal soldiers began hauling the trunks out and a Federal Colonel from Kentucky spotted one with initials "J.E.B.S." stenciled on the outside. "Whose trunk is that?" he demanded, and Flora, "as quietly as my excessive agitation would permit," replied "It is mine and it contains my husband's uniform and letters. Shall I unlock it so you may examine the contents?"

The Federal officer's voice became more dignified and he asked "Are you the widow of General Stuart?" Flora whispered "yes," and the officer replied "Madam, there are *some* gentlemen in the Federal army," and ordered that the trunk be carried upstairs unopened.

The Federals spent the next two days destroying everything associated with the saltworks, down to the kettles in which soil was boiled to produce salt, and at one point Flora tried to appeal directly to General Stoneman to prevent the burning of a small mill that stood so near the family home that it was likely to set everything ablaze. Stoneman refused her request, so she turned to the Kentucky colonel again. He commanded the rear guard, which had the responsibility for burning the mill and other structures. His command was the last to leave and as they rode away the little mill and the Stuart home were still standing.[2]

After the war she opened a school in Saltville, and in 1878 she moved to Staunton to teach at a Methodist school. In 1880 she became principal of Staunton's Virginia Female Institute, an Episcopal school for girls chartered in 1844. She stayed on for 19 years, retiring in 1899 after her daughter, Virginia Pelham Stuart Waller, died and Flora took her three children to raise. In 1907 the school was renamed Stuart Hall in her honor.

She lived another 16 years, surrounded by the three grandchildren and many reminders of her husband, including the framed flag she'd sewn for him in 1862 and which she was still intending to repair, at Jeb's urging, in May 1864. True to Jeb's request—a part of his will—she raised their children in Virginia, and she always preferred to be addressed as Mrs. J.E.B. Stuart. On May 6, 1923 she leaned down to pick up a toy dropped by one of her great-granddaughters on the front porch of the home of her son-in-law, Page Waller, where she was then living. She lost her balance, fell down four stone steps, hit her head and was unconscious for four days before dying on May 10, 1923, two days short of the 59th anniversary of Jeb's passing. She was buried in Hollywood Cemetery next to him and Little Flora.

Heros Von Borcke was promoted to Lt. Colonel in December, 1864, and was sent on a diplomatic mission to England by President Davis. He was there when he learned of the collapse of the Confederacy, so he returned to Prussia. He wrote and published his memoirs of the war in 1866, with editing assistance from John Reuben Thompson, noted Southern journalist, editor and poet.

The same year he returned to the military and fought in the Austro-Prussian war as a staff officer for Prince Friedrich Karl of Prussia, for which he was awarded the Order of the Red Eagle, a highly coveted medal for gallantry awarded from 1705 until 1918. He retired from the army in 1867, married, had three sons, bought an estate and inherited another and lived in the family castle of Giesenbrügge, proudly flying a Confederate battle flag from its battlements.

In 1884 he returned to the United States and was met at the pier by former members of Stuart's staff who were startled, but not necessarily surprised, to see that he had swelled to almost 400 pounds. He returned after visiting many of his old comrades, including Rooney Lee and Wade Hampton. In 1895 he died in Berlin from sepsis caused by the wound he received on June 19, 1864. During World War Two his gravestone was destroyed by the Soviet army, but the Sons of Confederate Veterans acquired and erected a new one over his grave in 2008.

Henry Brainard McClellan served on the staff of Robert E. Lee for three months and then on the staff of Wade Hampton from August 11, 1864 until the end of the war. He was paroled in Greensboro, North Carolina on April 26, 1865, returned to Cumberland County where he probably taught school until 1869, when he moved to Lexington Kentucky and became a professor at the Sayre Female Institute, where he remained as principal and professor until his death. He was active in Confederate veterans' affairs, wrote extensively, defended Stuart's memory and honor, published *The Life and Campaigns of Major General J. E. B. Stuart* in 1886, and died of a stroke in 1904. He is buried in Lexington Cemetery.

William Willis Blackford stayed with the newly formed 1st Regiment Engineer Troops after leaving Stuart's staff, although they often served more like infantry than anything else. In July he had a large cross constructed of cedar with the slightly inaccurate inscription "Here fell Gen. J.E.B. Stuart, May 12, 1864" (instead of May 11) to mark the spot of Stuart's wounding at Yellow Tavern, but then the Battle of the Crater occurred and he was ordered to Petersburg to help construct counter mines, so that he left the job of erecting the cross to others. He served through Petersburg and marched with the army to Appomattox, still riding his horse Magic. Like many others, the news of the surrender was unexpected and appalling. "I heard . . . something about 'the terms of surrender.' It struck me like an electric shock. . . . The effect was like a stunning blow, and for a moment I felt dazed . . . ."

His regiment of engineers was immediately adjacent to General Lee's tent the day of the surrender, and Blackford witnessed a side of Lee that few ever saw, and which clashed with the "Magnificent in Defeat" moniker with which he has been labeled:

> General Lee seemed to be in one of his savage moods and when these moods were on him it was safer to keep out of his way; so his staff kept to their tree except when it was necessary to introduce the [Federal] visitors. Quite a number came; they were mostly in groups of four or five and some of high rank. It was evident that some came from curiosity, or to see General Lee as friends in the old army. But General Lee shook hands with none of them. It was rather amusing to see the extreme deference shown by them to General Lee. When he would see Colonel Taylor coming with a party toward his tent he would halt in his pacing and stand at "attention" and glare at them with a look which few men but he could assume. They would remove their hats entirely and stand bareheaded during the interview while General Lee sometimes gave a scant touch to his hat in return and sometimes did not even do that. I could not hear what was passed, but the interviews were short.

After being paroled he rode Magic to Abingdon, his home, and soon resumed work as Chief Engineer with the Lynchburg & Danville Railroad. Later he operated a Louisiana sugar plantation, was Professor of Mechanics and Drawing as well as Superintendent of Buildings and Grounds at the Virginia Agricultural and Mechanical College, which became Virginia Tech. In 1881 he went to work for the Baltimore & Ohio Railroad until 1890, when he quit in order to pursue "oyster planting experiments" on Lynhaven Bay. Blackford died of "apoplexy" (a stroke) at his home in Princess Anne County on May 1, 1905, and was buried in Sinking Spring Cemetery in Abingdon. His marvelous memoirs were not published during his lifetime, but Dr. Douglas Southall Freeman saw to their release in book form as *War Years with Jeb Stuart* in 1945.

Blackford undoubtedly saw and visited Frank Robertson after the war, as both were engineers for Stuart and both lived in Abingdon. Following Stuart's death Robertson served on the staff of Rooney Lee until the end of the war. He married in 1868, fathered four daughters, and spent the rest of his life farming near Abingdon. Despite having heart trouble and precarious health during the war, he lived to the age of 85, dying on August 10, 1926.

Dabney Ball returned to the ministry after the war, serving in Methodist and Episcopal churches in Baltimore and Roanoke. However, he lost two children and his health failed, so he accepted a transfer to California for a year, returned to Baltimore, lost his wife of 30 years, and then died on February 15, 1878.

Andrew R. Venable transferred to Rooney Lee's staff after Stuart's death, and then became adjutant for Wade Hampton. In August he participated in Hampton's "beefsteak raid" that secured several hundred head of cattle for Lee's army, but he was then captured at Petersburg in October 1864. After a short stay in the Old Capitol Prison in Washington he was transferred by train to Fort Delaware in Pennsylvania, but along the way he jumped through an open window on the outskirts of Philadelphia and escaped. While hiding in Philadelphia he wrote his fiancé, Ariadne Stevens, in Baltimore, and she came to Philadelphia, where they were married. It is probable that no other Confederate soldier, particularly one as well-connected as Venable considered, much less accomplished, getting married in the heart of enemy territory while hiding from the enemy after escaping from prison.

After staying with Southern sympathizers and posing as an oil promoter, he worked his way back south and ultimately rejoined Hampton. In March 1865 he was assigned to the staff of Brig. Gen. John Echols in Western Virginia and was there when the war ended. He returned to his estate near Farmville, "Milnwood," and worked as a farmer and businessman. He was instrumental in arranging for the construction of the equestrian statue of Stuart in Richmond that was unveiled on May 30, 1907. He died at his home on October 15, 1909.

Theodore Garnett's rank as a lieutenant lapsed with Stuart's death, but he was re-commissioned to that rank as an aide for Rooney Lee. On March 15, 1865 he was promoted to captain and became assistant adjutant general for Brig. Gen. William P. Roberts, who was then commanding a brigade in Rooney Lee's cavalry division. After Appomattox he entered the University of Virginia and graduated with a law degree in 1866. In 1870 he was elected county judge in Suffolk, and in 1873 he went into practice in Norfolk, where he remained until his death in 1915. He was very active in Confederate veteran activities, and his tombstone identifies him as an aide to Stuart.

Chiswell Dabney, the youngest member of Stuart's staff, first became a farmer and ultimately an Episcopalian minister after the war, the latter not being what one might have expected during the days when he was a favorite of the young ladies at various parties and balls attended or arranged by Stuart. He also married within Stuart's military family, wedding Lucy Fontaine, sister of Col./Dr. John Fontaine, Stuart's staff surgeon and attending physician when he died. Joining the ministry did not occur officially until 1900, after he became more and more involved in church affairs and then became an ordained deacon in 1896. He was assistant rector at Emmanuel Church in Chatham, Virginia and became rector of Pruden parish in 1918. He died in 1923 at the age of 79 and is buried in Chatham.

Following Stuart's death, Alexander R. Boteler probably served for a short period as an aide-de-camp for Governor and Major General William "Extra Billy" Smith. In July 1864, his family home, "Fountain Rock," was burned by Federals under Maj. Gen. David Hunter, and in November he became the presiding judge of the Confederate military court and remained there until Appomattox. After the war he helped found Shepherd College in 1871, and in 1876 was a commissioner for West Virginia to the Centennial Exposition in Philadelphia. In 1881 he was appointed to the Tariff Commission by President Chester A. Arthur. In 1882 he became an Assistant U.S. Attorney and in 1884 became clerk of pardons in the Department of Justice. He wrote various books, illustrating one with his drawings, and painted portraits of famous Confederates such as Jefferson Davis, Robert E. Lee and Wade Hampton, despite having never received any formal training in art. After resigning from the Department of Justice in 1889 he lived in Shepherdstown until his death in 1892, and is buried there.

William Henry Hagen served as an aide-de-camp on Hampton's staff after Stuart's death, and was paroled at Greensboro, North Carolina, along with Major McClellan, on April 26, 1865. He returned to his home in

Shepherdstown, West Virginia, and was known as "Major" Hagen, although there is no record of his having been promoted beyond lieutenant. He became president of a cement mill, and then operated a hotel in Shepherdstown beginning in the late 1870s. In 1882 he traded the hotel for a small boardinghouse and lived a peaceful life with his wife until his death on June 18, 1895 at the age of 74.

After Yellow Tavern, John Esten Cooke became adjutant for Brig. Gen. William Pendleton and remained in that position until the end of the war. In 1867 he married Mary Francis Page of Clark County, Virginia, and the couple had a daughter and two sons, raising them at the Cooke family home, "The Briers." He was unable to make a living as a writer, and tried farming, at which he was only slightly more successful. When his wife died in 1878 he was forced to split up his family in order that they could be cared for properly, sending the daughter to live with his wife's sister. In the summer of 1886 he contracted typhoid fever but refused to acknowledge the illness until he fainted and was put to bed. He died the next day, September 17, 1886, and was buried in the Old Chapel Cemetery in Clarke County, Virginia.

Cooke was a hopeless romantic and the death of Stuart nearly broke his heart. He buried his silver spurs at Appomattox and returned to his writing, characterizing the heroes of the Confederacy—Jackson, Pelham, Stuart, Ashby and others as knights of old. As his biographer, John O. Beaty, pointed out, he was in a unique position, more so than perhaps anyone, of serving with and observing the major leaders of the Army of Northern Virginia from Manassas to Appomattox. Thus, his written record of what they did and said might have become one of the earliest and potentially most popular publications concerning the South during the war. Instead, he created an imaginary Virginia staff officer, Colonel Phillip Surry, who lived in a mansion named Eagle's Nest, and mixed accounts of the real Confederate leaders with stylized fiction involving Surry, written in the vein of Sir Walter Scott. The effect, rather than enhancing novels by inclusion of credible facts, was dilution of unique non-fiction by mixing it with increasingly unpopular romanticism.

Like Stuart, Cooke never received the promotion he believed he deserved, and his biographer opined that this was probably intentional because some of his many articles were critical of certain Confederate leaders. The last of his books was *The Maurice Mystery,* published in 1885.

When Cooke was promoted to captain in August 1862, Jeb gave him one of his uniform jackets to have altered and to wear. Whether with premeditation or not, Cooke kept the jacket as Stuart had worn it instead, and after the war displayed it proudly on the wall of his study at The Briers, an artifact of the time and man he most admired in life.

Stuart's daughter, Virginia Pelham Stuart, married Robert Page Waller, who was known as Page, and gave birth to three children, Matthew Page Waller, Virginia Stuart Waller, and Flora Stuart Waller, but died at age 34 in 1898 following the birth of Flora. The three children were then raised by their grandmother, Mrs. J.E.B. Stuart, who often lived in the home of Page Waller. Virginia was buried in Elmwood Cemetery in Norfolk.

James Ewell Brown Stuart, Jr. attended V.M.I., studied to be an engineer, and worked as a banker. When the Spanish American War broke out in 1898 he enlisted and became a captain. Following the war President Roosevelt appointed him Collector of Customs at Newport News, Virginia, and during World War I he served in France in the Supply Department as a civilian. He married Jo Phillips and they had three daughters and two sons, one who died in infancy, both named Jeb Stuart III. He retired from business in 1927, and lived in Long Beach, Long Island, New York and then in Istolpoga, Florida, where he died in 1930. He and his wife are buried in Section 7, Site 9002, in Arlington National Cemetery. The proud tradition of naming a son James Ewell Brown Stuart in each generation has continued. The most recent, J.E.B. Stuart VI, was in his early 20s and working at the Sheriff's office in Goochland Virginia as of July 2013.

On May 30, 1907, the statue honoring Jeb Stuart that the Richmond City Council had resolved to design and erect in May 1864 was finally unveiled in Richmond. Fifty thousand people attended the ceremony, and the dedication address was given by Theodore Stanford Garnett, Jeb's former aide-de-camp.

After acknowledging the identity and character of those to whom he spoke, Garnett said that he was there "[in] response to a call as inspiring as the bugles of Stuart on the field of battle. . . to attempt the impossible task which has been assigned to me by my old comrades," which was to place the statute originally planned 43 years previously for Stuart—a man of a type whom no one living would look upon again.

Garnett then told the audience a condensed story of Stuart's life from birth through West Point and pre-war experiences to the war, at which point he began describing, in glowing terms, what Stuart accomplished during all of the major campaigns of the war. Getting to those campaigns about which he might have inserted a smidgeon of apology or criticism, he described Fleetwood [Brandy Station] as involving "a succession of most gallant and desperate charges [by which Stuart] wrested victory from the jaws of defeat." Of Gettysburg he said, "The fact that it took Stuart one day longer than he expected to fight his way to Carlisle, Pennsylvania, arriving on the field of Gettysburg on the second day of the battle, has been used to account for the failure of the Army of Northern Virginia to keep up its unbroken score of victories . . . " [but] "to say that the battle would have been won if Stuart had arrived a day earlier is to tribute to him greater than his most ardent admirers could claim."

The address continued for the equivalent of 16 pages, and if the rule of thumb for screenplays applied, the length of the speech would have been only 16 minutes. Even at 20 or 30 minutes it was not too long or tedious for a spring day in May and that crowd. They were still unaccustomed to even the entertainment offered by radio, let along television, movies or Disney theme parks. They'd come for a flowery speech and Garnett did not let them down.

Almost predictably, Garnett closed with a poem, which, in the program accompanying the event was entitled "Stuart," although a modern Internet search reveals its use in connection with other great men for whom statues have been erected. It was the sort of old-fashioned, flowery rhyme Stuart would have enjoyed, not only in style and sentiment but in the use of archaic terms like "fit plinth in sooth!" It read as follows:

> I've called his name, a statue stern and vast,
> It rests enthroned upon the mighty past,
> Fit plinth for him whose image in the mind
> Looms up as that of one by God designed.
> Fit plinth, in sooth! the mighty past for him,
> Whose simple name is Glory's synonym.
> E'en Fancy's self in her enchanted sleep
> Can dream no future which may cease to keep

His name in guard, like sentinel, and cry
From Time's great bastions: "It shall never die!"

But his name, even if a synonym for glory, *shall* die, of course. It has lived much longer than most famous men, literally passing through and to five generations since 1864.[3] Still, the number of people who recognize the name today is a mere fraction of the number who did in 1907, and those were a fraction of his admirers in 1864. It is the way of the world that we live, we die, and we are forgotten, most sooner than others. Stuart was no Alexander the Great or Aristotle or Shakespeare or anyone who humans have the audacity to label immortal. What Jeb Stuart did and why he did it carries very little weight and has very limited meaning in the first quarter of the 21st Century. Those who have read this account of his life to this point are, in fact, of a quickly diminishing breed.

Yet for those whose pulse quickens at the thought of riding a galloping horse in battle or depending on a saber to fight an enemy; for those who as children brandished wooden lathes as sabers or carried a bath towel on a well rod as a regimental banner; for those who marvel at what men risked and did a century and a half ago; for those who still wonder at what might have been . . . the story of Jeb Stuart will live on a little longer.

As Garnett said, "we shall ne'er look upon his like again."

NOTES

1 *Jeb*, as sung by Bill Coleman on the music C.D. *Chantilly Remembrance* (Cold Comfort Productions, 1998).

2 Marrow Stuart Smith, Sean M Heuvel, ed., *Life After J.E.B. Stuart: the Memoirs of his Granddaughter*, pp. 27-28 (Lanham, Md: Rowman & Littlefield Publishers, Inc., 2012).

3 Jeb Stuart Jr. lived from 1860 to 1930. The first Jeb Stuart III was born in 1887 but died in 1888, and a second son, born in 1897, was given the same name. He died in 1990. Jeb Stuart IV was born circa 1936 and is still living, as is Jeb Stuart V, born circa 1963, and Jeb Stuart VI, born circa 1995.

BIBLIOGRAPHY

PRIMARY SOURCES, PUBLISHED

Alexander, Edward Porter, Gallagher, Gary W., ed., *Fighting for the Confederacy: The Personal Recollections of General Edward Porter Alexander* (Chapel Hill: University of North Carolina Press, 1989).

Beale, Richard L.T.. *History of the 9th Virginia Cavalry in the War Between the States* (Richmond: B. F. Johnson Publishing Co., 1899).

Blackford, W.W., *War Years with JEB Stuart* (New York: Charles Scribner's Sons, 1945).

Cooke, John Esten, *Mohun, or the Last Days of Lee and His Paladins: Final Memoirs of a Staff Officer Serving in Virginia* (New York: F.J. Huntington, 1869).

Blassingame; John W., ed., *Slave Testimony: Two Centuries of Letters, Speeches, and Interviews, and Autobiographies* (Baton Rouge: Louisiana State University Press, 1977).

Blue, John, Oats, Dan, ed., *Hanging Rock Rebel: Lt. John Blue's War in West Virginia and the Shenandoah Valley* (Shippensburg, PA: Burd Street Press, 1994).

Bowen, Rev. J.R. *Regimental History of the First New York Dragoons* (Ann Arbor, Mich.: J.R. Brown, 1900).

Chestnut, Mary, *A Diary from Dixie* (New York: Appleton & Co. 1906).

Cooke, Helen Grinnan, *Notes of Times at Brampton, Shackleford Family Papers* (1980).

Cooke, John Esten, *Surry of Eagle's Nest: Memoirs of a Staff Officer Serving in Virginia* (Philadelphia: Bunce & Huntington, 1866).

Cooke, John Esten, *Wearing of the Gray* (Bloomington: Indiana University Press: 1959).

Cooke, Phillip St. George *Cavalry Tactics or Regulations for the Instruction, Formations and Movements of the Cavalry of the Army and Volunteers of the United States* (Philadelphia: J.B. Lippincott & Co., 1862).

Douglass, Henry Kyd, *I Rode with Stonewall: The War Experiences of the Youngest Member of Jackson's Staff* (Chapel Hill: University of North Carolina Press, 1968).

Freemantle, Arthur, Lt. Col., *Three Months in the Southern States* (New York: John Bradburn, 1864).

Garnett, Theodore Stanford & Trout, Robert J., ed. *Riding With Stuart: Reminiscences of an Aide-De-Camp* (Shippenburg, PA: White Mane Publishing Co., 1994).

Gallagher, Gary W., ed., *Fighting for the Confederacy: The Personal Recollections of General Edward Porter Alexander* (Chapel Hill: University of North Carolina Press, 1989).

Garnett, Theodore S., *J.E.B. Stuart (Major General), Commander of the Cavalry Corps, Army of Northern Virginia, C.S.A.: An Address Delivered at the Unveiling of the Equestrian Statue of General Stuart at Richmond, Virginia, May 30, 1907* (New York & Washington: The Neale Publishing Company, 1907).

Grymes, J. Randolph, ed., *The Fanny Hume Diary of 1862: A Year in Wartime Orange, Virginia* (Orange, VA, 1994).

Hoole, Wm. Stanley, *Lawley Covers the Confederacy* (Tuscaloosa: Confederate Publishing Co., Inc., 1964).

Hoole, Wm. Stanley, *Vizetelly Covers the Confederacy* (Tuscaloosa: Confederate Publishing Co., Inc., 1957).

Hubbell, Jay B., ed., "The War Diary of John Esten Cooke," *Journal of Southern History*, Vol. 7 (November 1941).

Johnson, Robert Underwood, ed., *Battles and Leaders of the Civil War* (Norwalk, Conn.: Easton Press, 2002).

Jones, John B., *A Rebel War Clerk's Diary* (Philadelphia: J.B.Lippincott & Co., 1866).

Kidd, James Harvey, *Personal Recollections of a Cavalryman With Custer's Michigan Cavalry Brigade in the Civil War* (Ionia, MI, Sentinel Printing Co., 1908).

Longstreet, James, *From Manassas to Appomattox: Memoirs of the Civil War* (Philadelphia: J. B. Lippincott & Co., 1896).

Maurice, Federick, ed., *An Aide-De-Camp of Lee: Being the Papers of Colonel Charles Marshall, Sometime Aide-de-Camp, Military Secretary, and Assistant Adjutant General on the Staff of Robert E. Lee, 1862–1865* (Boston: Little Brown, 1927).

McClellan, Henry B, *I Rode with Jeb Stuart: The Life and Campaigns of Major General J.E.B.Stuart* (Bloomington: Indiana University Press, 1958).

McDonald, Capt. William N., *A History of the Laurel Brigade: Ashby's Cavalry of the Army of Northern Virginia and Chew's Battery* (Baltimore: Sun Job Printing, 1907).

Mitchell, Adele H., ed., *The Letters of Major General James E.B.Stuart* (Stuart-Mosby Historical Society: 1990).

Mosby, John Singleton, *Mosby's War Reminiscences: Stuart's Cavalry Campaigns* (New York: Dodd, Mead & Co., 1898).

Mosby, John Singleton, *Stuart's Cavalry in the Gettysburg Campaign* (New York: Moffatt Yard, 1908).

Moyer, H. P., *History of the Seventeenth Regiment Pennsylvania Volunteer Cavalry* (Lebanon. Pennsylvania, 1911).

Pollard, Edward Alfred, *The Lost Cause: A New Southern History of the War of the Confederates, Comprising a Full and Authentic Account of the Rise and the Progress of the Late Southern Confederacy—the Campaigns, Battles, Incidents and Adventures of the Most Gigantic Struggle of the World's History, Drawn from Official Sources and Approved by the Most Distinguished Confederate Leaders* (New York: E.B. Treat & Co. 1867).

Ross, Fitgerald, *A Visit to the Cities and Camps of the Confederate States* (Edinburgh & London: William Blackford & Sons, 1865).

Sheridan, Phillip Henry, *Personal Memoirs of Phillip Sheridan,* Vol. 1 (London: Chatto & Windus, Picaddilly, 1888).

Smith, Marrow Stuart; Heuvel Sean, W., ed. *Life After J.E.B. Stuart* (Lanham, MD: University Press of America, 2012).

Southern Historical Society Papers:

Dorsey, Col. "Gus" W. Dorsey, "Fatal Wounding or General J.E. B. Stuart," Vol. 30, p. 237 (1902).

Jones, J. William, "The Kilpatrick-Dahlgren Raid Against Richmond." Vol. 13, pp. 515–560 (1889).

Lee, Gen. Robert E., "Letter dated April 15, 1868 to Willam M. McDonald," Vol. 7, pp. 445–46 (1879).

Lee, Maj. Gen. Fitzhugh, "Speech of General Fitz. Lee, Army of Northern Virginia Banquet, October 28, 1875," Vol. 1, p. 99 (1876).

McKim, Randolph Harrison, "Stuart's Cavalry in the Gettysburg Campaign, A Reply to the Letter of Col. John S. Mosby," Vol. 37, pp. 21–37 (1909).

Mosby, John Singleton, "Longstreet and Stuart," Vol. 23, pp. 238–247 (1895).

Mosby, John Singleton, "Stuart and Gettysburg," Vol. 23, pp. 348–353 (1895).

Mosby, John Singleton, "Stuart's Cavalry in the Gettysburg Campaign," Vol. 37, pp. 21–37 (1909).

Poindexter, W.B. "Midnight Charge, and the Death of General J.E.B.Stuart," Vol. 32, p. 117 (1904).

Schuricht, Lt. Hermann, "Jenkins' Brigade in the Gettysburg Campaign. Extracts from the Diary of Lieutenant Hermann Schuricht, of the Fourteenth Virginia Cavalry," Vol. 24, pp. 339–351 (1896).

Talcott, Col. T. M. R., "Stuart's Cavalry in the Gettysburg Campaign, A Reply to the Letter of Col. John S. Mosby," Vol. 38, pp. 197–210 (1910).

"The Death of Major General J.E.B.Stuart," Vol. 7, p. 107 (1879).

"The Wounding and Death of General J. E. B. Stuart—Several Errors Corrected," Vol. 7, p. 140 (1879).

Trout, Robert J., *With Pen & Saber: The Letters and Diaries of J.E.B.Stuart's Staff Officers* (Mechanicsburg, PA: Stackpole Books, 1993).

United States War Department, *The War of the Rebellion: a Compilation of the Official Records of the Union and Confederate Armies, Official Records of the Union and Confederate Armies* (Washington: Government Printing Office, 1880–1901).

Von Borcke, Heros, *Memoirs of the War for Confederate Independence* (Nashville: Southern Classics Series, 1999).

Worsham, John H., *One of Jackson's Foot Cavalry: His Experience and What He Saw During the War 1861–1865, Including a History of "F Company," Richmond, Va., 21st Regiment Virginia Infantry, Second Brigade, Jackson's Division, Second Corps, A. N. Va.* (New York: The Neale Publishing Co., 1912).

PRIMARY SOURCES, UNPUBLISHED
Garnett Family papers, University of Virginia.
J.E.B. Stuart Papers, http://6whitehorses.com/cw/index.html.
J.E.B.Stuart Papers, Pearce Civil War & Western Art Museum, Corsicana, Texas
Stuart Papers, Virginia Historical Society, Richmond
CONTEMPORARY NEWSPAPERS & PERIODICALS
Century Magazine
Charleston Mercury
Chicago Tribune
Confederate Veteran magazine
Daily Evening Bulletin, San Francisco
Harper's Weekly
Journal of the Military Service Institution of the United States
National Tribune, Washington, D.C.
New York Times
New York Tribune
Philadelphia Weekly Times
Richmond Bulletin, The
Richmond Dispatch
Richmond Examiner
Richmond News-Leader
Richmond Sentinel
Richmond Times-Dispatch
Richmond Whig
Saturday Evening Post
Southern Bivouac
Washington Times

SECONDARY SOURCES
Akers, Monte, *Year of Glory: The Life and Battles of Jeb Stuart and His Cavalry, June 1862–June 1863* (Havertown, PA, 2012).
Beaty, John O., *John Esten Cooke, Virginian* (New York: Columbia University Press, 1922).

Bill, Alfred Hoyt, *The Beleaguered City: Richmond 1861–1865* (New York: Alfred A. Knopf, 1946).

Boatner, Mark Mayo III, *The Civil War Dictionary* (New York: David McKay Co., Inc. 1959).

Brennan, Patrick, "It Wasn't Stuart's Fault," *North & South* magazine, Vol. 6 (July 2003).

Bridges, David P. *Fighting with JEB Stuart: Major James Breathed and the Confederate Horse Artillery* (Arlington, VA: Breathed Bridges Best, 2006).

Busey, John W. & Martin, David G. Martin, *Regimental Strengths and Losses at Gettysburg* (Hightstown, N.J.: 2005).

Callihan, David L. "Jeb Stuart's Fateful Ride," *Gettysburg Magazine,* Vol. 4 (January 2001).

Davis, Burke *JEB Stuart: The Last Cavalier* (New York: Rhinehart & Co. 1957).

Downey, Fairfax, *Clash of Cavalry: The Battle of Brandy Station* (New York: Van Rees Press, 1959).

Fahr, Matthew, "Civil War reaches 150th anniversary; Armada soldier left his mark," *Armada Times,* May 02, 2011.

Falcon, Hal, Ph.D., *How to Analyze Handwriting: What Does My Handwriting Tell You?* (New York: Cornerstone Library, 1984).

Gallagher, Gary W., ed., *The Spotsylvania Campaign* (Chapel Hill: University of North Carolina, 1998).

Glatthaar, Joseph T., *General Lee's Army: From Victory to Collapse* (New York: Free Press, 2008).

Guttman, Jon, "Battle of Yellow Tavern," *America's Civil War* (January 2000).

Johnson, Clint, *In the Footsteps of J.E.B. Stuart* (Winston-Salem, NC, 2003).

Kehlbeck, Keith, *Gone to God: A Civil War Family's Ultimate Sacrifice* (Rolling Meadows, IL: 2013).

Klein, Maury, "J.E.B. Stuart's Life: What Should We Think of the General?" *Civil War Times Illustrated,* Vol. 25 (September, 1986).

Knepper, Robin, "'Banjo Sam' Gets Marker: Orange Remembers 'Banjo Sam' Sweeney, one of Confederate J.E.B. Stuart's Musicians, *The Free Lance Star* (June 13, 2010).

Krohlick, Marshall D., "Lee vs. Stuart: The Gettysburg Altercation," *Virginia Country's Civil War,* Vol. 2 (1984).

Krick, Robert E. L., *Staff Officers in Gray: A Biographical Register of the Staff Officers in the Army of Northern Virginia* (Chapel Hill: University of North Carolina Press, 2003).

Longacre, Edward G., "Major General J.E.B. Stuart: Last Stand of the Last Knight," *Civil War Times,* (June 2004).

Lynghaug, Fran , *The Official Horse Breeds Standards Guide* (MBI Publishing, 2009).

Maxwell, Jerry, *The Perfect Lion: The Life and Death of Confederate Artillerist John Pelham* (Tuscaloosa: University of Alabama Press, 2011).

McClure, A.K., *Abraham Lincoln and Men of War-Times: Some Personal Recollections of War and Politics During the Lincoln Administration* (Philadelphia: The Times Publishing Co., 1892).

Nesbitt, Mark, *Saber and Scapegoat: J.E.B.Stuart and the Gettysburg Controversy* (Mechanicsburg, PA: 1994).

Patton, Robert H., *The Pattons: A Personal History of and American Family* (New York: Crown Publishers, 1994).

Perry, Thomas D., *Ascent to Glory: The Genealogy of J.E.B. Stuart* (Ararat, VA: 2008).

Perry, Thomas D., *God's Will Be Done: The Christian Life of J.E.B. Stuart* (Ararat,VA: Laurel Hill Publishing, LLC, 2011).

Perry, Thomas D. with Moore, William T., *Whatever May Be My Fate May You Be Happy: J.E.B.Stuart, Bettie Hairston, and the Beaver Creek Plantation* (Ararat,VA; Laurel Hill Publishing, LLC, 2011).

Power, J. Tracy, *Lee's Miserables: Life in the Army of Northern Virginia from the Wilderness to Appomattox* (Chapel Hill: University of North Carolina Press, 1998).

Pryor, Elizabeth Brown, *Reading the Man: A Portrait of Robert E. Lee Through His Private Letters* (New York: Penguin Group, 2007).

Ramage, James A., *Gray Ghost: The Life of John Singleton Mosby* (The University Press of Kentucky: 2010).

Rhea, Gordon C., *The Battles for Spotsylvania Court House and the Road to Yellow Tavern, May 7–12, 1864* (Baton Rouge: Louisiana State University Press, 1997).

Riggs, David F., *East of Gettysburg: Custer vs. Stuart* (Ft. Collins, CO: Old Army Press 1970)

Robinson, Warren C., *Jeb Stuart and the Confederate Defeat at Gettysburg* (Lincoln: University of Nebraska Press, 2007).

Schullz, Duane, *The Dahlgren Affair: Terror and Conspiracy in the Civil War* (New York: W. W. Norton & Co. 1998).

Shaara, Michael, *The Killer Angels* (New York: Random House, 1974).

Thomas, Emory M., *Bold Dragoon: The Life of J.E.B.Stuart* (New York: Harper & Row, 1986).

Thomason, John, *JEB Stuart* (New York: Charles Scribner's Sons, 1930).

Trout, Robert J., *Galloping Thunder: The Stuart Horse Artillery Battalion* (McChanicsburg, PA: Stackpole Books, 2002).

Trout, Robert J. Ed. *In the Saddle with Stuart: The Story of Frank Smith Robertson of Jeb Stuart's Staff* (Gettysburg: Thomas Publications, 1998).

Trout, Robert J., *The Followed the Plume: The Story of J.E.B. Stuart and his Staff* (Mechanicsburg, PA: Stackpole Books, 1995).

Trout, Robert J., *With Pen & Saber: The Letters and Diaries of J.E.B. Stuart's Staff Officers* (Mechanicsburg, PA: Stackpole Books, 1993).

Trudeau, Noah Andre, "Battle of Gettysburg: Major Eugene Blackford and the Fifth Alabama Sharpshooters," *America's Civil War* (July 2001).

Walker, Frank S., *Remembering: A History of Orange County, Virginia* (Orange, VA: Orange County Historical Society, 2004)

Walker, Paul D., *The Cavalry Battle that Saved the Union: Custer vs. Stuart at Gettysburg* (Gretna, LA: Pelican Publishing Co. 2002).

Warner, Ezra J., *Generals in Gray: Lives of Confederate Commanders* (Louisiana State University Press, 1959).

Wert, Jeffry D., *Cavalryman of the Lost Cause: Biography of J.E.B. Stuart* (New York: Simon & Schuster 2008).

Wertz, Jay & Bearss *Smithsonian's Great Battles & Battlefields of the Civil War: A Definitive Field Guide* (New York: William Morrow and Co., 1997).

Wittenburg, Eric J., *Gettysburg's Forgotten Cavalry Actions: Farnsworth's Charge, South Cavalry Field, and the Battle of Fairfield, July 3, 1863* (New York: Savas Beatie, 2011, 2013).

Wittenburg, Eric. J. & Petruzzi, J. David, *Plenty of Blame to Go Around: Jeb Stuart's Controversial Ride to Gettysburg* (New York: Savas Beatie, 2006, 2011).

Wittenburg, Eric J. *Protecting the Flank at Gettysburg: The Battles for Binkerfoff's Ridge and East Cavalry Field, July 2–3, 1863* (El Dorado Hills, CA: Savas Beatie, 2012, 2013).

Yates, Bernice-Marie, *JEB Stuart Speaks: An Interview with Lee's Cavalryman* (Shippensburg, PA: 1997).

Zimmerman, Daniel, "J.E.B. Stuart: Battle of Gettysburg Scapegoat," *America's Civil War* (May 1998).

INTERNET SITES

Battle of Mine Run, http://civilwarwiki.net/wiki/Battle_of_Mine_Run.

Brown, Allen, "Col, Dahlgren's Leg at the Washington Navel Yard," *Landmarks,* http://allenbrowne.blogspot.com/2012/05/col-dahlgrens-leg.html (May 17, 2012).

Civil War Talk, http://civilwartalk.com/threads/jeb-stuart.48184/page-3.

"Col. Ulric Dahlgren.; Curious Story Regarding the Disposition of his Remains." *The Richmond Bulletin,* Aug. 5. 13, 1865, http://www.nytimes.com/1865/08/13/news/col-ulric-dahlgren-curious-story-regarding-the-disposition-of-his-remains.html?pagewanted=2.

Find a Grave, http://www.findagrave.com/cgi-bin/fg.cgi?page=gr&GRid=8754439.

Friends of Gettysburg, http://www.friendsofgettysburg.org/FriendsofGettysburg/ The-GreatTaskBeforeUs/TheGreatTaskBeforeUsDetails/tabid/99/ItemId/297/September-14th-2011-Robert-Swan.aspx.

Early Methods for the Surveillance and Control of Glanders in Europe, by J. Blancou, http://www.oie.int/doc/ged/D8902.PDF.

Hall, Clark B., "A Curious Affair:" The Battle of Morton's Ford, February 6, 1864," http://www.brandystationfoundation.com/cse-columns-pdf/mortons-ford.pdf.

National Registry of Historic Places Inventory—Nomination form for Brampton, Madison County, Va. (1985); http://www.dhr.virginia.gov/registers/Counties/Madison/056-0001_Brampton_1985_Final_Nomination.pdf.

Miller, John, "A Short History of Jenkins' Brigade during the Pennsylvania Campaign," *Emmittsburg Area Historical Society,* http://www.emmitsburg.net/archive_list/articles/history/
civil_war/jenkins_brigade.htm.

O'Connell, Dan, "The Bristoe Campaign," *TOCWOC: A Civil War Blog,* http://www.brettschulte.net/CWBlog/2012/04/10/the-marching-campaign-bristoe (March 25 to April 10, 2012).

Raid Around Richmond—From *The Daily Richmond Enquirer,* May 13th, 1864, http://www.myfamily.com/group/nc3rdcavalry/discussions/85106149.

Siegel, Chuck, *Battles in Madison County in September/October 1863: A Mini-Tour,* http://www.rvcwrt.org/madison.html.

Stone Sentinels, http://www.gettysburg.stonesentinels.com/AOPCavCorps.php.

Wittenberg, Eric J., "Ulric Dahlgren in the Gettysburg Campaign," http://www.gdg.org/
Gettysburg%20/Magazine/dahlgren.html.

Yellow Tavern: http://www.historynet.com/battle-of-yellow-tavern.htm.

MISCELLANEOUS

Coleman, William, *Chantilly Remembrance* music C.D. (Cold Comfort Productions, 1998).

Roode, Patricia K., *J.E.B. Stuart and the Battle of Gettysburg: Was He Responsible for Lee's Defeat?* Senior's Honors Thesis, History Dept., Rutgers University, April 2011

INDEX